Key Concepts in
Social Gerontology

Recent volumes include:

Key Concepts in Community Studies
Tony Blackshaw

Key Concepts in Public Health
Frances Wilson

Key Concepts in Anti-Discriminatory Social Work
Toyin Okitikpi

Key Concepts in Ethnography
Karen O'Reilly

Key Concepts in Mental Health, Second Edition
David Pilgrim

The SAGE Key Concepts series provides students with accessible and authoritative knowledge of the essential topics in a variety of disciplines. Cross-referenced throughout, the format encourages critical evaluation through understanding. Written by experienced and respected academics, the books are indispensable study aids and guides to comprehension.

JUDITH PHILLIPS, KRISTINE AJROUCH
and SARAH HILLCOAT-NALLÉTAMBY

Key Concepts in
Social Gerontology

Los Angeles | London | New Delhi
Singapore | Washington DC

© Judith Phillips, Kristine Ajrouch, Sarah Hillcoat-Nallétamby, 2010

First published 2010

SAGE Publications Ltd
1 Oliver's Yard
55 City Road
London EC1Y 1SP

SAGE Publications Inc.
2455 Teller Road
Thousand Oaks, California 91320

SAGE Publications India Pvt Ltd
B 1/I 1 Mohan Cooperative Industrial Area
Mathura Road
New Delhi 110 044

SAGE Publications Asia-Pacific Pte Ltd
33 Pekin Street #02-01
Far East Square
Singapore 048763

Library of Congress Control Number: 2009929965

British Library Cataloguing in Publication data

A catalogue record for this book is available from the
British Library

ISBN 978-1-4129-2271-5
ISBN 978-1-4129-2272-2 (pbk)

Typeset by C&M Digitals (P) Ltd, Chennai, India
Printed in India at Replika Press Pvt. Ltd
Printed on paper from sustainable resources

contents

contents

v

key concepts in social gerontology

acknowledgements

The authors would like to express their sincere thanks to the people who have contributed towards the development and production of this book:

- Jodie Croxall (Social Policy PhD student, Centre for Innovative Ageing (CIA), Swansea University) for her invaluable contributions to sourcing and collating materials and to initial drafts of the 'death and dying', 'bereavement', 'family relations' and 'independence' concepts. Christine Dobbs (PhD, Social Psychologist, CIA) for her help in preparing early drafts of the 'disability', 'palliative care', 'dementia', 'frailty' and 'biographical approaches'. Her contributions towards the end of the project renewed our energy and fuelled our hopes that we might just finish on time!
- Rachel Hazelwood, who stepped in at the end to relieve us from the daunting task of collating our contributions and liaising with our publishers. Had Rachel not been on board – who knows – perhaps we would have pressed the 'delete' rather than the 'send' button, and our publishers might still be waiting!
- Our referees Toni Antonucci, Svein Olav Daatland, Dale Dannefer, and Clemens Tesch-Roemer for agreeing to advise and review our work as it progressed. Their thoughtful comments and insightful reactions helped us refine ideas and develop a more inclusive approach.
- Vanessa Burholt (Director, Centre for Innovative Ageing, Swansea University), whose encouragement to Sarah made the writing enterprise a goal to be achieved.
- Kristine Ajrouch acknowledges in particular the Eastern Michigan University (EMU) for granting a Spring/Summer Research Award in 2007 to write this book. The collegial atmosphere at EMU provided an accommodating writing environment in the midst of multiple, competing teaching and service responsibilities. And finally, much love and appreciation to Abraham, Ali, and Rachelle Ajrouch, who each supported me daily in their own way over the years as this book occupied various periods of our life together.
- Sarah Hillcoat-Nallétamby would like to thank New Zealand for having let her go … to discover Welsh cakes, the seaside and the beginning of yet another new horizon. Thank you Judith and Kristine for inviting me to join with you to co-author this book.

Introduction: Social Gerontology – 'New Science, New Concepts'

Social gerontology is a relatively new and dynamic scientific field reflecting increasing interest in ageing across the world.

Throughout the centuries, old age and ageing have been ever-present, but have received minimal attention from social thinkers. Education and research in ageing have not been a high priority in terms of research funding or policy, until relatively recently. As James Birren states, 'gerontology is an ancient subject but a recent science'. Gerontology as a subject area is becoming increasingly global, with predominantly undergraduate programmes in the USA and Australia and postgraduate courses in the UK.

Demographic ageing has raised issues for policy and practice as well as creating new and increasing markets for business and commerce. Consequently, the need for an evidence base for policy decisions or best practice, or for reviewing the market, has led to an increased interest in research in ageing. New research questions are being asked, new theories in ageing are developing and new researchers are crossing disciplinary boundaries with novel methods to study ageing.

A social perspective and analysis of ageing, which this book addresses, stands alongside biological and clinical perspectives in helping us understand the processes of ageing. The multidisciplinarity of gerontology is emerging as a 'new science' (Walker, 2008). With this comes particular challenges of discipline recognition embedded within gerontology, and difficulties of drawing the boundaries of 'the social'.

Traditionally, social gerontology has concentrated on the study of the social, economic and demographic characteristics of older people and an ageing population; however, in recent years the definition has expanded to include health, technology and overall lifestyle. The gerontological concepts in this book are therefore taken from a range of disciplines.

Over the last 25 years the social perspective has grown in importance and is reflected by the burgeoning literature and courses in social gerontology. Such courses attract students of social work, occupational therapy, nursing and, geriatric medicine, and students come from backgrounds in sociology, psychology, biology, design, planning and geography.

This book addresses the need for concise, lucid knowledge on what constitutes the 'building blocks' of social gerontology. It provides a review of the core concepts, both classic and emerging, in this subject area.

Students embarking on their journey into social gerontology will find this book particularly relevant, providing a readily accessible guide to key concepts in the discipline. It will cover both theoretical and practical work in the area, presenting concepts that reflect well-established and contested issues, as well as new concepts emerging through cutting-edge research.

Additionally, new research programmes focusing on ageing (e.g. ESRC 'Growing Older' and the 'New Dynamics of Ageing' programmes in the UK, and training programmes funded by the National Institute of Ageing in the USA) have produced a new generation of researchers. There is a need, therefore, for accessible information on the key issues and concepts in gerontology that draws from sound evidence-based research.

It is not only in relation to growing agendas of research but also the impact gerontology has on policy and practice that is also increasing. Ageing is a global issue, as demographic change critically demonstrates. Policy needs an evidence base because governments across the globe are looking for solutions to the challenges of an ageing population and for sound evidence on the effectiveness of policies and practices.

A further consequence of new research in the area is that new concepts have been developed and applied. The field is a dynamic one, drawing on ever-increasing subject areas (e.g. criminology, technology). Over the last 20 years the literature on social gerontology has burgeoned. From a relatively small number of publications, today there are books and journals on every aspect of social ageing. Alongside there has been a growth in courses and programmes on gerontology run by social scientists from a variety of different fields, thus providing a rich tapestry of teaching on gerontology.

In summary, this book will be of particular interest to:

- Students in a variety of undergraduate and postgraduate social science programmes, particularly in gerontology, who need an easily accessible and an appropriately priced book.

- Social and health care students and practitioners: the book will be of interest and relevance as both a core text and reference book for qualified social workers and nurses who are in practice.
- Academics across a wide range of disciplines interested in ageing: the book will provide a valuable source of reference to academic staff and researchers.
- Specialists such as planners (environmental aspects of ageing) and geneticists (biology of ageing): the book will introduce a new audience to aspects of ageing.

The book is organised alphabetically and covers 50 of the key concepts in social gerontology, drawing on a discussion of each concept – its history, application, its usefulness to theory and research as well as its significance in practice. It goes beyond a simple definition of the concept to look at how it has shaped the discipline of social gerontology today and provides a critical evaluation of its application. At the end of each chapter a short list of references is provided. Cross-referencing between concepts is a feature of the book, enabling students to get a broader perspective of the concept. The book is intended to inform debate on particular issues and to set the scene for further exploration of the key issues in ageing. The 50 concepts have been carefully selected on the basis of the currency with which they are used in teaching and research in gerontology. Our selection too is based on the disciplines from which we come – geography and social work (JP); social policy, family sociology and demography (SH-N); and sociology (KA) – and our perspective is primarily western. We are conscious that our chosen concepts have different meanings and understandings in other cultures and the reader should be sensitive to this when assessing different applications of the concept. For example, we have used the terms 'elders' and 'older people' to reflect the cultural contexts in the USA and the UK. Some of the concepts in the book may not focus exclusively on social gerontology, either because they are underrepresented or are newly introduced into gerontology, with a good example being global ageing.

REFERENCES

Walker, A., Address given at the ERA AGE conference in Brussels, February 2008.

Advocacy

> *A process to help older people ensure that their rights and choices are exercised and to enhance self-determination.*

It can be the most vulnerable members of society, such as older people with frailty or physical disability, who find themselves in circumstances where they need an advocate to enable them to make informed choices, to understand the options available to them and to remain in control of their own lives. Advocacy does not involve only services and systems, but also means to help reduce a sense of helplessness, vulnerability, isolation and victimisation (Jones, 2004).

Dunning (1998: 200) defines advocacy as 'People making a case for themselves and advancing their own interests, or representing others and supporting them to secure and exercise their rights on an individual or collective basis. The concept is especially important where people are disadvantaged or discriminated against and are at risk of mistreatment or marginalisation.' At a broader, societal level, advocacy therefore touches upon fundamental principals – social inclusion, equality and social justice (Action for Advocacy 2002).

Advocacy involves two main sets of roles – instrumental and expressive (Dunning, 2005; Wright, 2006). Instrumental roles are more formal and are about 'doing' (e.g. being a spokesperson or representative) whereas expressive roles are more informal and are about 'being' (e.g. a confident, witness or enabler). There is, however, disagreement about the exact form advocacy should take and how it should be practised. Advocacy has many functions and can take various forms. It has been linked with concepts of empowerment, user participation, citizenship, independence and dignity as well as choice. As some advocate, it should be linked to a human rights approach and a broader vision of personhood rather than just a health and social care agenda or consumerism (Dunning, 2005). Crisis or issue-based advocacy, citizen advocacy and self-advocacy are three common models, along with peer (sharing a common experience) or paid advocacy. Professional advocacy is carried out by professionally qualified and paid workers;

lay advocacy can be carried out by family or friends; citizen advocacy is being independent of services, and self-advocacy is 'speaking up for yourself' (Dunning, 1998).

A number of studies into older people's use of advocacy services found that older people had difficulties in understanding what is meant by the term advocacy (Dunning, 2005; Scourfield, 2007; Wright, 2006). The term was regarded as being problematic, confusing or even off-putting for some older people. It was sometimes associated with the legal system, mediation or more general kinds of help and support. Awareness of the presence, purpose and benefits of advocacy is generally acknowledged as being poor, not only by older people but also by other groups that work with older people.

Jones (2004: 7) notes that in the UK in the 1980s and 1990s advocacy services grew as independent voluntary organisations in order to meet the advocacy needs of vulnerable people. Some of these services are generic, working across all vulnerable groups in their community; others support specific groups, for example people with learning difficulties. An underpinning concept is that such services are organisationally independent from the statutory services, and that they focus on the wishes and needs of the client. However, interest in the rights and representation of older people has been a more recent departure. The motivation for advocacy has developed as the need to combat abuse and age discrimination has increased, yet this was slow in developing in relation to older people.

Phillipson (1993: 183) provides some early definitions of advocacy and identifies three general themes of advocacy. It is a way of: meeting human needs, increasing power and participation and responding to intergenerational conflicts.

Dunning (1998: 201–02) further suggests that interest in advocacy with older people stems from other interrelated developments and concerns: the ageing of the population, with the consequential lack of family to act as 'natural advocates'; the legislation, which has placed an emphasis on advocacy and representation; the role of advocacy in the protection of vulnerable adults and the need for advocacy at times of transition when their views may not be heard.

This interest is well illustrated in the UK where successive governments have placed an emphasis on citizens' advocacy and embraced it in major strategies such as 'Valuing People' (Department of Health, 2001), the Health and Social Care Act 2001, the *National Service Framework for Older People* (2001) and the *Care Homes for Older People:*

National Minimum Standards (2003). *Care Homes for Older People: National Minimum Standards* incorporates the provision of information about external agents (such as advocates) in one of those standards. It also indicates an expectation that, in the event of a complaint where an older person lacks capacity, that person should have access to available advocacy services. In 2002 the *Advocacy Charter* was developed as a set of core principles for advocacy and following on from this *A Code of Practice for Advocates* was produced in 2006, both by the organisation Action for Advocacy. However, funding has not readily flowed from such commitments.

Scourfield (2007: 18–19) links the development of advocacy in the UK with New Labour's modernisation agenda and the desire for public policies directed towards older people to promote empowerment, independence, well-being, choice, inclusion, participation, citizenship and dignity. Similarly, there has been a bottom-up emphasis in advocacy originating from diverse disability and mental health service user groups, which have emphasised the importance of advocacy in obtaining rights, inclusion and social justice.

Again, the UK group Action for Advocacy (2008) notes the recent recognition by government of the role of advocacy in safeguarding people's rights and promoting increased choice and control over their lives. However, despite this notable rise and prominence of advocacy in recent government legislation and policy, only a handful of people in specific situations actually have the right to access and advocate, and services are still patchy.

According to Atkinson (1999), although advocacy exists in principle for all user groups, it is far from universal in practice and is not there for everyone who needs it. Access to advocacy is often decided by a combination of factors: historical, geographical and financial. Access starts with the existence of a project in an area, but people need to know about it, who and what it is for, how to reach it and what to expect from the service (Margiotta et al., 2003: 32).

In the UK, advocacy services are also unevenly distributed across the country, with different schemes offering different types of services. Furthermore, there is a growing acceptance that services need to be properly mapped and joined up, not only with each other, but also with similar endeavours such as mediators, councillors and law centres.

A recent survey of advocacy services in Wales (UK) by Age Concern Cymru (2007) suggests that the provision of advocacy services is currently struggling to meet the needs of older people. The report asserts that

advocacy

7

without advocacy, vulnerable older people are more likely to be at risk of abuse, to be unaware of their rights and how to act on them, and are less likely to have their voices heard and their wishes respected.

One of the most prohibitive factors to commissioning advocacy with older people is the lack of a requirement for it in primary legislation. In the UK the Older People's Advocacy Alliance (OPAAL) suggests that this lack of legislation not only makes it more difficult to raise and identify funds for advocacy, but it also weakens the requirement for local authorities to make sure that advocacy is available.

Dunning (1998) suggests that advocacy is a process of empowerment and might accordingly be located within debates around the concepts of power and participation. The concept of advocacy has a direct application in practice with a variety of local and national schemes. Margiotta et al. (2003: 45–6) put forward ten themes that should underpin good practice in advocacy services. These include: 'building up trust; well trained coordinator and volunteer advocates; effective communication between health and social care professionals so the advocate is understood; independence of the advocate; a one-to-one relationship in which the advocate represents their partner alone; allegiance; unpaid with the consequences of no allegiance to an employer; a long-term relationship and citizen advocates to be drawn from diverse backgrounds; and finally standards of practice and monitoring of the service.'

Older people are not a homogeneous group and may need different advocacy at different times (Dunning, 2005). The evidence suggests that the capacity and quality of what is available can also be patchy. Some groups are not well covered with advocacy services, such as older people from black and ethnic minority groups. Advocacy in relation to people with dementia has raised issues of communication, consent and ethics, and has highlighted the need for a person-centred approach, reflecting on the older person's history.

See also: Ageing, Care, Dementia, Disability, Frailty, Independence

key concepts in
social gerontology

REFERENCES

Dunning, A. (1998) Advocacy, empowerment and older people, in M. Bernard and J. Phillips (eds), *The Social Policy of Old Age*. London: CPA Publications. Chapter 12: 200–221.

Dunning, A. (2005) *Information, Advice and Advocacy for Older People: Defining and Developing Services*. York: Joseph Rowntree Foundation.

Age Integration

Where people's entry, exit and performance in basic social institutions such as education, work and retirement are no longer constrained by age.

Age integration refers to a structure where roles in various institutional settings may vary, and are not dictated by whether one is young, middle aged or old. It is often contrasted with the term 'age segregation', which draws attention to the social barriers that exist with regard to age norms and related acceptable roles in education, work or leisure activities.

Age integration is a concept that was presented as an ideal type of societal structure by Riley and Riley (1994a, 1994b) to address the problem of structural lag. Almost two decades ago Matilda White Riley (1988) introduced the concept of structural lag, suggesting that (1) the ageing process changes as society changes; and (2) discrepancies exist between an increasingly healthy older population and the ability of societal institutions to provide meaningful, adequate pathways for continued social activity. In other words, life expectancies are greater than ever, accompanied by good health, yet the absence of role opportunities continues to pose a challenge to ageing societies. Highlighting the significance of the social environment to mental and physical health, the structural lag concept encapsulates the disconnection between growing numbers of 'long-lived' people and the lack of available role opportunities (Riley, 1988; Riley and Riley, 1989). Trends in population ageing and morbidity compression are societal-level transitions that suggest a need for re-evaluating how we think about ageing, and hence the idea of age integration emerged as one pathway by which to alleviate the problem of structural lag.

The notion of age integration builds from earlier work suggesting that societies adopt a system whereby individuals have flexibility with regard to the time they spend in activities of work, education and leisure (Best, 1980; Rehn, 1977).

Age integration would lead to the possibility of more flexibility in roles across the life span. Today it is more acceptable for the young to occupy educational settings, the middle aged to dominate in the workplace, and then older individuals to pursue leisure activity. Using ideal typologies, Riley and Riley (2000) suggest breaking down structural barriers that exist with regard to age norms and related acceptable roles in education or work, and instead propose an age integrated structure in society where roles in education and work may vary, not dictated by whether one is young, middle aged or old. The concept of age integration suggests that full-time work would give way to part-time work, with such responsibilities spread across all ages. Ideally, institutions become integrated as well. Workplaces begin to provide educational facilities for employees or provide child care. Or at the other pole, people increasingly begin to work from home, hence integrating work, family and leisurely pursuits. Riley and Riley (1994a) also suggest that values will change in an age-integrated society. New meanings will arise out of flexible life experience, where economic competition and achievement will lose meaning and be replaced by value in high-quality social relations, contributions to society and personal fulfilment.

Naturally, potential abuses could emerge from a society organised around the concept of age integration. Entitlement programmes to support older people may receive negative attention, jeopardising the security afforded to older people who simply do not wish to work, or are prohibited from working due to health challenges. The tenets of age integration offer a novel approach to the way society is organised, yet challenges remain as to how to ensure that the labour of elders (and children) are not exploited.

Age integration provides an interesting approach by which to organise major societal institutions, and some suggest that social relations provide a pathway by which to achieve such integration. Hagestad and Uhlenberg (2005) address the topic of age integration by arguing that structural lag persists in part because of the ongoing cycle between age-specific settings/activities and negative attitudes/behaviours towards elders. They suggest that social networks in particular possess qualities that both perpetuate the cycle and offer the potential to break it.

Consider the following situation: A 30 year-old woman takes her 74 year-old grandmother on a vacation to their ancestral homeland. One evening, the granddaughter and her husband plan an evening out at a lively nightclub, where festivities do not being until 11 pm. Knowing they will be gone until 4 am, the young woman informs her grandmother it is best she does not accompany them, as it will be too late a night for the older woman. Her grandmother instantly gets dressed for the evening and insists on joining them. The young woman and her husband reluctantly take her along, where they join other family members.

As the evening progressed, it was the young woman and her age peer relatives who could not remain awake, falling asleep at the table. The 74 year-old woman later chastised her granddaughter for assuming that it was she who would not be able to stay awake.

Families are often portrayed as the ideal age-integrated context, ensuring regular and frequent interactions between generations and also suppressing any potential for conflict regarding aged-based welfare policy (Attias-Donfut, 2000; Walker, 2000). The family frequently serves as a conduit between the older individual and role opportunities with other social institutions (Hagestad and Uhlenberg, 2005; Hareven, 1994, 2000). Family relations, and in particular the affective nature of family relations, have the potential to provide initial clues into creating diverse roles for people across the life course.

Obstacles to continued roles may occur through either formal rules or informal taken-for-granted assumptions. Social relations that unfold within a family context may represent the only truly age-integrated network in which people are enmeshed, and hence provide an ideal setting to contemplate the changing characteristics of population ageing. The idea of age integration holds promise for how societies might effectively address the situation of increasing numbers of older people who are healthy.

See also: *Ageing, Family Relations, Population Ageing, Social Relations*

REFERENCES

Attias-Donfut, C. (2000) Cultural and economic transfers between generations: one aspect of age integration. *The Gerontologist*, 40: 270–272.

Best, F. (1980) *Flexible Life Scheduling*. New York: Praeger.

Hagestad, G. O. and Uhlenberg, P. (2005) The social separation of old and young: a root of ageism. *Journal of Social Issues*, 61: 343–360.

Hareven, T. K. (1994) Family change and historical change: an uneasy relationship, in M. W. Riley, R. Kahn and A. Foner (eds), *Age and Structural Lag: Society's Failure to Provide Meaningful Opportunities for Work, Family and Leisure*. New York: Wiley. pp. 130–151.

Hareven, T. K. (2000) *Families, History, and Social Change*. Boulder, CO: Westview Press.

Rehn, G. (1977) Towards a society of free choice, in J. J. Watts and R. Rose (eds), *Comparing Public Policies*. Wroclaw: Ossolineum.

Riley, M. W. (1988) The ageing society: problems and prospects. *Proceedings of the American Philosophical Society*, 132: 148–153.

Riley, M. W. and Riley, J. W. (1989) The lives of older people and changing social roles. *Annals of the American Academy of Political and Social Science, The Quality of Ageing: Strategies for interventions*, 503: 14–28.

age integration

11

Riley, M. W. and Riley, J. W. (1994a) Structural lag: past and future, in M. W. Riley, R. L. Kahn and A. Foner (eds), *Age and Structural Lag: Society's Failure to Provide Meaningful Opportunities for Work, Family and Leisure*. New York: Wiley. pp. 15–36.

Riley, M. W. and Riley, J. W. (1994b) Age integration and the lives of older people. *The Gerontologist*, 34: 110–115.

Riley, M. W. and Riley, J. W. (2000) Age integration: conceptual and historical background. *The Gerontologist*, 40: 266–270.

Walker, A. (2000) Public policy and the construction of old age in Europe. *The Gerontologist*, 40: 304–308.

Ageing

A process whereby people accumulate years and progressively experience changes to their biological, social and psychological functioning as they move through different phases of the life course.

Four dimensions of ageing are commonly identified: chronological, biological, psychological and social ageing. Chronological ageing refers to the number of years since someone was born, but is generally not recognised as an adequate measure of the extent of ageing because, as a process, it is thought to vary between individuals. Chronological age also provides individuals with a means of distinguishing roles and relationships in terms of the behaviour and expectations that are linked to different chronological groupings. Biological ageing, often known as senescence (declines of a cell or organism due to ageing) and sometimes functional ageing, refers to biological events occurring across time which progressively impair the physiological system so that the organism becomes less able to withstand disease, ultimately increasing its susceptibility to death. From this perspective, the ageing process stems from several physiological factors, and is modified throughout the life course by environmental factors (such as nutrition), experiences of disease, genetic factors and life stage. Psychological ageing focuses upon changes that occur during adulthood to an individual's personality, mental functioning (e.g. memory, learning and intelligence) and sensory and perceptual processes. Social ageing refers to the changing experiences that individuals will encounter in their roles and relationships with other people and as members of broader social structures (such as a religious group) as they pass through different phases of their life course. As an individual experience, social ageing affects perceptions of who we are, but can also be shaped or 'constructed' by social and cultural contexts which dictate the normative expectations about the roles, positions and behaviour of older people in society. While all three dimensions of biological, social and psychological ageing generally interact, the pace at which each dimension is experienced may be different for the same individual.

Finally, population ageing, sometimes referred to as societal ageing, is a process whereby a group (such as a country or an ethnic group) experiences the progressive increase in the actual numbers and proportion of older people within its total population. This change, brought about largely by socio-economic improvements in health and living standards, progressively reduces mortality and fertility, resulting in increased life expectancy and fewer births, and ultimately, an increase in the older population in relation to younger age groups. Population ageing has long-term implications for governments in terms, for example, of the cost of health and social care for an increasingly important number of older people.

Our fascination with understanding the processes of ageing, the decline of the ageing body and the quest to prolong life has been a source of inquiry for thousands of years, and has been represented in various civilisations through the antediluvian, hyperborean and foundation themes – believing that in the past individuals lived much longer, that in some parts of the world people do actually live very long lives and, lastly, that certain substances have the capacity to prolong life. The search for the causes of ageing in western culture appear as early as the Greco-Roman period, with Hippocrates' theory of ageing, which was based on the idea that an innate heat was essential to life, and that as people aged, it would diminish as part of the natural course of life. Later, Aristotle carried this theory further by comparing the innate heat to a fire, and hence to something that could be extinguished or exhausted. The onset of the scientific era spurned further inquiry, for example with Bacon's quest to identify the laws governing the ageing process during the 1600s and later during the 1700s with Benjamin Franklin's interest in rejuvenation. Galton's data, collected during the 1800s, demonstrated that many human attributes varied depending upon age, and during the 1900s, biologists such as Pearl contributed to an investigation of the hereditary nature of longevity (Birren and Clayton, 1975). During the first part of the twentieth century, large-scale studies of the ageing process were largely of medical orientation, but its social dimensions were also beginning to draw interest; in the UK, for example, in 1947 the Rowntree Committee's study on the *Problems of Ageing and the Care of Older People* was published (The Nuffield Foundation, 1947).

These developments formed the basis of what was to become the scientific study of ageing during the 1970s, which has subsequently emerged as a multidisciplinary field. Psychological perspectives have improved understanding of how attitudes towards ageing influence later life experiences, and how older people themselves perceive and interpret the ageing process. A particular focus has been on establishing how older people deal with the experience of ageing and what strategies they adopt to cope with changes to health, psychological functioning, social relationships and material circumstances. Theoretical advances suggest that as they age, people become selective about the activities they undertake, developing strategies to optimise their abilities (Baltes and Baltes, 1990) or actively changing the environment in which they live, readjusting their goals to make them easier to achieve. More recently, there has been an interest in exploring the place of communication in the ageing process which is both an individual and an interactive process (Nussbaum and Coupland, 2004).

Bernard et al. (2000) suggest that the study of social ageing has recently benefited from the work of critical gerontologists who have raised awareness of the role that the welfare state may play in increasing economic dependency and social marginalisation in later life, and from postmodern theorists who have challenged the conception of the ageing experience as one characterised by a progressive loss of meaning to life, also highlighting the pervasiveness of ageist attitudes and expectations. Bernard et al. suggest that along with biographical perspectives, which have helped to demonstrate how diverse the ageing experience is and how it mirrors a lifetime of other experiences, these different strands have highlighted many implications of the ageing experience, particularly for women, in areas such as employment, income, wellbeing, and the various dimensions of caring.

Among the numerous advances in the biology of ageing have been attempts to distinguish physiological from pathological ageing and the development of 'biomarkers' as a means of measuring the rate of ageing.

Several theories, notably theories of the evolution of ageing, seek to explain the effects of senescence on the body, why ageing occurs, what genes contribute to the process and how the human genome is affected by natural selection. It is now established that manipulating both the environment and the genetic make-up of human beings can alter life expectancy and the maximum duration of the life span, innovations which raise the question of whether the process of biological ageing itself can be delayed or even reversed. Studying how genetics may influence the ageing process and longevity raises several questions, notably why the human organism should need to age once it has fulfilled its functions of reproduction (an evolutionary perspective) and whether it will be possible or desirable to intervene and change the rate of ageing and its causes (Moody, 2006).

A more recent focus on ageing has been to view it as a dynamic rather than a static process, as people move through different stages and transitions of the life course. This has led to a growing diversity of methodological approaches in the field, including longitudinal and event history analyses which track the paths or transitions that individuals and groups follow as part of the ageing process, and help distinguish age, period or cohort effects. The increased availability of large, often cross-nationally comparable data sets has also meant that significant developments have been made in distinguishing both culturally specific and historically determined aspects of the ageing process (Morgan and Kunkel, 1998). In the field of biological ageing, for example, the development of longitudinal studies has been used to identify physiological functions or 'biomarkers', biological indicators which help identify the key features of the basic ageing process, such as a person's ability to hear.

In addition to theory and method, ageing has been the object of interventions in various fields. Health interventions, such as exercise programmes for example, have been designed to address the physiological declines resulting from disuse of the body; and from psychology, intervention strategies are now available to help older people learn and remember better. Research on the brain, behaviour and ageing has highlighted the importance of interventions which facilitate environmental stimulation for older people, in the case of stroke victims for example, and the use of environmental prosthetics now provides a means of adapting the physical environment to fit the needs of older people who experience sensory deficits. From a social policy perspective, the engagement of policy makers, planners and legislators has enabled the development and implementation of strategies to address, in particular, issues of ageism and age discrimination which intensify with the ageing process.

Hence, as a complex, multidimensional phenomenon, the concept of ageing brings with it many questions – ranging from how societies can challenge ageism or use intervention strategies most effectively to maximise cognitive and functional capacities, to understanding whether the biological and environmental determinants of ageing can be fully understood and mastered in order to provide the means of resolving an age-old desire, that of prolonging the duration of human life. What seems to underpin all these questions, however, is whether our goal should be to promote the quality of the ageing experience or rather to pursue the long-standing quest of prolonging human life.

See also: *Ageism, Cohort, Longevity, Population Ageing*

FURTHER READING

O'Hanlon and Coleman (2004) provide a very good review of the different approaches to understanding attitudes to ageing.
O'Hanlon, A. and Coleman, P. (2004) Attitudes towards ageing: adaption, development and growth into later years, in J. Nussbaum and J. Coupland (eds), *Handbook of Communication and Ageing Research* (2nd edition). Mahwah, NJ: Lawrence Erlbaum Associates. pp. 31–63.

REFERENCES

Baltes, P. B. and Baltes, M. M. (1990) *Successful Ageing: Perspectives from the Behavioural Sciences.* Cambridge: Cambridge University Press.
Bernard, M., Chambers, P. and Granville, G. (2000) Women ageing: changing identities, challenging myths, in M. Brenard, J. Phillips, L. Machin and V. Davies (eds), *Women Ageing: Changing Identities, Challenging Myths.* London: Routledge. pp. 1–22.
Birren, J. and Clayton, V. (1975) History of gerontology, in D. Woodruff and J. Birrenn (eds), *Ageing: Scientific Perspectives and Social Issues.* London: D. van Nostrand Company. pp. 15–27.
Moody, H. (2006) *Ageing: Concepts and Controversies* (5th edition). Thousand Oaks, CA: Pine Forge Press.
Morgan, L. and Kunkel, S. (1998) *Ageing: The Social Context.* Thousand Oaks, CA: Pine Forge Press.
The Nuffield Foundation (1947) *Survey Committee on the Problems of Ageing and the Care of Old People.* London: Oxford University Press.
Nussbaum, J. and Coupland, J. (eds) (2004) *Handbook of Communication and Ageing Research* (2nd edition). Mahwah, NJ: Lawrence Erlbaum Associates.

key concepts in
social gerontology

Ageing in Place

Growing older without having to move home.

Ageing in place is a concept that allows people to live independently by receiving services as needs change. As such it represents a transaction between an ageing individual and his or her residential environment that is characterised by changes in both the person and environment over time, with the physical location of the person being the only constant (Lawton, 1989).

Remaining in one's home for as long as possible has become synonymous with well-being, quality of life, independence and autonomy, and is often discussed in conjunction with 'attachment to place' and 'meaning of home'. Home as a place of shared memories and resources is a strong reason why people prefer to age in place. Two factors have caused ageing in place to emerge as a salient concern of gerontological policy makers. The first is the explosive growth of homeownership after the Second World War; the second is that 'home has re-emerged as a key site for the provision and consumption of care' (Wiles, 2005: 81).

Two of the main commentators of place attachment are Rowles and Rubenstein. Graham Rowles' (1978) study *Prisoners of Space* focuses on the insidedness of place in terms of *social insidedness* and *physical insidedness*, the former describing the habitual social exchanges within the home and the latter the familiaristic and routine of the home environment. Taking a more micro approach in the meaning of home, Rubenstein (1989) links people and place through *social-centred* (norms and relationship to others), *person-centred* (the expression of the life course in the environment) and *body-centred processes* (relating to the body). All three enable an understanding of the meaning of home to older people and the policy thrust to 'age in place'.

Means (2007: 66–7) suggests that 'ageing in place' has been the policy of all UK governments at least as far back as the agricultural and industrial revolutions and traces developments from the 'workhouse' until the present day – 'ageing in place' can, therefore, be argued to be a seamless and almost endless policy commitment' (Means, 2007: 67). Developments in community care in the 1980s reinforced ordinary housing as the location for care rather than the institution. This drive was partly due to the cost of institutional care and the notion that community care would be less expensive primarily because it rested on the commitment of women as carers within the family to provide care.

Yet as Wiles (2005) argues, with greater political and public interest in the idea of 'ageing in place' we need a critical engagement with the idea of home as a social and spatial context for ageing. Homes require emotional, physical and social work to become sites of care and to be desirable. As Milligan (2005) also points out, 'home' can also include a care-home setting.

It is not only policy, but also its translation into practice that has driven this concept. There are many housing initiatives/interventions that support the concept of 'ageing in place', and to support older peoples' usual preferences to 'stay put' in their homes rather than having to move into institutions. These include: 'housing with care for later life', 'Assisted Living', 'Staying Put Programmes' and 'Independent Living'. These allow older people to remain as tenants, owners or leaseholders, with an additional 'care component' attached which can address a spectrum of needs from very low to very high dependency levels that might have formerly resulted in an admission to residential care. Thus, these initiatives/ interventions are often promoted as 'Homes for Life'. However, although by definition, most of these schemes offer the chance to 'age in place', for many of them you must first move into a new residence to 'start ageing', that is many Independent Living, Assisted Living schemes offer the chance to 'age in place' but an older person must move there first.

Other initiatives involve governments developing home maintenance and modification services. These recognise that many older people, especially if they are frail, have concerns about dealing with tradespeople, specifically including the financial side of repairs (care and repair/ handy-person schemes) and equity release schemes. These programmes are all aimed at allowing older people to remain at home for as long as possible through physical modification or equipment and increasingly through the use of technologies in the home. However, such schemes may be less than ideal.

'Lifetime Homes and Lifetime Neighbourhoods' is a concept which is also based on the positives of the concept of 'ageing in place'. Standards introduced in the UK in 2008, for example, for all new housing are based on the premise that all such housing should be accessible and adaptable for everyone throughout their lives and as needs change. A National Strategy for Housing in an Ageing Society (*Lifetime Homes and Lifetime Neighbourhoods* [Department for Communities and Local Government, Departmant of Health and Department for Work and Pensions, 2008]) draws attention to the importance of design and standards in achieving ageing in place at both a micro (housing) and macro (eco-town) level.

The advantages of living and growing older in place are that people may have lived in the same place all their lives and prefer to remain within their community. There is also a continuity in the sense of privacy and control in one's own home. The disadvantages of ageing in place as a goal are that it is used as a blanket policy with little consideration of the suitability of that place. Even though there is evidence of lack of fit between the person and their environment, some studies show that even in deprived communities older people have a preference to stay put (Scharf et al., 2002). However, in many suburban communities, for example where public transportation is lacking, ageing in place may not be the ideal or may require infrastructure that is suited to an ageing population. Although older people may 'stay put', the environment around them can also change as in-migrants settle or industry is built around them.

Technologies have increasingly enabled older people to age in place. A number of 'smart' homes and technologies are emerging which are aimed specifically at ageing in place (Lawson et al., 2007), such as wireless remote technologies. However, most are often demonstration projects and cost prohibits their general mainstreaming, and it is particularly difficult to retrofit many homes. Acceptability of such technologies is also an issue (Lawson et al., 2007).

Critics argue that ageing in place has been described as a slogan, a non-theoretical commonsense concept, seen as a single cure for all problems (Means, 2007). Yet research (Means, 2007) illustrates the problematic nature of ageing in place for certain groups of people – those who are homeless, who may never have an attachment to place or a specific home; those in the private rented sector who may lack security; and those with dementia, whose quality of life may be improved by a move to alternative accommodation. As Lawton (1977: 277) comments, 'no matter where an older person lives … the physical environment should maximize the person's independence, choices, opportunities for social interaction, privacy, safety and security'. Ageing in place therefore should be one of many options, not the only choice (Means, 2007).

Heumann and Boldy (1993: 26) see limitations to the concept:

In some cases, the building is sound, but too large or contains too many barriers for a frail person to manage and special adaptation for a single individual is cost prohibitive.

Sometimes, the building is adequate, but the surrounding neighbourhood is dangerous or deteriorated by nearby environmental pollutants, loss of public infrastructure, or high crime rates.

Even when housing and social environments are conducive to ageing in place, the local economy may not be able to accommodate its elderly population, if the only option is visiting support services to persons scattered throughout the community. This can be true for some urban areas as well as the more obvious situation in rural areas.

If 'ageing in place' is to become a reality, then a wide variety of housing choices that fit the needs of the local ageing population and serve the full continuum of assisted independent living and, secondly, a comprehensive and holistic approach to the support needs of an ageing individual and ageing community need to be in place. In the British context, the provision of home care even for older people with complex needs or reciprocal care (childcare for shopping) is crucial if 'ageing in place' is to be a sustained concept working in practice.

Focusing on 'place' also gives us a better understanding of the concept. The individual's perception of the environment is crucial in terms of their actions within it. Moving the concept to the 'theory of place' also broadens it to a more macro level, focusing on neighbourhoods and communities where social interaction can be accommodated in the definition of ageing in place. The concepts of space and place, as developed by geographers, could lead to a more nuanced debate around 'ageing in place' (Andrews et al., 2007), viewing place as a kind of dynamic, negotiated and complex process (Wiles, 2005) with meaning (Tuan, 1977) and which shapes the intimate relationships between people.

The concept of 'ageing in place' can refer to attachment to more than one place and can be a complex process with regard to migration, whereby 'the older adult continually re-integrates with place in the face of change and uncertainty through creative and social actions that foster meaning and identity' (Andrews et al., 2007: 52).

The concept of 'ageing in place' has been considerably influential in gerontology as well as mainstream policy on care for older people, yet it requires careful investigation in relation to its almost universal acceptance as a good thing for older people.

See also: *Ageing, Assisted Living, Care, Dementia, Housing, Independence, Quality of Life*

REFERENCES

Department for Communities and Local Government, Department of Health and Department for Work and Pensions (2008) *Lifetime Homes, Lifetime Neighbourhoods: A National Strategy for Housing an Ageing Society.* London: Department for Communities and Local Government.

Rowles, G. (1978) *Prisoners of Space.* Boulder, CO: Westview Press.

Scharf, T., Phillipson, C. Smith, A. and Kingston, P. (2002) *Growing Older in Socially Deprived Areas: Social Exclusion in Later Life.* London: Help the Aged.

Wiles, J. (2005) Conceptualizing place in the care of older people: the contributions of geographical gerontology. *International Journal of Older People Nursing* in association with *Journal of Clinical Nursing,* 14(8b): 100–108.

Ageism

The practice of evaluating individuals or groups identified as old in a negative manner.

Ageism is increasingly an issue that older adults face (Butler, 1990; Palmore, 2001). Often compared to the other 'isms' that exist, including racism and sexism, ageism is unique because, as Palmore (2001) rightly points out, every individual has the potential to experience discrimination or prejudice based on their age if they live long enough. It produces an 'othering' effect that lumps all those considered old into a category defined, first, as different and, secondly, as inferior. More importantly, it suggests that all old people are alike, hence obscuring differences that exists among and between older persons.

The origins of ageism are discussed in both psychological and social terms. For instance, ageism as a product of psychological forces is put forth in the theory of terror management. Martens, Goldenberg and Greenberg (2005) suggest that the unconscious concern with death and frailty motivates individuals to use cultural systems of beliefs to maintain a positive sense of self. As a result, individuals devalue old age as a means to cope with the threat of death. Others highlight the social origins of ageism, emphasising the importance of social roles (Cuddy et al., 2005; Hagestad and Uhlenburg, 2005; Kite et al., 2005). Moreover, the interactional dynamic of ageism is acknowledged, including research that suggests that the more individuals watch television, the more likely they are to perceive elders in negative terms (Donlon et al., 2005).

The existence of ageism runs through academic efforts as well. Disengagement theory, or the proposition that as people age they willingly withdraw from social life (and wider society supports such a withdrawal) was the first theory developed in the field of social gerontology (Cummings and Henry, 1961). It was later challenged by competing theories postulating that growing older does not necessitate social withdrawal and indeed may include many positive experiences (e.g. activity theory, continuity theory, etc.). The most recent critique suggests that the language that social gerontologists use to refer to their topic of study may promote ageism within the field (Palmore, 2000). The most common words used to reference the general topic of inquiry are loaded with negative connotations. Palmore critiques the use of the following terms: ageing, old, elderly. The term *ageing* is synonymous with decline, often encompassing a range of situations including deterioration, chronic illness and a failure to thrive. The word *old* derives from the Latin root *alere*, which means to grow or nourish; however, the connotations are usually negative, equated with words such as antiquated, archaic, frail and behind the times. Finally, the word *elderly* implies frailty, disability and/or senility. In response, Palmore suggests that social gerontologists be cautious with the language they apply to their areas of research. In particular, he advocates that people use the word they mean to convey, for example senile instead of old, or deterioration instead of ageing. Additionally, Palmore suggests neutral or positive terminology that social gerontologists may want to consider adopting in their scientific writing. Suggested neutral terms include: *older persons, retired person, grandparent* or *persons over 60*, for example. Words with positive connotations one may want to consider in ordinary writing or conversation include *senior, elder* or *veteran*.

Other suggestions to combat ageism draw from the social aspects of chronological age. Bytheway (2005) argues that research that uses chronological age to classify people is central to the aim of documenting and challenging ageist policies, attitudes and behaviours. On the other hand, chronological designations obscure heterogeneity within age groups, and promote distance between those chronologically identified as the oldest-old, for example, and the rest of the population. Bytheway ultimately suggests finding other ways besides chronological age to study ageing, including a focus on role transitions, or to subscribe to subjective age identities (i.e. allow the research participants themselves to define old age). Hagestad and Uhlenburg (2005) suggest that choronological age informs policy decisions in post-industrial society, leading to spatial, institutional and cultural separations between age groups. Such separation leads to age segregation which constitutes an important phenomenon for understanding the existence and prevalence of ageism within a society. Social networks, both structurally and functionally, are identified as playing a key role to potentially reinforce or ideally to eradicate ageist attitudes and behaviours.

Bias against individuals or groups because of chronological age also differs from classic 'isms' because it generally operates as an unacknowledged force in the wider society. Whereas racism and sexism are to some extent recognised as a problem, even if not all have the ability to identify their own individual bias against another race or gender, ageism is rarely publicly discussed. Ageism represents a pervasive, yet rather uncritically analysed force that exists within societies.

A survey instrument listing 20 types of ageism has been developed to measure its prevalence in various societies (Palmore, 2001). Specifically, it provides a means to answer three questions: What is the prevalence of ageism in various societies? Which types of ageism are more prevalent? Which subgroups of older people report more ageism? A small study carried out using this instrument gathered data from 84 persons between the ages of 60 and 93. The survey found that 77% of the respondents reported experiencing ageism at least once, and over half of the incidents were reported to have occurred 'more than once'. The most frequently reported types of ageism involved being subjugated to prejudiced attitudes, including disrespect and assuming that health problems were caused by age. Very few reported outright discrimination. No differences emerged with regard to gender or age (above or below age 75); however, those with lower levels of education reported higher incidents of ageism.

This may aid in reducing the prevalence of ageism in our society, yet weaknesses with this measure exist. Cohen (2001) points out that the item asking about whether an elder has 'been poked fun at' because of their age is too broad to be meaningful. For instance, humour in the form of jokes may be used to relieve tensions surrounding a sensitive issue as well as to denigrate a group. The one statement elders are asked to respond to does not differentiate between those two aims. Furthermore, the items developed detect perceptions of ageism, and hence do not pick up on whether or not it objectively occurred. For instance, Cohen suggests that an elder may be the recipient of an ageist attitude/act, but may not recognise it as such. Additionally, the instrument captures more outright, explicit expressions of ageism. More prevalent are the implicit, subtle forms of ageism, both those negative, unconscious thoughts and attitudes that individuals carry within (including self-stereotypes) as well as enacted negative behaviours towards an older person (Levy, 2001). Levy raises the significance of implicit ageism, and the difficulty of measuring it.

Ageism is addressed most often in advanced industrialised societies. Still needed are critical applications of ageism and the study of age bias in cultures where tradition orders the greater part of arrangements for older individuals.

See also: *Ageing, Disability, Frailty, Gender, Geronotology*

REFERENCES

Butler, R. (1990) A disease called ageism. *Journal of the American Geriatrics Society*, 38: 178–180.

Bytheway, B. (2005) Ageism and age categorization. *Journal of Social Issues*, 61: 375–388.

Cohen E. S. (2001) The complex nature of ageism: What is it? Who does it? Who perceives it? *The Gerontologist*, 41(5): 576–577.

Cuddy, A. J. C., Norton, M. I. and Fiske, S. T. (2005) This old stereotype: the pervasiveness and persistence of the elderly stereotype. *Journal of Social Issues*, 61: 267–286.

Cumming, E. and Henry, W. E. (1961) *Growing Old: The Process of Disengagement.* New York: Basic Books.

Donlon, M. M., Ashman, O. and Levy, B. R. (2005) Re-vision of older television characters: a stereotype-awareness intervention. *Journal of Social Issues*, 61: 307–320.

Hagestad, G. O. and Uhlenberg, P. (2005) The social separation of old and young: the root of ageism. *Journal of Social Issues*, 61: 343–360.

Kite, M. E., Stockdale, G. D., Whitley, B. E. and Johnson, B. (2005) Attitudes toward younger and older adults: an updated meta-analytic review. *Journal of Social Issues*, 61: 241–266.

Levy, B. R. (2001) Eradication of ageism requires addressing the enemy within. *The Gerontologist*, 41(5): 578–579.

key concepts in social gerontology

Martens, A., Goldenberg, J. L. and Greenberg, J. (2005) A terror management perspective on ageism. *Journal of Social Issues*, 61: 223–240.

Palmore, E. (2000) Ageism in gerontological language. *The Gerontologist*, 40(6): 645.

Palmore, E. (2001) The Ageism Survey: first findings. *The Gerontologist*, 41(5): 572–575.

Ambivalence

> *Feelings of tension, contradiction and uncertainty experienced by people when they are caught between competing pressures to deal with the social, personal and family needs or expectations of support from others.*

In concrete terms, ambivalence may occur in family relationships when individuals want to be autonomous but also realise that they are dependent on others – for older people this may equate to a situation where they lose physical autonomy but want to remain living independently at home. Equally, ambivalence may occur when people's normative attitudes and behaviour are brought into question with regard to the relationships they have with other family members – should someone continue to provide support to an older parent who is chronically ill or should this be the responsibility of more highly skilled professionals? Likewise, an individual may feel ambivalent about the most appropriate behaviour or attitude to adopt if they find themselves assuming a role which is incompatible with their own personal needs – being a carer for an older person at the same time as being a paid worker in the labour force, for example.

The notion of ambivalence has recently become the subject of renewed investigation by social gerontologists interested in the field of family relationships, particularly those between parents and adult offspring, but it has been the object of sociological, postmodern and feminist theorising for much longer. Sociological ambivalence refers to incompatible normative expectations, attitudes and beliefs which place people in situations where they experience contradictory expectations about the social roles and statuses they occupy. These contradictions are

ambivalence

25

perceived to be a natural part of human nature essentially because all social relations have both rational and ambiguous dimensions – freedom and constraint or independence and dependence, for example. From a postmodern perspective, ambivalence reflects the expectation that changes in society will make social relationships less certain, more diverse and more complex so that we will have increasingly contradictory expectations about life – people will want to exercise personal autonomy and freedom of choice for example, but will also expect support from social institutions such as the welfare state (Lüscher and Pillemer, 1998). Feminist theoretical traditions highlight the conflicting and contradictory nature of contemporary family relations and role expectations, which in themselves point to ambivalence – for example, the recognition that women's household labour and caring activities can be both oppressive and alienating but also meaningful if seen as acts of caring and dedication to others. In the field of psychology, ambivalence is recognised in contexts where individuals experience simultaneous but opposing sentiments for someone, like love and hatred.

Over the past two decades, the concept of intergenerational ambivalence has been introduced to the field of intergenerational relations in an attempt to address criticism of the intergenerational solidarity–conflict model developed by Vern Bengtson et al. (2002) which has provided the theoretical and empirical basis for the analysis of family ties between older parents and their adult children. This model has been criticised for portraying intergenerational relations in terms of two poles or extremes of either harmony or conflict and for overlooking the possibility that social ties between family members may be characterised by uncertainty and risk. With the elaboration of the concept of ambivalence, primarily associated with the work of Lüscher and Pillemer (1998), a second framework known as the intergenerational ambivalence model has now emerged. Here ambivalence is seen as an organising concept which can be used to describe the contradictory nature of family relationships (Pillemer and Lüscher 2004). These authors have argued that ambivalence needs to be understood in terms of two dimensions, sociological ambivalence and psychological ambivalence. The former situates the concept in relation to social structures at the macro level which are influential in shaping normative expectations about roles or status for example, while psychological ambivalence relates to experiences at the subjective, micro level in terms of cognitions, emotions and motivations. Refined in this way, the concept of intergenerational ambivalence suggests that parents and adult children will experience contradictions in their relationships because they encounter feelings of harmony and conflict simultaneously.

Subsequently, the concept of intergenerational ambivalence has been refined as a heuristic model of social relations (Lüscher, 2002), portraying families at the macro level as institutions which transmit broader societal values and beliefs to their members. As such, families have the capacity to either reproduce, or conversely, change these values and beliefs; structural ambivalence therefore occurs when both reproduction and innovation co-exist. Similarly, but on the scale of micro-level interactions, intersubjective ambivalence will occur when family members experience both convergent and divergent feelings–wanting to identify with the family, but also wanting to preserve an individual and separate identity from it.

The concept of intergenerational ambivalence has been the subject of further empirical investigation, notably in the recent cross-national comparative study Old Age and Autonomy: the role of service systems and intergenerational family solidarity (OASIS), which focused in part on establishing how individuals and families cope when older members are at risk of dependency (Lowenstein and Ogg, 2003). Drawing on various data sources, other studies have provided empirical investigation or validation of the concept: in the context of divorce for gay and lesbian relationships (Connidis and McMullin, 2002); in relation to the life course (Hillcoat-Nallétamby and Phillips, 2007); establishing typologies of parent-adult child relationships (van Gaalen and Dykstra, 2006); estimating levels of ambivalence in these relationships (Phillips et al., 2003); studying parent care by adults in Germany (Lorenz-Meyer, 2004); testing the solidarity–conflict and ambivalence frameworks in relation to quality of life for older people (Lowenstein, 2007); and assessing its relevance in multi-cultural, non-western contexts (Hillcoat-Nallétamby, under review).

The conceptual and theoretical bases of the intergenerational ambivalence model have been the subject of some debate and criticism among social gerontologists, so much so that it was the subject of a special edition of the *Journal of Marriage and Family* in 2002. Lüscher himself points to ways in which the study of ambivalence in relation to intergenerational relations can be advanced: shifting the focus from only one individual to an individual within a group with the aim of clarifying the interplay of social roles; considering ambivalence in a structural context of more than two generations and conceiving it in regard to specific activities; and addressing the concept's shortcoming as a static notion, which fails to take into account life course transitions. Connidis and McMullin (2002) argue that sociological ambivalence needs to be reconceptualised. Drawing on the theoretical traditions of critical theory and symbolic interactionism, they have argued that ambivalence needs to reflect the tensions and contradictions inherent to the structured dimensions of social relations (e.g. gender, race, age), how these contradictions are reproduced at the micro level, for example in family relations, and how as actors and agents of social change, people respond to them as they manage their relationships with others. This criticism points to the argument that ambivalence can be viewed as a bridging concept which aptly describes social interactions as the sum of both individual action (or agency) and the effect of structured social relations. Bengtson et al. (2002) have challenged Connidis and McMullin's theoretical reconceptualisation, arguing that it neither manages to link individual agency and social structure, nor reflects any significant developments of established theory and concepts such as the traditional symbolic interactionist approaches to role theory.

Whether the concept of ambivalence actually differs from that of conflict, and can even be accommodated in the existing solidarity–conflict framework, has also been a subject of debate (Bengtson et al., 2002). Lüscher argues that because social relations pass through temporal processes during which relationships are renegotiated, redefined or remain unresolved, they will be characterised by periods of indecision. From this perspective, the concept of ambivalence is thus different from conflict because its suggests 'pending conflict', that is, an unresolved tension between competing forces which arise over time, whereas conflict suggests a final state in which tensions and conflicts have been overcome. However, other empirical research (Giarrusso et al., 2005) indicates that the concept of ambivalence could in fact be accommodated within the existing conceptual dimensions of the solidarity framework with ambivalence operationally defined as the intersection of affection and conflict.

In sum, the notion of ambivalence represents a multifaceted concept. From sociological to psychological ambivalence, spanning both macro and micro levels, ambivalence has come to form part of a broader theoretical paradigm of intergenerational relations, and has been refined even further to represent both its intersubjective and structural characteristics. As both its historical and contemporary developments suggest, ambivalence remains a subject of some ambivalence in its own right, evoking what appears to be a debate about theoretical and empirical validity characterised by both conflict and consensus.

See also: Care, Family Relations, Gender, Generations, Life-course Perspective, Quality of Life, Social Relations

FURTHER READING

For a full discussion of the concept of ambivalence in the context of intergenerational solidarity, see *Journal of Marriage and Family*, 64(3) (2002).

REFERENCES

Bengtson, V., Giarrusso, R., Mabry, J. B. and Silverstein, M. (2002) Solidarity, conflict, and ambivalence: complementary or competing perspectives on intergenerational relationships? *Journal of Marriage and Family*, 64(3): 568–576.

Connidis, I. and McMullin, J. A. (2002) Sociological ambivalence and family ties: a critical perspective. *Journal of Marriage and the Family*, 64(3): 558–568.

Hillcoat-Nallétamby, S. (under review). Exploring intergenerational relations in a multicultural context: the example of filial responsibility in Mauritius. *Journal of Cross-Cultural* Gerontology.

Lowenstein, A. and Ogg, J. (eds) (2003) *Old Age and Autonomy: The Role of Service Systems and Intergenerational Family Solidarity*. Final Report. Haifa: Centre for Research and Study of Ageing, University of Haifa, Israel.

Lüscher, K. and Pillemer, K. (1998) Intergenerational ambivalence: a new approach to the study of parent–child relations in later life. *Journal of Marriage and the Family*, 60: 413–425.

Pillemer, K. and Lüscher, K. (eds) (2004) *Intergenerational Ambivalences: New Perspectives on Parent–Child Relations in Later Life*. Elsevier Ltd.

van Gaalen, R. I. and Dykstra, P. (2006) Solidarity and conflict between adult children and parents: a latent class analysis. *Journal of Marriage and Family*, 68: 947–960.

Assisted Living

> A living arrangement where older people can benefit from different levels and types of support to assist them in retaining independence.

A single consensual definition of 'assisted living' does not exist and many definitions lack a clear focus on the services to be provided and the needs to be met by assisted living. Several features, however, such as 'flexible care, self contained dwellings and a homely feel to the building' are essential in a definition (Hanson et al., 2006: 1).

The concept is used in the USA rather than the UK, although a number of housing with care initiatives growing in the UK would come under this definition, such as retirement community living, sheltered housing, co-housing, extracare facilities, continuing care retirement communities. In the UK, for example, the following categorisations can be made of 'assisted living' contexts:

Designated housing: general stock for rent, usually bungalows, designated for independent older people.

Conventional sheltered housing: a generally independent population housed in self-contained units, usually rented but with some leasehold, but sharing communal facilities and staffed by a scheme manager.

Abbeyfield houses: a distinct form of sheltered housing, all units rented, including a house manager and cleaning and catering staff, with a predominantly older female, but more independent, population.

Extra-care in sheltered housing: a form of sheltered housing with additional care facilities to cater for a population with mixed dependencies, usually with other services and activities provided. 'Extracare housing is a development of sheltered housing that aims to meet the housing, care and support needs of older people, while helping them to maintain their independence in their own private accommodation' (Darton et al., 2008: iv). In the UK, extra-care models of housing are primarily from the public and registered social landlord sector.

Mixed dependency extra-care housing: similar to the above type of extra-care housing but with a mixed population, roughly split as a third with no current care needs, a third with low to moderate care needs and a third with moderate to high care needs.

Lifestyle extra-care housing: an aspirational form of extra-care housing providing for a mixed dependency population but also providing a diverse programme of recreational, social and cultural activities.

High dependency extra-care housing: a form of extra-care housing where the majority of residents, older than in other settings, have moderate to high levels of care needs.

Registered care homes: accommodation and staffing that meets care standards to house a population with care needs short of nursing homes.

Nursing homes: licensed facilities that provide nursing or personal care services to people who are infirm or chronically ill, though not necessarily an older population, again meeting care standards.

Assisted living can range from small three-resident properties to retirement communities. Other definitions stress the importance of independence with assisted living being for people who need assistance with the activities of daily living but wish to live as independently as possible – this can be alone within a complex or with others.

The common link is the emphasis on supported independence, the range of services, individuality, privacy, dignity, choice and homeliness. Some will have communal restaurant facilities in addition to individual kitchens, etc. Generally, most schemes are also distinguished by their use of telecare.

However, the diversity and confusion of provision under the broad heading of assisted living have caused concern. In the USA, for example, a Senate Special Committee on Aging called a workshop to develop guidelines for policy, regulation and operations and to classify such definitions. Heumann and Boldy (1993), in their typology of assisted living, look at predisposing factors (social values such as self-actualisation, the type of assisted living ownership and the degree of governmental support and services) as well as environmental dimensions such as the degree of communal space and integration within the neighbourhood.

The development of assisted living in the UK came in part as a response to the inability of sheltered housing to meet the health and social care needs of an increasing older population. Sheltered housing (*see* Housing entry) dominated the provision of housing for older people from the late 1950s to the mid-1980s, yet became increasingly difficult to let. Tenants were in need of extra services and a number of models emerged in response to this, replacing the traditional forms of sheltered housing such as warden-controlled bungalows or flats with communal facilities. These initial schemes were originally called category 2 schemes (between sheltered housing and residential care, i.e. Part 3 of the National Assistance Act 1948 which placed a duty on local authorities to provide residential care for older people) yet have been replaced by what is now termed 'Extra-care' – housing with care – although there are several differing definitions of extra-care.

Additionally, the promotion of community care with less reliance on residential care led to the development of other solutions and to the blurring of the boundary between housing and care (Oldman et al., 2002), with older people each having their own front door but with an additional call on help and support.

In the UK context, the development of such schemes has been fostered through the government's favoured emphasis on independence, the personalisation of service and on keeping people at home for as long as possible. Additionally, such schemes also enable the joining up of health and social care as well as service user choice and empowerment and the prevention of entry to long-term care.

The growth in such schemes as extra-care has come from market demand, where it is seen as more consumer-focused than more medical types of provision such as nursing home care. However, this creates a dilemma where schemes are 'sold' to attract people with the aim of maintaining fitness and an active lifestyle, possibly with the anticipation of future needs, yet the increasing care needs of an ageing cohort can create very different emphases in a community. Maddox (2001: 436) draws attention to the *appropriateness* of such facilities for older people with declining function. The distinctiveness which he draws attention to focuses on the 'implicit and often explicit' roots of such housing in communitarian values and in ecological and developmental theory. Assisted living can secure the maximum quality of life for older people through its distinctive set of living arrangements.

In an evaluation of extra-care schemes in England, Darton et al. (2008) found that those who moved into extra-care schemes were less physically and cognitively impaired than those moving into care homes (30% compared to 75% going into residential care and 85% nursing care); 4% were cognitively impaired compared to 39% moving into care homes.

Although assisted living may enable people to 'age in place' (*see* Ageing in place entry), more inclusive admission and discharge criteria and concomitant staffing and funding are necessary if ageing in place is to underpin the philosophy of assisted living (Chaplin and Dobbskeepel, 2001). Evidence from some US states, for example, shows that policies need to be revised to enable assisted living to embody ageing in place, particularly for those with dementia, as the cultural diversity of an area used to be reflected in the schemes. Considering the needs of black and ethnic minority groups in the design process is also important.

One advantage of extra-care is the continued involvement of family carers (Gaugler and Kane, 2007; Institute of Public Care, 2007), although a contentious issue is the use of facilities by the surrounding community (Hanson et al., 2006). Satisfaction with assisted living facilities includes participation in the decision-making process regarding the move to assisted living, the quality of staff and resident interaction, as well as the quality of the operation and satisfaction that the philosophy of assisted living is borne out in practice (Edelman et al., 2006). A study into the factors that underpin success in the UK found that the following were important: philosophy and outcome aims; types of scheme; design; service delivery model, including assistive technology; community role; partnership approach – strategic and operational and value for money (Institute of Public Care, 2007).

In the UK, the Department of Health (2008) has drawn up good practice guidelines for meeting the housing and care needs of older people living in extra-care schemes:

- Living at home – not in a home.
- Having one's own front door.
- The provision of culturally sensitive services delivered within a familiar locality.
- Flexible care delivery based on individual need.
- The opportunity to preserve or rebuild independent living skills.
- The provision of accessible buildings with smart technology that make independent living possible for people with physical or cognitive disabilities, including dementia.
- Building a real community, including mixed tenures and mixed abilities, which is permeable to the wider community and benefits from a variety of provisions available to all citizens.
- An Extra-care Housing Toolkit has also been developed as a structured approach to developing policy and locally based initiatives.

The development of both medium-sized and large (village) extra-care schemes is expected to continue. However, there is a danger that local authorities will see extra-care housing as a form of accommodation suitable for all when it is not suitable for everybody. Viewing extra-care as an alternative to residential care therefore needs to be evaluated.

Given the perceived increase in dementia over the next 50 years, the issue of where people should live and whether such schemes can evolve to accommodate people with dementia, or who are above a particular health threshold, is a key area for discussion. The UK report by the Institute for Public Care (2007: 4) suggests that a more appropriate term for extra-care housing should be 'prolonged residence' rather than 'home for life'. The same report also concludes that in many circumstances extra-care is able to offer people an alternative to residential care. It can improve or maintain feelings of well-being and support a good quality of life.

While practitioners are looking to extra-care models, its evolving role and the possibility of meeting changing lifestyle choices is still somewhat unclear.

Co-housing is a further model which has developed elsewhere, such as the in USA, Denmark and the Netherlands (Brenton, 2001), where mutual support, empowerment and self-determination are prevalent. Here groups of friends or neighbours may develop their own collective housing, based on a common purpose.

Assisted living and extra-care do give a focus for new research agendas and the potential for theory building around successful ageing, but as Maddox (2001) comments, there is a dearth of large-scale and longitudinal studies.

See also: *Ageing in Place, Care, Cohort, Dementia, Housing, Independence, Long-term Care, Quality of Life, Retirement, Successful Ageing*

FURTHER READING

Croucher, K., Hicks, L. and Jackson, K. (2006) *Housing with Care for Later Life.* York: Joseph Rowntree Foundation.

Darton, R., Bäumker, T., Callaghan, L., Holder, J., Netten, A. and Towers, A.-M. (2008) *Evaluation of the Extracare Housing Fund Initiative: Initial Report.* Personal Social Services Unit (PSSRU) Discussion paper 2506/2 May 2008, University of Kent.

Heuman, L.F. and Boldy, D.P. (1993) *Ageing in Place with Dignity: International Solutions Relating to Low Income and Frail Elderly.* Westport, CT: Praeger.

Institute of Public Care (2007) *Raising the Stakes: Literature Review.* Oxford and Bath: Institute of Public Care.

Maddox, G. (2001) Housing and living arrangements: a transactional perspective, in R. Binstock and L. George (eds), *Handbook of ageing and the Social Sciences.* New York: Academic Press.

Oldman, C., Heywood, F. Means, R. (2002) *Housing and Home Later Life.* Buckingham: Open University Press.

Bereavement

The situation of individuals who anticipate or experience the loss of someone significant through that person's death, and the subsequent adjustments made as a result.

While there are numerous and sometimes even conflicting definitions associated with bereavement, for example the terms *grief, mourning* and *bereavement* are commonly used interchangeably, it is frequently understood to mean the objective situation of individuals who have experienced the loss of someone significant through that person's death (Stroebe and Schut, 2001).

During the course of their lifetime, every individual will experience bereavement following the loss of a friend, family member or other loved one. While most people will be deeply affected by this experience, until the last two decades, the study of the bereaved has not represented a significant area of investigation in the field of human and health sciences, and in particular, ageing. However, socio-demographic transformations, particularly increased life expectancies and changing patterns of mortality, have made deaths outside the older age ranges a relatively rare occurrence and this has altered the contemporary profile of those experiencing bereavement. In contrast to the beginning of the last century, in the western context at least, when a significant proportion of deaths were caused primarily by infectious diseases and occurred to those whom we would consider today as in mid-life or younger, most deaths today occur among older people and are caused primarily by chronic illnesses (i.e. heart disease, cancer, respiratory diseases). Thus, deaths now typically occur after individuals have experienced a full and complete life, and as a result experiences of death and bereavement have become largely confined to the latest stages of the life course. Indeed, many people now reach middle age without having any direct experience of bereavement.

In response to these transformations, the social practices associated with bereavement have undergone many changes. No longer is bereavement a 'shared' or communal experience, as was the case when the care of the dying as well as deaths themselves took place in the community and at home. Today, formal organisations and services have, for the most part, taken over the practices associated with death (e.g. the removal and disposal of the body), effectively removing these experiences from the family and broader social group. Indeed, it may even be argued that bereavement has become increasingly 'bureaucratised', and, as a consequence, people are less able to deal with the aftermath of the loss of a loved one.

Although bereavement has always been part of the human experience, in the West scholarly interest in the phenomenon has by and large been dominated by the psychoanalytical concept of grief work first postulated by Freud in the early 1900s. As its name implies, grief work is based on the premise that the bereaved should 'work through' their grief; they must think through and face the reality of their loss, express their feelings and detach emotionally from the deceased in order to become reinvested in life. The concept of grief work has been elaborated upon by various theorists. Both Kübler-Ross (1969) and Bowlby (1980) suggested that responses to grief can be seen to follow distinct sequential stages or phases, and Worden (1982) argued that the bereaved should be set the task of actively working through these stages in order to make a complete adjustment. Although using differing approaches, these psychoanalytical theories each detail the basic course that a person will normally follow after bereavement, viewing it as a process involving a predictable and orderly pattern of responses to a person's death. However, more contemporary theorists have shifted the focus towards the ways in which individuals adapt to the disruption of affectional bonds (e.g. in attachment theory).

Although all these theories have been extremely influential in terms of the way bereavement is understood and addressed, scholars increasingly recognise that at any stage of life bereavement is a highly complex experience with various social, economic, physical and psychological consequences, and this has led to the burgeoning of multidisciplinary research interests. For example, recent work has focused on the financial implications of the death of a life partner (Corden et al., 2008). Likewise, as later life and the experience of old age bring with them the complexities specific to ageing, notably an increased likelihood of physical and mental health problems, interest has focused on understanding the bereavement experience in terms of its impact in several life domains. These have included understanding the changing nature of social roles for the bereaved, when the death of a spouse or life partner may mean losing a confidante or companion in everyday activities; changes to life circumstance such as reduced financial security, precipitated by the sudden loss of spousal or partner income; and an increased risk of social isolation because of a potentially more restricted social network of people to call upon for help, when a spouse, family members or close friends die or other family members move away. It is recognised that the potential for social isolation among older people is greater than for other age groups because of the likelihood that they will experience multiple losses within a short period of time (i.e. they may lose more than one friend or family member). Such experiences it is thought can rekindle memories of earlier losses with the consequence that older people may encounter a 'bereavement overload', with bereavement becoming a constant feature of their lives (Parkes, 1997). Some studies of older adults have also found that bereavement magnifies the risk of psychological disturbances, such as increased symptoms of anxiety, depressive symptoms and major depressive episodes (Gallagher et al., 1983), as well as new or worsened physical illnesses and even an increased risk of death. However, Genevro's extensive (2004) review of the outcomes of bereavement, although not focusing exclusively on older people, is more cautious in it conclusions, noting, for example, that uncomplicated or normal bereavement does not appear to be associated with enduring negative outcomes although this may not be the case for complicated or traumatic grief experiences.

Given that older people are more likely to experience bereavement than other age groups, it is surprising to note that, until recently, bereavement has not warranted much attention by social gerontologists or policy makers (Croxall and Hillcoat-Nallétamby, 2007). Although there are notable exceptions (e.g. Bennett and Vidalhall, 2000), literature in the area of older people and bereavement tends to be restricted to a narrow range of topics, namely spousal loss, the gendered dimension of the experience and its epidemiological consequences. Sidell (1993) suggests that this apparent indifference to the study of the bereavement experiences of older people reflects what he calls 'gerontophobia', that is, a desire to dissociate ageing from death in order to counter further negative connotations associated with this field of inquiry. Whether gerontologists agree with this statement is debatable, but until the 1990s many of the gerontology textbooks did not even include chapters on the subjects of death, dying and bereavement, and very few articles in the *Gerontologist* and the *Journal of Gerontology* discussed them.

bereavement

Likewise, the provision of bereavement services in the health field has, historically speaking, been limited, particularly in the UK context, although the modern hospice movement since the 1960s has actively supported the bereaved. Some explanation for this rests with the longstanding assumption that bereavement is a 'private' experience – the domain of kinship groups and friends – and this goes some way to explaining the underdevelopment of formalised service provision and support in this area. Interestingly, however, Genevro (2004) concludes from her review of research on the education and training of healthcare professionals since the 1980s that while there are few studies of good quality on this theme, from a comparative perspective, the United Kingdom is possibly more advanced in training opportunities in the area of bereavement and grief for doctors during their careers.

Historically, then, bereavement does not appear to have been a prominent feature of social or health policy and while the increased emphasis on end-of-life care is beginning to bring bereavement needs to the fore, they are still largely delivered in a medical context (i.e. hospitals, hospices). This raises the question of whether those beyond this environment actually receive any organised support.

In conclusion, while it may be argued that the issues surrounding bereavement in later life have been a neglected area of gerontological inquiry, there is a further explanation to be explored. The needs of older bereaved people have perhaps suffered from assumptions that, compared to other, younger age groups, they somehow have a natural ability to be able to cope with these experiences. In other words, normative or ageist expectations are perhaps at play here and may be reflected in both the relative neglect of scholarly interest in the topic of bereavement in later life, and in a paucity of formal service provisions designed to meet the needs of bereaved older people.

See also: *Ageing, Care, Death and Dying, Gender, Gerontology*

FUTHER READING

Hansson, R. and Stroebe, M. (2002) *Bereavement in Late Life: Coping, Adaptation, and Developmental Influences*. Washington: American Psychological Association.

Scrutton, S. (1995) *Bereavement and Grief: Supporting Older People Through Loss*. London: Arnold.

REFERENCES

Croxall, J. and Hillcoat-Nallétamby, S. (2007) Living on after death: bereavement and social welfare needs. *Mortality*, 12, Supplement, S27, pp. 1–98.

Kübler-Ross, E. (1969) *On Death and Dying*. London: Tavistock.

Parkes, C. (1997) Bereavement and mental health in the elderly. *Reviews in Clinical Gerontology*, 7: 47–53.

Sidell, M. (1993) Death, dying and bereavement, in J. Bond, P. Coleman and S. Peace (eds), *Ageing in Society: An Introduction to Social Gerontology*. London: Sage. pp. 151–179.

Stroebe, W. and Schut, H. (eds) (2001) *Handbook of Bereavement Research: Consequences, Coping, and Care*. Washington, DC: American Psychological Association.

Worden, J. W. (1982) *Grief Counseling and Grief Therapy: A Handbook for the Mental Health Practitioner*. New York: Springer.

Biographical Approaches

> **Biographical approaches draw on people's life histories as a means of understanding their present and future needs and aspirations.**

Biographical, life history and reminiscence approaches have become popular in health and social care (Bornat, 1999). The strengths of biographical approaches are twofold. In a health setting, the approach can be beneficial for service users, for example by giving them voice, and for the service provider by helping them identify needs that may otherwise remain unrecognised.

Who we were in the past shapes who we are today, and we all have unique life histories. At the same time, it is often the case that older people are viewed as a homogeneous group, despite a wealth of research indicating quite the opposite (Clarke, 2000). Biographical approaches allow us to tap into an individual's attitudes, beliefs, and their sense of self. Indeed, when faced with life changes, as is often the case in older people confronted by physical or cognitive decline, there is a strong tendency to interpret the circumstances in the context of the past life as a whole. Only by understanding the meaning that an individual has placed on his or her social world and life history are we able to appreciate more fully their current lives, their wishes and fears, and their future aspirations.

Bornat and Walmsley (2008) note that there are several methodologies of and various purposes behind biographical approaches in research. In broad terms, the activity itself can be research-based, that is undertaken to solve a problem, or practice-based, for example undertaken within the realm of health or social care. Furthermore, the process can be top-down, for example where a practitioner observes, or bottom-up, where the patient or service user sets the agenda and shares his or her autobiography. Methods can include discourse analysis, life history, case notes and patient histories, autobiographies and life story books.

The history of biographical approaches is relatively short. Indeed, compared with just 20 years ago, these approaches have become quite commonplace (Bornat and Walmsley, 2008), especially in the areas of health and social care. An early proponent of the biographical approach was Johnson (1976), who questioned the validity of employing a series of pre-formulated questions in order to assess an individual's need. Just 10 years later he was proposing the biographical approach as a means to measuring care needs in the community setting (Johnson et al., 1988). The argument that an individual's needs are not merely social or medical has shaped our understanding of what the patient-centred approach might be. Needs are specific to each individual, and it is through the narrative that an individual can communicate these (implicitly or explicitly) to the healthcare professional. Indeed, it has been suggested that gerontology has legitimised biographical investigation as a social function, and the approach is being used increasingly in childhood and early adulthood research (Chamberlayne et al., 2000).

Biographical approaches view later life as a continuing process, not as a stage or single event. As Clarke (2000: 429) points out, it can be a time of 'ongoing development and self-determination, rather than a time of withdrawal and disengagement'. Additionally, an individual is the sum of his or her past, and the past comprises many story-lines, for example education, family and work (Johnson, 1976). The telling of a life story can help unravel the past – including the recent past – *and* help assess the present and articulate future worries, fears and goals. However, there are ethical issues concerning empowerment, ownership and appropriation (for a detailed discussion, see Bornat and Walmsley, 2008).

While biographical approaches are extremely important tools in the practice environment, their uses in the research environment should not be underestimated. As with other forms of data collection, biographies can provide answers to research questions. In turn, these answers can inform social and health policy. One classical example is Edgerton's (1967, cited in Bornat and Walmsley, 2008) study of those discharged from an institution for people with a learning disability. He concluded that a benefactor was key to whether rehabilitation into the community was successful or not. This finding was novel, yet today the role of citizens' advocates (i.e. Edgerton's benefactors) is deemed as pivotal in social and health care provision.

These approaches have significance for practice on several counts. They can benefit the narrator by (1) empowering them, (2) assisting them in indentifying their needs and (3) allowing them to engage in reminiscences. Giving voice is an empowering experience, and examining together with the listener the meaning that the narrator has given his or her life may help to accommodate change, alleviate fears and promote future aspirations. Further, the telling of a life story can have a cathartic value (Elford et al., 2001) – although, as Clarke and her colleagues (2003) point out, the empathetic listener should be able to discourage the narrator from discussing distressing issues. The narrator can feel valued and this, in turn, can enhance the perceived quality of life as well as the quality of interpersonal relationships.

Biographical approaches can benefit healthcare professionals by helping them see the 'person behind the patient', and thus improving that relationship and giving a more complete picture on which to base assessments and provide interventions. Those healthcare staff involved in the life-story process report better relationships with the patient, and there is a positive effect upon patient care (Bornat and Walmsley, 2008; Clarke, 2000).

These approaches can also improve social and health care provision, forming a substantial stepping stone towards patient-centred care. Indeed, they have been used to examine specifically older users and their perceptions of service provision and delivery, and also in dementia care (Bornat, 1999; Clarke et al., 2003).

Finally, biographical approaches can benefit society as a whole. A strong body of evidence suggests that this line of work helps to challenge our perceptions of older people (Clarke et al., 2003), and it may ultimately help decrease the threat of stereotyping and counterbalance the perceived loss of self that is sometimes experienced in the institutionalised care setting (Surr, 2006).

See also: Care, Dementia, Disability, Gerontology, Quality of Life

REFERENCES

Bornat, J. (ed.) (1999) *Biographical Interviews: The Link between Research and Practice.* London: Open University Press, Centre for Policy on Ageing.

Care

Providing or receiving assistance in a supportive manner.

The above definition conveys some of the essential and divergent components of 'care' – it is embedded within a relationship, value-laden, active as well as passive, powerful as well as disempowering. Consequently, it has many different associations, both positive and negative. Early UK and North American literature in relation to care for older persons was loaded with negative and patronising stereotypes of dependency in later life. The predominant discourse focused on the burden and stress faced by family carers (mainly daughters) in caring for older parents. This has changed over the last decade as part of a movement to reflect the positives of later life and the reciprocal elements of care.

Care can be seen as a holistic notion pervading all human relationships and activity. Care is a central part of life, binding together families, friends and communities. It is embedded in social relations. Care therefore also embodies love, solidarity, exchange, altruism and spirituality.

Care as a concept in the UK gained prominence during the feminist movement in the 1960s. The gendered nature of 'caring' for women by women in both public and private spheres received both empirical and theoretical attention from feminist researchers over a number of years. In the UK, Janet Finch and Dulcie Groves' edited collection, *A Labour of Love* (1983) and Gillian Dalley's *Ideologies of Caring* (1988) were influential in the initial awareness-raising of the issues female carers faced in their caregiving roles. A criticism of these and other early writers, however, focused on their lack of concentration and analysis on aspects such as age, sexual orientation or disability. They concentrated exclusively on the organisation and experiences of white, non-disabled, heterosexual carers. Consequently, they stereotyped situations in which carers were found – out of the labour market, independent rather than interdependent and in reciprocal relationships, providing care in the domestic 'home' setting. They also ignored the fact that most care was provided by older people themselves to other older people. An examination of the facts suggests a different picture of men and women experiencing difficulties as they juggled work and family life, with older people giving considerable reciprocal support to their carer, financially, emotionally and practically.

Care involves reciprocity and *inter*dependency; components that have been picked up in more recent debates which have focused on the concept of citizenship, rather than gender alone. This notion has become synonymous with the emphasis on 'social rights'. One of the most influential writers on this broader front is Joan Tronto, who argues that care is a political as well as moral concept. Tronto (1993) outlines four ethical elements in 'an ethic of care': attentiveness, responsibility, competence and responsiveness, all of which need to be present and integrated if good care is required.

There are a number of distinctions in the care literature. These include the nature of care (personal, financial, emotional, medical or social), different types of carer (by age, gender, sexual orientation, class and race) or care recipient (older person, person with a learning disability, with mental health problems), time spent in the caregiving role (new carer or long-term carer), amount of care provided (under or above 20 hours; 50 hours plus) and role relationship (daughter, son, spouse). Census data consistently show differences between carers on all these dimensions. There are also differences in the location of care (in the formal 'professional' sector or informal 'family' based care).

Formal care is seen to be paid and formally organised, while informal care is unpaid and associated with family care, carried out in the home. Despite these divisions, there are a number of commonalities between these two locales of care. Women play the major role in both the formal

care

and informal organisation of care. Additionally, the tasks in both the formal and informal care are often intimate, involving bodywork which can be seen as 'dirty work' and of low status. Many jobs in the formal sector are regarded as unskilled; in informal care, all work is seen as unskilled. And in both there are major issues about availability and quality. For both formal, but more so, informal care, the work is hidden and silent.

Increasingly, literature on both sides of the Atlantic has concentrated on the nuances of care, highlighting diversity. The experiences of providing care have been seen to be different in relation to ethnic groups. The assumption that those in ethnic minorities care for their own has now been widely established as a myth. Ethnic minorities face particular difficulties in relation to finance, health, opportunities for social participation, and appropriate support, particularly from professionals who do not share a similar language and culture. Accessibility to sensitive services also differs between rural and urban areas, with accessibility being a particular problem. Differences also arise in relation to the situation of carers who are new to their role and those who have established long-standing care commitments or where transition into the care role has been gradual rather than new, for example with an older person with dementia as opposed to someone who may require intense support overnight through a stroke (Yeandle et al., 2007).

Care of and by older people is most often discussed within the relationship of the family. With the changing structure, nature and roles within the family the traditional patterns of care are changing. Spouse care, predominantly focusing on women taking on care roles, has shifted to look at male carers. Friends as carers are also increasingly apparent in providing care. The evolution of care networks (including all the above) comprising different relationships has also been the subject of increasing research, with key questions being asked as to whether support networks necessarily translate into care networks, particularly when personal care is required (Keating et al., 2003).

The location of care has dramatically shifted over the last century, with care being provided in the community rather than in institutions. In the UK it has also increasingly meant the private sector taking on more responsibility for formal care services and the introduction of large (some US) companies in the market for residential care. Different issues and concepts are emerging through this arena of care, such as 'risk and abuse', the recruitment and retention of the care workforce, and the integration of health and social care.

Our analysis of care has to take into consideration the effects of globalisation on care networks and provision. Increasingly, care is being provided at longer distances. Care chains are extending globally, with extreme examples of 'astronaut families' cited, that is families placing their older relatives in another country to become recipients of care services in another state. More common, however, are movements of migrants back to their homeland at regular intervals to provide care or global exchanges of money to secure care services elsewhere. The consequences of globalisation will be experienced differently through gender, class and ethnic inequalities (Chappell and Penning, 2005).

Increasingly, work, and not just home, location has to be factored into the equation for carers who are juggling work and care for an older person. Evidence from both the UK and Canada shows that carers are commuting long distances to provide hands-on care, often around the working day (Martin-Matthews and Phillips, 2008). Such carers can be at increasing risk of stress if there is little support from formal services, others in the family or if they have unsympathetic line managers and employers. The long-term consequences of providing care, particularly if carers are outside the labour market, are also evident for carers, although there is still little longitudinal data to identify those carers and care recipients who are particularly at economic risk.

Care as a concept is complex and diverse and poses a number of challenges for the twenty-first century. It is still a key gender issue. The challenge is to move care into the public sphere while avoiding the prospect of women remaining predominantly in low-status activity. The public face of 'care' in the form of care work needs to be moved higher up the agenda. Parallel to this, care is socially constructed and is packaged and sold by the private sector. The challenge here is to unify the concepts of private and public care with the need for good quality care to be readily available and affordable to the increasing numbers of older people who may potentially need care.

See also: Disability, Gender, Housing, Long-term Care, Religion/Spirituality, Social Relations

care

FURTHER READING

Phillips, J. (2007) *Care: Key Concepts*. Cambridge: Polity Press.

Care Management

> **The process linking older people's needs to tailor-made service provision.**

Several definitions of the term 'care management' (or 'case management' as it is referred to in the USA) exist. In the UK it is seen as a system and a process whereby different services, such as health, social care and housing, can work together for the benefit of the older person. Challis et al. (1995: 38) define care management as 'the process of identifying and organising more individualised and appropriate packages of care to vulnerable individuals requiring long-term care, usually in their own homes'. Functions (coordination), goals (better use of resources; promoting client well-being), core tasks (assessment and care planning), characteristics of recipients (multiple needs), and a multi-level response (linked practice and agency levels) are all key characteristics of care management (Challis et al., 1995).

In the UK, care management was at the heart of the 1990 Community Care Act promoting the move away from institutional care to more intensive coordinated home care support and enabling the separation of the purchaser (assessment) and provider of services. Closely linked to the care management process was needs-led assessment, which was the driver in the process of tailoring services to individual needs. As the White Paper stressed, the aim was 'to make proper assessment of need and good care management the cornerstone of high quality care' (Department of Health, 1989: 5). Funding anomalies which promoted institutional care over home care were also behind the move to care management. There was a perception that older people were moving unnecessarily into residential care, particularly into the private sector, using social security funding. Although care management is not defined by legislation, the official guidance which followed the UK's National Health Service and Community Care Act of 1990 mapped out the core tasks of the process. Six objectives followed from this:

- Ensuring that the resources available are used in the most efficient way to meet individual needs.
- Restoring and maintaining independence by enabling people to live in the community wherever possible.

- Working to prevent or to minimise the effects of disability and illness.
- Treating those who need services with respect and providing equal opportunities for all.
- Promoting individual choice and self-determination, and building on existing strengths and care resources.
- Promoting partnership between users, carers and service providers in all sectors, together with organisations of and for each group (Department of Health, 1990: 23).

The early development of the concept came through the Personal Social Services Unit at Kent University (PSSRU), with a number of demonstration projects such as the Kent Community Care Project. Yet the implementation of care management was not straightforward. The pilot studies on which the model was based were difficult to extrapolate on a wider scale. Social workers operating care management had reduced workloads and some older people with more complex multiple needs were excluded from the studies. Social work itself was seen as being devalued, with assessment, previously the domain of social work, being shared with community nurses and occupational therapists (Bradley, 2005). There was also a critique of the transferability of the concept from the US context, from where it originated and is known as 'case management'. 'Case management', which implied that people are 'cases' with their lives to be 'managed', came to be seen as both negative and paternalistic. Although hailed as a cost-effective alternative for people with complex needs who required long-term care, two features were necessary in the effectiveness of care management from the US perspective: an integrated care system (missing in the UK) and a dependence on the informal sector of care. In the US, therapeutic models of case management exist, with a focus on counselling, advocacy and the importance of the relationship in the process.

The policy was also driven by the budgetary pressures of an ageing population. However, the evidence did suggest that older people who would otherwise have entered residential or nursing care could remain at home at similar or lower cost than would have been the case without care management (Weiner et al., 2002).

In evaluating care management 20 years on, Challis et al. (2007: 26) draw attention to *specialisation* in care management, which is a focus on specific user groups rather than a generic process for all users, and *targeting* in care management, which is the process by which vulnerable adults with complex needs receive the level and forms of care they require, which will differ from those with less complex needs. Although this may have led to success in care management, budgetary devolution and a multidisciplinary approach are two key areas which have not been realised in practice (Challis et al., 2007: 28). Research in 2002 has shown that there has been considerable variability in care management arrangements since implementation. This has arisen through delay and a lack of clarity and specificity at the start; a focus on all users of services rather than a targeted approach; variability in what is reported as care management in terms of a process or role, and whether social work skills were part of the process (Postle, 2002). Faced with such confusion, care management has turned into an administrative tool with an emphasis on eligibility and priority, risk and paperwork (Means et al., 2003), rather than a concentration on users and their needs. On a more positive note, users and carers did feel more involved in the process of assessment and care planning than previously (Warburton and McCracken, 1999).

In a US review of care management, Kane and Kane (2001: 418) suggest that success is mixed at best. Tensions exist for social workers, with the dual role of advocate versus gatekeeper and cost controller. The divide between health (often operating the medical model) and social care (operating a social model) has also led to separate systems operating in relation to one individual.

Given the increased managerialist agenda and government influence over the professions in the UK, it is not unusual that care management has evolved into a system-focused practice, with older people linked to a job description rather than a professional qualification. The lack of time for value-driven and theory-based, as well as critically reflective, practice, key components of social work, has been eroded in many social workes' practice (Adams, 1998).

Despite its difficulties there is optimism that care management can meet its objectives. It has enabled older people to remain at home and has attempted to introduce equity in the provision of services (Horder, 2008). Care management has also led to a raft of other activities around older people, such as the commissioning of services and advocacy, and the identification of unmet needs at a more strategic level. Furthermore, it also 'enshrines many elements of good professional practice' as well as proving an enduring structure (Horder, 2008: 136). Social work has also had to grapple with uncertainty in the role and tensions between limited resources and unlimited needs.

See also: Advocacy, Care, Disability, Housing, Independence, Long-term Care

FURTHER READING

Lymbery, M. (2005) *Social Work with Older People: Context, Policy and Practice.* London: Sage. Chapter 8.

Means, R., Richards, S. and Smith, R. (2008) *Community Care.* Basingstoke: Palgrave Macmillan.

Phillips, J., Ray, M. and Marshall, M. (2006) *Social Work with Older people* (4th edition). Basingstoke: Palgrave Macmillan.

REFERENCES

Adams, R. (1998) *Quality Social Work.* London: Macmillan.

Bradley, G. (2005) Movers and stayers in care management in adult services. *British Journal of Social Work*, 35: 511–530.

Challis, D., Darton, R., Johnson, L., Stone, M. and Traske, K. (1995) *Care Management and Health Care of Older People: The Darlington Community Care Project,* PSSRU, University of Kent, Canterbury.

Challis, D., Hughes, J., Jacobs, S., Stewart, K. and Welner, K. (2007) Are different forms of care-management for older people in England associated with variations in case-mix, service-use and care-managers' use of time? *Ageing & Society*, 27: 1, January. pp. 25–48.

Department of Health (1989) *Caring for People: Community Care in the Next Decade and Beyond.* London: HMSO.

Department of Health (1990) *Community Care in the Next Decade and Beyond.* London: HMSO.

Horder, W. (2008) Care management, in M. Davies (ed.), *The Blackwell Companion to Social Work* (3rd edition). Oxford: Blackwell. pp. 129–139.

Kane, R. and Kane, R. (2001) Emerging issues in chronic care, in R. Binstock and L. George (eds), *Handbook of Ageing and the Social Sciences* (5th edition). London: Academic Press. pp. 406–425.

Means, R., Richards, S. and Smith, R. (2003) *Community Care: Policy and Practice* (3rd edition). Basingstoke: Palgrave Macmillan.

Postle, K. (2002) Working between the idea and the reality: ambiguities and tensions in care managers' work. *British Journal of Social Work*, 32(3): 335–352.

Warburton, R. and McCracken, J. (1999) An Evidence-based Perspective from the Department of Health on the Impact of the 1993 Reforms on the Care of Frail Elderly People' in M. Henwood and G. Wistow (eds), *With Respect to Old Age: Long Term Care-Rights and Responsibilities* (Volume 3). London: The Stationery Office.

Weiner, K., Stewart, K., Hughes, J., Challis, D. and Darton, R. (2002) Care management arrangements for older people in England: key areas of variation in a national study. *Ageing and Society*, 22: 419–439.

care management

Civic Engagement

> *A range of specific, organised actions and behaviours intended to connect individuals to one another in the quest to address public concerns.*

Civic engagement broadly refers to involvement in community and public efforts, with the ultimate goal of improving the quality of life in society. It includes taking part in community programmes, public affairs and participation at some level in politics. Such activity may consist of volunteering to help someone in need, attending a neighbourhood association meeting, or simply voting. The formation of associations to address various needs in society is perhaps a classic representation of civic engagement. Networks of civic engagement foster connections between and among individuals, producing norms that uphold a sense of generalised reciprocity as well as overall social trust (Putman, 1995). Yet, a clear definition of civic engagement is still lacking. Brought into question are matters such as: how frequently does one have to be active in civic affairs to be identified as 'engaged'? For example, if one votes once every four years in the US presidential elections, may we then state that that person is engaged in civic matters?

More importantly, when considering the issue of civic engagement among older adults, the term has traditionally indicated formal volunteering, a narrow focus which makes invisible other forms of civic engagement to which older adults may commit, such as voting, staying informed about public matters, caregiving, or informal social relations (Martinson and Minkler, 2006). Martinson and Minkler, in the US context, trace the development of civic engagement among older adults as formal volunteering to the 1960s, when an array of organised volunteering opportunities were established by the government as a means to address poverty among elders. Programmes were developed to provide a small stipend to older adults who engaged in formal volunteering activities meant to address the needs of youth and elders in need. Moreover, older adults have a history of organising for political ends in the USA, including the formation of the Grey Panthers who are intent on addressing age discrimination.

Participation in volunteering activity by older persons increased dramatically in the last decades of the twentieth century (Chambré, 1993). Nevertheless, volunteering may provide active engagement for some elders, while others may find that it competes with filial obligations and other personal commitments (Knoke and Thomson, 1977; Rotolo, 2000). Further, volunteering may not benefit all older people equally (Martinson and Minkler, 2006; Musick et al., 1999). Accounting for the diversity in the ageing experience (race, class, gender) is necessary to assess the benefits of formal volunteering for older adults, particularly to guard against the possibility that formal volunteering becomes a replacement for social welfare (Martinson and Minkler, 2006).

Previous research investigating the effects of volunteer work overwhelmingly documents positive effects. Beneficial consequences have included both physical and mental health outcomes. Among those in late life, personal characteristics correlated with volunteering suggest that volunteers usually have higher education levels, are physically healthier and have better psychological well-being compared to persons who choose not to volunteer. Most research regarding volunteer involvement indicates a positive effect, yet some have acknowledged the likelihood of a selection bias, that is, people who are healthy are more likely to volunteer and are generally likely to be more positive, engaged and satisfied with life. Though the relationship between volunteering and well-being may not always be linear, and indeed may be bi-directional, there is evidence that even small amounts of volunteer involvement can lead to positive outcomes for some individuals.

Recently, however, research has suggested that at least some non-volunteers are just as healthy as their volunteering peers. Individuals who engage in volunteer activities may simply be in environments where there are more volunteering opportunities, where they are actively recruited to volunteer and/or where they feel it is their social obligation to volunteer (Chambré, 1993).

Previous studies that examine the role of volunteering in later life generally include some aspect of social relations as a control measure due to its documented association with health and well-being. Social relations appear to exert some influence, but results are mixed. For instance, Li and Ferraro (2005) find that the extent to which an older person has contact with friends, neighbours or relatives influences whether or not they are likely to volunteer. Predictably, more social contact is correlated with volunteering. Morrow-Howell et al. (2003) hypothesised that elders with low levels of social integration would demonstrate more positive effects of volunteering on health, but found no evidence to support that contention. It may be that older adults who do not formally volunteer, but have larger networks, benefit from the encounters they have with those network members, hence eschewing the need for a public social role such as volunteering. Likewise, older adult volunteers with larger networks may feel burdened by the competing demands that individuals within their large network and volunteering simultaneously make on their time.

Most recent thoughts on civic engagement and older adults are that the growing numbers of elders in society will provide an 'untapped' social resource, yet this assumption potentially excludes those unable or unwilling to formally volunteer. Moving beyond attitudes and behaviours, some are redefining civic engagement as a formal 'role' for retired older adults. Recent empirical work suggests that civic engagement could extend beyond volunteerism among retirees to include paid work in organisations intent on pursuing civic goals, such as faith-based organisations, educational institutions or social service agencies (Kaskie et al., 2008). In other words, civic engagement among older adults should be defined as a role that involves participation with some organisation – paid or voluntary – that has a direct impact on the community and involves a commitment of at least one day per week. Such activity may include teaching/mentoring, caregiving, or some other service provision, and involves a greater commitment than most volunteer opportunities. This emerging definition of civic engagement moves beyond the traditional connection to volunteering, includes paid work and also builds on the notion that retirement involves a life-course transition, complete with new expectations and skills. The accumulation of life experiences generates skills and knowledge that uniquely position retired older adults, who now find themselves with more time, to provide critical and valuable support to their local communities.

Traditional civic engagement connects people to others, creating social capital. Some have noted a shift in the traditional form of civic engagement at the end of the twentieth century, with the emergence of organisations developed for a cause. These organisations, referred to by Putnam (1995) as 'tertiary groups', do not serve the classic function of binding the individual to others, though they may gain influence in the political arena. The emergence of the American Association of Retired Persons (AARP) represents an example of this shift in civic engagement forms. The numbers of individuals who belong to this organisation are enormous (and growing), but they differ from traditional forms in that members do not necessarily know one another nor do they come in contact with one another in the name of the organisation. Putnam explains that membership of such organisations generally consists of paying dues and occasionally reading a newsletter, yet community attachment does not emerge from these sorts of memberships. They may share the same interests, yet are not connected to one another.

Civic engagement among older adults constitutes an avenue for participation in pubic life. Traditionally conceptualised as formal volunteering, the prevailing view is that such engagement adds a positive element to the quality of life in later years. Yet, diversity in the ageing experience suggests that volunteering may not benefit all older adults. Moreover, the form and practice of civic engagement are changing to include paid work and membership of organisations that do not necessarily foster connections between individuals. The shape of civic engagement opportunities is likely to continue to change over the coming years as the proportion of elders increases within and across societies.

See also: *Ageing, Care, Gender, Quality of Life, Retirement, Social Relations*

REFERENCES

Chambré, S. M. (1993) Volunteerism by elders: past trends and future prospects. *The Gerontologist*, 33(2): 221–228.

Kaskie, B., Imhof, S., Cavanaugh, J. and Kulp, K. (2008) Civic engagement as a retirement role for ageing Americans. *The Gerontologist*, 48(3): 368–377.

Knoke, D. and Thomson, R. (1977) Voluntary association membership trends and the family life cycle. *Social Forces*, 56(1): 48–65.

Li, Y. and Ferraro, K. F. (2005) Volunteering and depression in later life: social benefit or selection processes? *Journal of Health and Social Behavior*, 46: 68–84.

Martinson, M. and Minkler, M. (2006) Civic engagement and older adults: a critical perspective. *The Gerontologist*, 46: 318–324.

Morrow-Howell, N., Hinterlong, J., Rozario, P. A. and Tang, F. (2003) Effects of volunteering on the well-being of older adults. *The Journals of Gerontology. Series B: Psychological and Social Sciences*, 58B: S137–S145.

Musick, M. A., Herzog, A. R. and House, J. S. (1999) Volunteering and mortality among older adults: findings from a national sample. *The Journals of Gerontology. Series B: Psychological and Social Sciences*, 54B(3): S173–S180.

Putnam, R. D. (1995) Bowling alone: America's declining social capital. *Journal of Democracy*, 6(1): 65–78.

Rotolo, T. (2000) A time to join, a time to quit: the influence of the life cycle transitions on voluntary association membership. *Social Forces*, 78(3): 1133–1161.

civic engagement

Cohort

A group of individuals or couples who share a common event, such as birth or marriage, during a particular period of time, usually a year.

Cohorts normally experience the same demographic event (birth, divorce, marriage, education, for example), so we therefore talk of birth cohorts – individuals born in the same year – and marriage cohorts – those who married in the same year, and so on. Cohorts are said to 'age' as they advance continuously from one age group to another across their life span.

Cohort analysis, sometimes referred to as longitudinal analysis, uses data to track cohorts of individuals across time throughout their lives or at successive later dates on the basis of their common demographic experience. For example, a marriage cohort can be followed from the time they marry through successive periods to assess how many couples divorce, or to establish the risk of them divorcing after a certain period of time. Some studies adopt an inter-cohort approach because they aim to compare differences between two or more cohorts, while others will focus on intra-cohort variations, those within a given cohort. One of the main methodological challenges of cohort analysis is to be able to distinguish whether observed trends reflect cohort differences (whether cohort effects have an impact on one age group in a population), changes in age-specific behaviour (where age effects refer to an individual's experience of the passing of time) or the influence of particular historical circumstances or events (known as period effects, which have an impact on everyone at a particular point in time) as these three variables are not independent of each other (Hardy and Waite, 1997). This has led to the development of various research designs adapted to the study of ageing as a process, and which involve, for example, the collection of longitudinal, time-lagged and sequential data which enable researchers to control for the confounding effects of cohort, age or period (Jamieson, 2002; Victor et al., 2007), and to the development of complex statistical modelling techniques.

The concept of cohorts has become a central aspect to our understanding of how the ageing process can change over time, how cohorts can vary significantly from each other and what inter-linkages there may be between social change and individual ageing. Jamieson (2002) argues that, as a multidisciplinary field, social gerontology focuses on understanding changes to individual lives in the context of changing social structures, and that central to these processes is the passing of both individual and historical time. It is when individual and historical time are studied together that it becomes important to distinguish cohort, period and age effects.

Several macro-level factors contribute to cohort changes and differences, including: the composition of each cohort (e.g. their size or distribution by gender); changes to the ways in which a society and its institutions are organised, such as changes to the allocation of financial resources at retirement; technological changes such as the availability of new drugs; and, finally, how the links with other surviving cohorts who are in different phases of the life course are structured (e.g. increasing employment among women may affect the type and frequency of support that older cohorts can expect from their offspring) (Uhlenberg and Miner, 1995).

The sociologist and demographer Norman Ryder (1965), interested in cohort change or succession and how it was linked to social change, argued that people belonging to a certain age group at a given point in time were also members of a specific birth cohort which had a particular or unique location in history. He argued that new cohorts, as they progressively replaced members in the age categories of preceding cohorts (part of the process of cohort succession), could potentially provide the opportunity for social change to occur because they would bring with them characteristics (e.g. an unusually large cohort) that were different from those of preceding cohorts. For Ryder, comparing different cohorts would provide a powerful strategy for studying and understanding social change. Later on, the concepts of cohort and age strata became central to Riley's (1971) work on age stratification, a macro-social level of theory, reflecting the idea that age is a factor which influences how societies structure themselves and how individuals are organised into groups or strata based on age, moving from one age stratum to another during a lifetime (Hammarstrom, 2004). Riley uses the concept of cohorts to identify individuals who age together, through biographical time (their own personal ageing history) and historical time (the unique historical background they share as they age). This perspective links the life course of individuals and the historical background within which ageing occurs. As cohorts age, moving through specific historical periods, they will pass through age structures which reflect expectations and experiences about the roles and behaviour people are

cohort

expected to abide by and adopt. Cohort members therefore influence these structures but are also influenced by them. Riley and colleagues' later work in 1999, known as 'the ageing and society paradigm', explains variations between age groups and birth cohorts as the interplay between cohort flow (the movement through time of individuals born in the same year), the individual ageing experience and historical change. In sum, the age stratification perspective aims to understand the inter-linkages and interdependencies between the individual ageing process, age cohorts and social structures by considering individuals as members of age strata, cohorts and the historical periods in which they live (Hardy and Willson, 2002).

Building on age stratification theory, the concept of a cohort is also central to the life-course perspective, associated in particular with the work of Elder, which connects individual life trajectories (a micro-level focus) to broader societal changes and structures (macro-level focus), as well as focusing on short-term transitions such as completing education or moving from marriage to divorce. The life-course perspective focuses on the nature and timing of these transitions from one status or position to another and how these movements are organised in terms of characteristics such as age. This perspective is useful when studying differences in ageing across cohorts and whether there is consistency among cohort members as they make these transitions. By emphasising the temporal nature of roles and analysing events such as retirement as sequences which will be shaped by social structure, but also by what individuals do themselves, the life-course perspective offers an individualised perspective to life-course events as they unfold across time. This is in contrast to the aggregate representations of these experiences offered by the concept of cohort analysis.

Although cohort analysis has served in the development of theoretical and methodological approaches in the field of gerontology, this approach has been criticised on several grounds (Baars et al., 2006). At the micro-level of human interaction, for example, it fails to capture the lived experience of ageing, and overlooks the meaning of, and interpretations given to, age and the ageing process by older people themselves. Another criticism is that because the concept is based on studying people as part of aggregated categories, their individual differences can be overlooked, complex realities may be oversimplified and age groups may be viewed as homogeneous categories if analysed only in terms of their collective characteristics.

These criticisms notwithstanding, there have been numerous large-scale studies which have relied on the identification of birth cohorts to track and investigate particular aspects of human behaviour and development. Two such studies in the UK are the cohort-based English Longitudinal Study of Ageing (ELSA) and the cohort longitudinal study, the *2000 Millennium Birth Cohort Study*, both of which will track cohorts of individuals to see how their lives are affected by their health, education, economic, family and employment histories. ELSA began with a sample of 12,000 men and women aged 50 or more who will subsequently be re-interviewed at regular intervals, and the Millennium study has involved interviewing the parents of a population of 18,800 babies born during the 12 months of 2000, and subsequent waves of the survey will enable these cohorts to be followed throughout their lives. Another landmark study designed to track the lives of successive birth cohorts and generations of kin members has been the *Longitudinal Study of Generations* (LSOG), initially developed by Vern Bengtson in 1971 at the University of Southern California, Los Angeles. The study documents the intergenerational relations of 300 three-generation families comprising grandparents, middle-aged parents and grandchildren, and aims to investigate continuity and change in family intergenerational relations across time, as well as examining how the well-being of individuals in the family is influenced by broader social changes. The study has since been extended to include a fourth generation of great-grandchildren, and six more surveys have been completed, with the latest in 2001.

Although not immune to criticism, the concept of a cohort therefore provides a powerful conceptual and empirical tool for the study of change as individuals experience the ageing process across time.

See also: *Ageing, Gender, Generations, Gerontology, Life-course Perspective, Quality of Life*

cohort

REFERENCES

Baars, J., Dannefer, D., Phillipson, C. and Walker, A. (eds) (2006) *Ageing, Globalization and Inequality: The New Critical Gerontology*. Amityville, NY: Baywood Publishing Company, Inc.

Bengstson, V. (1971) *Longitudinal Study of Generations* (LSOG). Available at: www.usc.edu/dept/gero/research/4gen/index.htm (accessed 20 July 2009).

Riley, J. W. (1971) Social gerontology and the age stratification of society. *The Gerontologist*, 11: 79–87.

Ryder, N. B. (1965) The cohort as a concept in the study of social change. *American Sociological Review*, 30(6): 843–861.

Uhlenberg, P. and Miner, S. (1995) Life course and ageing: a cohort perspective, in R. H. Binstock and L. K. George (eds), *Handbook of Ageing and the Social Sciences* (4th edition). New York: Academic Press. pp. 208–225.

Convoy Theory

An interdisciplinary framework that seeks to explain how social networks and social support operate across the life course.

Convoy is a metaphor used to demonstrate the notion that individuals are surrounded by layers of people who provide support in times of need. Convoys include all aspects of social relations, encapsulating the significance of networks, with equal concern given to types of support and the quality such networks provide. It is perhaps best known in social gerontology through the seminal article written in 1980 by Robert L. Kahn and Toni C. Antonucci. In this piece the authors describe a theory that proposes social relations as multidimensional and developmental. Social relations include network characteristics and support aspects, each of which is influenced by personal and situational characteristics, which together influence health and well-being. The result of this theory has led to the development of the Convoy Model of Social Relations. A preliminary examination highlights the ways in which convoy characteristics vary by age (Antonucci and Akiyama, 1987). The classic model suggests that convoys can provide important mediating effects on health and well-being outcomes. The structure of a convoy often emerges from the support needs of a person, and whether or not the resulting support is adequate rests on convoy characteristics as well as the personal and situational characteristics of the individual.

Convoy theory has its roots in the work of anthropologist David Plath (1980), who coined the term to suggest that life may be understood as a 'career' of various relationships with significant others that shape identities and life experiences. A person's convoy includes those individuals involved in daily interactions that validate an individual's existence, but also from a developmental stance assume responsibility for an individual's ageing. In other words, the convoy is comprised of significant others who foster maturity and shape the ageing experience through supportive enactments. A person's convoy requires active management based on the focal individual's skill and initiative, and it contributes to the institutionalisation of the individual. Convoys, 'work in the processing of an individual human life' (Plath, 1980: 138). Yet, convoys are mutually influential in the sense that others shape the individual, but what happens to the individual – his or her successes and failures – also influences convoy members. According to Plath, convoys are dynamic, changing over the life course, and are meant to provide support. It references interpersonal relationships, highlighting the impact other individuals have on a person's lifetime trajectory. Plath terms this quality 'long-term engagements'. It also invokes meanings given to the self. Finally, socio-historical context is seen as a critical influence on the formation and evolvement of convoys. The work of Plath highlights the ways in which social interactions over time impinge on human development. Though developed in a Japanese context, it appears to be a universal concept, quite readily applied to various other cultural and national settings.

Methodological advancements to capture the characteristics of a person's convoy build from Plath's articulation of close relationships. The convoy is measured by asking individuals to imagine themselves in the centre of three concentric circles. They are requested to think of the people closest to them, the people most important in their lives (Antonucci, 1986). They are then asked to place those individuals into three groups, one group for each of the three circles in order of how much they mean to the individual. Respondents are instructed that there is no need to put down everyone they know. Individuals are told that the circle can be empty, full, or anywhere between empty and full. In the first circle surrounding the individual, they are asked to provide the first name and last initial of those people they feel so close to it is hard to imagine living life without them. In the second circle they are asked to place people to whom they may not feel quite that close, but who are still very important to them. Finally, in the third circle are placed people whom they have not already mentioned who are close enough and important enough in the respondent's life that they should also be positioned in their diagram. The result is a personal convoy that provides a basis for discerning various convoy characteristics including size, composition, contact frequency and geographic proximity. The utility of this method has been demonstrated in studies carried out with diverse cultural groups, including those of Bangladeshi origin living in England (Phillipson et al., 2003), the Japanese, Germans and French (Antonucci et al., 2001), as well as those of Arab ancestry living in both the USA and Lebanon (Ajrouch, 2005).

Over the years, convoy theory has been modified to consider various ways that social relations influence well-being. One development has been an elaboration of the mechanism or process through which health and well-being change because of social relations. The support-efficacy model, developed by Antonucci and Jackson (1987), suggests that social support influences health and well-being by conveying support to the target person, both contemporaneously and longitudinally, which in turn enhances the individual's feelings of self-efficacy and control. Efficacy enhancement can be generalised (e.g. you are a competent person), or it can be specific (e.g. you can achieve a significant improvement in diabetes self-care). This theoretical advance may be easily translated into intervention programmes aimed at older persons. For instance, informal support providers may be recruited to reinforce messages received from professionals or a formal support provider (i.e. physicians), and additionally provide affirming reinforcement when positive health behaviours are practised and/or aid in the practice of positive health behaviours. Identifying individuals with low social support may help to bring forth those people who are at risk for poorer adherence and health.

Convoy theory has also developed to include stress as an influence on well-being. In particular, a stress-buffering hypothesis has been advanced where convoy characteristics are thought to provide an important resource in times of stress, attenuating the stress–health link. For example, Antonucci et al. (2003) found that among men, social network size and perceived support from the child relied on most, buffer the negative effects of low education on health. More specifically, lower-educated men report better health, on a par with their higher-educated counterparts, when they have large networks and perceive support available from their child. Interestingly, this effect was evident only for men, and only among those in middle age. The buffering hypothesis provides a more specific understanding of the role convoys play in influencing well-being at different points in the life course and for different groups of people in society.

Finally, cross-national research employing the convoy model to study older populations has led to a renewed emphasis on the important effect socio-historical events and cultural norms have on convoy formation and change. For example, living in a country where war and political instabilities extend for long periods of time draws attention to how trust and interaction norms join together to influence the shape and nature of convoys. Moreover, emphases on the origins of support exchanges, whether stemming from instrumental or emotional needs, are likely to shape norms that inform convoy development and characteristics. Further investigation into these issues is needed.

Convoy theory draws from the traditions of phenomenology, anthropology, sociology and developmental psychology to elaborate the intricacies of social relations. This theory appears enormously applicable to a myriad of national and cultural settings. As a result, convoy theory provides a potential avenue for developing a more comprehensive understanding of how social networks and social support operate in similar ways, how they differ, and the extent to which they influence well-being across the life course.

See also: *Ageing, Gerontology, Social Relations, Social Support*

REFERENCES

Ajrouch, K. J. (2005) Arab American elders: network structure, perceptions of relationship quality and discrimination. *Research in Human Development*, 2(4): 213–228.

Antonucci, T. C. (1986) Social support networks: hierarchical mapping technique. *Generations X*, 4: 10–12.

Antonucci, T. C., Ajrouch, K. J. and Janevic, M. R. (2003) The significance of social relations with children to the Socio-Economic Status-Health Link in men and women aged 40 and over. *Social Science and Medicine*, 56: 949–960.

Antonucci, T. C. and Akiyama, H. (1987) Social networks in adult life and a preliminary examination of the convoy model. *Journal of Gerontology*, 42: 519–527.

Antonucci, T. C. and Jackson, J. S. (1987) Social support, interpersonal efficacy and health, in L. L. Carstensen and B. A. Edelstein (eds), *Handbook of Clinical Gerontology*. New York: Pergamon Press. pp. 291–311.

Antonucci, T. C., Lansford, J. E., Schaberg, L., Smith, J., Baltes, M., Akiyama, H., Takahashi, K., Fuhrer, R. and Dartigues, J. (2001) Widowhood and illness: a comparison of social network characteristics in France, Germany, Japan, and the United States. *Psychology and Ageing*, 16(4): 655–665.

Kahn, R. L. and Antonucci, T. C. (1980) Convoys over the life course: attachment, roles, and social support, in P. B. Baltes and O. Brim (eds), *Life-span Development and Behavior* (Volume 3). New York: Academic Press.

Phillipson, C., Ahmed, N. and Latimer, J. (2003) *Women in Transition: A Study of the Experiences of Bangladeshi Women Living in Tower Hamlets*. Bristol: The Policy Press.

Plath, D. (1980) *Long Engagements*. Stanford, CA: Stanford University Press.

Convoy theory

Cultural Ideals

Standards that a society or culture use to define the ways in which older adults should be treated and/or the ways in which older adults should behave.

Cultural ideals reflect consensus based on values among members of society. Ideals about ageing and old age tend to promote positive sentiments regarding social relationships, activity and health status. For example, the notion that old age will be a time of leisure, relaxation and travel represents one ideal found in the USA. Such shared goals become the standard against which individuals are compared, and to which individuals often compare themselves. The goal is to become like the ideal, though it is in reality achieved by only a few. Stemming from religious teachings, literature and media portrayals, ideals of life in old age rest on beliefs about how the world 'should be', often oversimplifying the challenges and realties associated with an ageing society. Three ideals will be discussed to illustrate the shape of these beliefs, as well as the potential risks they carry. It should be noted that ideals are culture-bound, and hence often take various forms depending on a particular society.

Standards about relations between older parents (and other older relatives) and children within families permeate ideals subscribed to across cultures and societies. The basic assumption advances that children will treat older parents with the utmost respect and care. The source of this value is often found in religious teachings. Taking as an example the context of the USA, historical documentation suggests cultural ideals about old age within the family stem from a Puritan tradition that old age represents a journey towards meeting God. Religious teachings emphasised that older adults receive respect and, moreover, supposed that they retain power over younger members. Family relations assumed a hierarchical character during the New England colonist era. Simply put, the young were to revere the old. Yet as Cole (1992) documents, the reality of old age during this period of American history proved to be much more complicated, often deviating away from cultural ideals. Old age was no guarantee of veneration by the young. Social factors, including gender wealth and race, shaped and influenced how older adults were treated. For instance, older women without families were often denigrated, mistreated and marginalised. Age alone did not guarantee veneration of the old by the young. Other historians commenting on different cultural contexts have made similar observations (Thane, 2005).

The notion that age alone constitutes the basis for relations between family members permeates cultures and societies around the world. For instance, ideals of filial piety exist in Asian contexts where Confucian and Buddhist teachings advocate reverence for older family members because of their earlier sacrifices while child rearing and due to life experiences. Yet, technological and educational developments have rendered older adult life experience less valuable within Asian cultures today. Moreover, the mere existence of the filial piety value does not guarantee that this ideal will be met. Nevertheless, it continues to represent a tradition to which many aspire, even if in an altered form from traditional conceptions (see Chow, 2001).

Cultural ideals are perhaps most dangerous when it is assumed they represent real-life experiences. For instance, in an edited volume on ethnic families in the USA, a chapter on Arab-Americans unequivocally states:

> It is a Western cultural *norm* that this category of the elderly belongs in nursing homes, away from the loving, affectionate, vivacious, enthusiastic atmosphere of the younger generation. ... It is inconceivable of a Middle Easterner to think of sending his parents to a nursing home or similar public institution. (Elkholy, 1988: 158)

This statement represents a belief about two different cultures, defined here as 'Western' and 'Middle Eastern'. Positioning an immigrant from Middle Eastern ancestry as morally superior to the West may serve to bolster self-image, but at the same time denies pragmatic realities. The inconceivability of accessing formal support from a public source proposed in the quote above is, first, a sentiment and not based on empirical observation; and secondly, oversimplifies the potential challenges and problems faced by an older immigrant with care needs in finding and making decisions about social support and caregiving.

In sum, cultural ideals surrounding family relations abound across all cultures and societies. It is important to recognise not only what they are, but also perhaps more significantly the potential obstacles they raise to accessing the best quality of life for older adults and their family members.

An ideal that emerged after the Second World War in the USA, the 'Golden Years', refer to a point in the life course where retired older couples live a life of luxury. Having worked hard and earned the right to leisure, this period is often hailed as the crowning glory of later life. This ideal underwrites a retirement industry in the USA, where the place one lives, along with the retirement image projected, come to represent the ultimate aspiration (McHugh, 2003). Yet, this image assumes that an older couple are somehow living in a vacuum, and supposes no interference from others. For instance, it does not account for the fact that adult children will sometimes re-enter an older couple's home life, needing to live with their parents once again because of job loss, divorce or health conditions. Moreover, health issues experienced by older adults themselves may limit opportunities to participate in the Golden Years. This ideal also supposes financial wealth and security. The reality suggests that many older adults cannot afford to live the Golden Years. Finally, many older adults may *not* want to live in a total state of leisure.

Recently, the image of the Golden Years is giving way to a more publicly engaged life in later years, where older adults wish to continue working and remain integrated with wider society. This includes high volunteerism and a preference for bridge jobs, or work that links the older adult between a career and retirement. Recognising ideals about old age projected through media outlets is an important part of identifying challenges associated with achieving the Golden Years ideal and learning to question cultural ideals generally.

Activity in later years constitutes an important ideal for American retirees. Ekerdt (1986) elaborated the dimensions of a busy ethic, which permeates ideals about life after retirement. This ideal serves many purposes, including a validation of retirement, a defence against obsolescence, and to align retirement within the overall American value system. Building from the work ethic, as well as the belief that activity staves off decline and is good for body and soul, the busy ethic serves the purpose of legitimating retirement. Interestingly, it is not necessarily the act of being busy that matters most. Instead, it is the belief that being busy is good and a goal to achieve. In sum, the busy ethic is an ideal where retirement in later life is socially, politically and morally validated.

The busy ethic constitutes an ideal and expectation representing values that draw from American society. Yet research on retirement in Britain and Australia appears to build on similar assumptions. In particular, Gee and Baillie (1999) explore retirement expectations in both countries and find the busy ethic a useful framework for discussing attitudes towards retirement among middle-aged adults in both contexts. In particular, continuity appears important with regard to retirement expectations, and work involvement may be translatable in retirement to a busy ethic. Though these countries are quite different from one another and the USA, the common language and historical origin may give reason for such similarities.

The threat of the busy ethic ideal is that it subtly coerces older adults to subscribe to a lifestyle that may not suit their situation. For instance, the busy ethic stems from the work ethic, and so cohorts of women who did not work outside the home may not feel the need to convey an image of 'busyness'. Instead, they may delight in not being busy with their traditional roles of cook, housekeeper and care person to small children. For example, a woman of 65 years, divorced with adult children living on their own, may decide that she no longer wishes to cook on the holidays, might hire an individual to clean her home once a week, and may not want to baby-sit her grandchildren. She would like to do nothing after having a life of caring for others. The autonomy to choose how to spend later years becomes overshadowed by an expectation and ideal to remain busy.

In sum, cultural ideals associated with the later years of life may provide shared societal goals which are meant to support a high quality of life. Yet, when the reality of life events interferes to prevent older adults from reaching such ideals, they risk harming an older adult's sense of self in his or her eyes, and in the eyes of others. Ideals of life in old age rest on beliefs about how the world 'should be', often oversimplifying the challenges and realities associated with an ageing society. A critical evaluation of ideals is necessary to ensure that alternative trajectories are equally acceptable and validated.

See also: *Cohort, Gender, Family Relations, Quality of Life, Retirement, Social Relations*

REFERENCES

Chow, N. S. (2001) The practice of filial piety among the Chinese in Hong Kong, in I. Chi, N. Chappell and J. Lubben (eds), *Elderly Chinese in Pacific Rim Countries.* Hong Kong: Hong Kong University Press. pp. 125–136.

Cole, T. R. (1992) *The Journey of Life: A Cultural History of Ageing in America.* New York: Cambridge University Press.

Ekerdt, D. J. (1986) The busy ethic: moral continuity between work and retirement. *The Gerontologist*, 26(3): 239–244.

cultural ideals

Elkholy, A. A. (1988) The Arab American family, in C. H. Mindel and R. Habenstein (eds), *Ethnic Families in America: Patterns and Variations*. New York: Elsevier. pp. 145–162.

Gee, S. and Baillie, J. (1999) Happily ever after? An exploration of retirement expectations. *Educational Gerontology*, 25: 109–128.

McHugh, K. E. (2003) The three faces of ageism: society, image, and place. *Ageing and Society*, 23: 165–185.

Thane, P. (2005) The age of old age, in P. Thane (ed.), *The Long History of Old Age*. London: Thames and Hudson. pp. 9–29.

Death and Dying

An irreversible event, biological death marks the end of physical existence, whereas social death refers to the gradual loss of an individual's social identity and functioning as they are progressively excluded from their social surroundings. Dying refers to the process leading to death and may involve spiritual, cultural and social dimensions.

In western societies, interest in death and dying has become increasingly prominent as we face the unprecedented experience of extended life duration, with the consequence that the 'end of life' has become a distinct and often prolonged phase of the life course. Death and dying, however, are debated subjects in terms of their definitions and meanings as socially, psychologically, medically and culturally determined processes. Exactly how the concept of dying should be defined, for example, will remain uncertain if we are unable to categorically state when the process has begun or who is best qualified to establish its onset. As a social construct, dying may represent a highly personal spiritual experience, or it may involve other people making it both an individual and group experience. How the dying trajectory is recognised will also depend upon the perceptions of those involved in the experience. Seale's (1998) concept of the 'dying role' illustrates this well when he argues that someone is likely to assume the identity of a dying person when they have been diagnosed with a medical condition which it is anticipated will have terminal outcomes. The dying role in this case is not initially linked to experiencing chronic illness or old age but acquires meaning through its medical significance.

The concept of death is often framed in terms of its social and biological meanings, and can also encompass the idea of a 'good' and a 'bad' death. Biological (or clinical) death, an event which cannot be reversed, is understood to be marked by the ending of physical life so that the human entity no longer exists. However, critics of the biological or clinical determination of death argue that it should be recognised as part of a broader set of social relationships which may continue to exist well after bodily death, often in the form of emotional and social attachments maintained perhaps through ritual or reminiscence (Kellehear, 2007). In contrast, social death, which can occur before clinical death, refers to a process whereby an individual is progressively excluded from their social surroundings as contacts and interactions with other decrease to the point where their social identity and functioning are eroded and they can no longer influence the lives of others around them. In a medical context, for example, social death may occur when health professionals no longer address the dying person directly, or when family and friends begin grieving in anticipation of death and gradually reduce or stop direct communication with the dying person. The concept of social death can also be linked to the broader concept of sequestration – the separating out or setting apart of things – and, in the field of gerontology, may be considered as synonymous with a form of marginalisation or the social exclusion of older people. The notion of a 'good' death suggests that its timing and occurrence are in some way appropriate; the death of an older person, for example, would probably be seen as more normal (because they have survived their life course) than one occurring to a younger person where it could be seen as premature. Equally, a 'good death' could mean being surrounded by friends and family and dying in familiar surroundings and a 'bad' death as perhaps ending one's life in a medicalised context devoid of personal contacts.

Although scholars have drawn attention to the relative absence of interest in death and dying in the field of gerontology until the 1960s (Sidell, 1993), and in the sociological strand of gerontological literature until the 1980s (Walter, 1993), the field of psychology has nonetheless increased our understanding, for example through research on people's attitudes when contemplating or confronting their own death, which has led to the development of the concept of 'death concern' or 'death anxiety'. Other studies have also demonstrated the importance of spiritual, cultural and interpersonal factors in shaping end-of-life experiences, and how they influence the grief and bereavement experiences of those who survive. One of the more salient theoretical developments in the field has been the identification and explanation of the ways in which people approach and face death and dying. Glaser and Strauss (1965), for example, through their work on the social organisation of dying and its psychological determinants, identified patterns of awareness of dying and trajectories of dying. One of the most well-known theoretical developments to these stage theories was elaborated by Kübler-Ross (1969), who offered insights into the psychological processes experienced by individuals dealing with terminal illness. Kübler-Ross identified five stages to dying and grief – denial, anger, bargaining, despair and acceptance. As part of a more general criticism of stage theories and their tendency to portray the experiences of dying and bereavement as a linear and uniform process, Kübler-Ross's work was also subsequently heavily criticised for its lack of methodological rigour, and oversimplistic interpretation of complex processes.

Historically speaking, gerontologists themselves appear to have shunned the issues of death and dying, perhaps in an attempt to rid the field of negative images of older people, the later stages of the life course and the ageing process itself. Others have argued that the failure or reticence of those working in the medical field to consider the social dimensions of death and dying has meant that critical discussion of the portrayal of death solely as a biological event is lacking, a situation which probably fails to help the general public who confront both its biomedical and social dimensions (Kellehear, 2007). Kellehear places these criticisms in a wider historical context, and points to the progressive sequestration of the death and dying experiences from society, arguing that dying has passed from being a group experience to becoming a highly private occurrence. In addition, he argues that both death and dying are now predominantly experienced in an institutional rather than a private domestic setting, with the consequence that they are increasingly defined through a medical discourse. Such criticisms raise questions about the power that health professionals have to establish when the dying process begins, how it may be identified, when it is close to occurring, even when it should end and lead to clinical death, but also whether the 'medicalisation' of these experiences mean that individuals are increasingly likely to feel estranged from them. Sociological and historical literature has captured this issue through the 'denial of death' thesis, which suggests that death has become an increasingly marginalised subject in contemporary society, leading to the segregation of the dying in society from other groups (Zimmermann and Rodin, 2004). From a more applied perspective, Lloyd (2004) has offered a convincing criticism of the difficulties in aligning the concept of a 'good death' within current social policy frameworks which emphasise the need to promote individual autonomy, choice and independence during the dying process, an orientation which contradicts the recognition of death and dying as a social process involving others.

Bearing these criticisms in mind, it would seem that there is little scope for expecting any significant developments to current service provisions or policy initiatives either for the dying or for those who accompany them through this process to its final stage of death. This, however, would be an inaccurate conclusion to draw. During the first decade of the twenty-first century in the UK, for example, the ethical dimensions of end-of-life and palliative care, and the circumstances of death have drawn particular attention, with leading advocacy groups for older people, notably Age Concern (2002) and Help the Aged (2002), publishing policy statements on death and dying. Reflected in these policy directives is a commitment to ensuring that people are able to experience a 'good death', that is, a process which provides the dying person with the means of understanding and remaining in control of their situation, which enables them to maintain dignity and have access to appropriate support. In short, the notion of a 'good death' is underpinned by principles which advocate empowerment of the dying, and which have been influential in the development of guidelines for those working in palliative and terminal care contexts. Furthermore, and undoubtedly because of the theoretical and empirical advances made in the field of ageing studies since the 1960s, the recognition that attitudes and approaches to death and dying are culturally diverse has created an awareness of the need for flexible and personalised approaches to dealing with these processes in a medical context.

It may therefore be said that although the field of gerontology, along with practitioners of the medical field, has been criticised for being slow or reticent to integrate the themes of death and dying into research and practice, and to recognise them as complex, psychological, social and cultural phenomena, there is evidence to suggest that these positions are changing. While the inevitability of death cannot be undermined, even as contemporary medical advances may seek to keep it at arm's length for as long as possible, gerontological interest in the process of dying and its outcome opens the way for clearer insights about how to improve our knowledge and understanding of this last phase of our 'life career', and ultimately enhances the dying experience for those concerned.

See also: Ageing, Bereavement, Gerontology, Palliative Care, Social Exclusion, Social Relations

REFERENCES

Glaser, B. G. and Strauss, A. (1965) *Awareness of Dying*. New York: Aldine.
Help the Aged (2002) *Making Decisions around the End-of-Life*. Help the Aged Policy Statement. London: Help the Aged.
Kellehear, A. (2007) *A Social History of Dying*. Cambridge: Cambridge University Press. Kübler-Ross, E. (1969) *On Death and Dying*. London: Routledge.
Lloyd, L. (2004) Mortality and morality: ageing and the ethics of care. *Ageing and Society*, 24: 235–256.
Seale, C. (1998) *Constructing Death: The Sociology of Dying and Bereavement*. Cambridge: Cambridge University Press.
Sidell, M. (1993) Death, dying and bereavement, in J. Bond, P. Coleman and S. Peace (eds), *Ageing in Society: An Introduction to Social Gerontology*. London: Sage. pp. 378–386.

Dementia

A clinical state, characterised by a loss of function in multiple cognitive domains and accompanied by a series of symptoms that accompany diseases or conditions that affect the functioning of the brain.

Diagnostic features of dementia include memory impairment and at least one of the following: loss of power to understand words (aphasia), complete or partial loss of the ability to perform complex muscular movements (apraxia), impaired ability to recognise objects and sounds (agnosia) and disturbances in executive functioning. In addition, the cognitive impairments must be severe enough to cause impairment in social and occupational functioning. Importantly, the decline must represent a decline from a previously higher level of functioning (American Psychiatric Association, 1994).

Commonly, dementia starts gradually and progresses over the course of several years. As well as the diagnostic criteria, symptoms can include confusion, mood swings and changes in personality (where a patient may become fearful or irritable) and behaviour (where, for example, the patient may wander or show personal neglect).

Generally, dementia is viewed as *mild* when the affected individual can manage independently, *moderate* when some support is needed to perform tasks of daily living, and *severe* when continual help and support are necessary. Although there are several types, the three main categories are *Alzheimer's* (the most common form, affecting around 417,000 people in the UK), *vascular* (the second most common) and *mixed* (where Alzheimer's and vascular are found together) (Kitwood, 1997).

Although the diagnostic criteria for dementia seem clear, actual diagnosis is not. As Kitwood (1997) notes, first, some diagnostic tools measure performance at one particular time, whereas it is essential to measure the decline in performance, that is, a decline between two points in time. Secondly, depression can express itself in cognitive impairment, and both dementia and depression involve neurological changes. There is therefore uncertainty as to whether the diagnosis should be based on clinical judgement or on psychological testing.

It has been proposed that 'dementia has probably replaced cancer as the most feared [disease] by older people' (Bond and Corner, 2001: 95). Others argue that the stigma surrounding dementia is decreasing gradually, and those who are given the diagnosis are receiving help in accepting the implications (Kitwood, 1997). As a result, we can see a shift towards a social model of patient-centred care.

In 1901, a 51-year-old woman admitted to the state asylum in Frankfurt, Germany, was presenting symptoms recognisable as some form of dementia, and was placed under the care of Dr Alois Alzheimer. *Post mortem*, her brain was studied by the psychiatrist Emil Kraepelin. Alzheimer presented the case in 1907, where he discussed both cognitive and non-cognitive features (e.g. hallucinations and behavioural deficits) of dementia. The last century saw a great advancement in diagnostic tools, such as CT scanning, thus enhancing our clinical understanding. However, by the late 1980s it was generally accepted that dementia is a descriptive term and it should refer to the whole person and not just the brain (Kitwood, 1997). A good illustration of how this principle has entered the policy domain in the UK is in the *National Service Framework for Older People* (Department of Health, 2001), where the Department of Health has committed itself to providing older people and their carers with person-centred care and services.

Although dementia is a medical condition, it can be an extremely distressing diagnosis to come to terms with. As it progresses, it can be a major challenge for significant others to witness, especially if they are also in a caregiving role. In addition, formal care-providers are particularly susceptible to strain in the dementia care environment. It is therefore essential that (1) the highest standards of psychosocial patient care are maintained, (2) strong and accessible networks exist to support the informal carer, and (3) formal carers receive up-to-date training and psychological support.

The late Professor Tom Kitwood made a significant contribution to ensuring that individuals living with dementia are treated as unique and worthy. Central to this is the notion of *personhood*, which he defined as 'as standing or status that is bestowed upon one human being by others. ... It implies recognition, respect and trust' (1997: 8). He argued that interpersonal and psychosocial factors can play a major role in the degree to which and the duration that a person with dementia can maintain relationships, utilise abilities and experience enjoyment. However, he suggested that the ill-being that dementia brings, first, takes our focus away from the 'inadequacy of our social arrangements' (1997: 40) and, secondly, we may see treatment comprising medication in the main rather than sympathy and psychological interventions – the latter for both the person with dementia and his or her caregiver(s).

There is, of course, an expansive range of current research areas investigating dementia from the clinical perspective, not least in the promising and novel area of stem cell research. However, against the backdrop of social gerontology, this section focuses on the psychosocial, and two common interventions are discussed here.

Generally, the goal of successful therapy in this context is to increase the quality of life of the person with dementia, and this is generally measured on the Quality of Life–Alzheimer's Disease (QOL–AD) scale. NICE (2006) recommends, for example, Cognitive Stimulation Therapy (CST) for individuals with mild to moderate dementia. CST comprises 14 sessions of activities that are aimed to stimulate and engage. The viability of CST was tested recently, and it was found that, although the level of cognitive functioning remained unchanged, the quality of life had improved (Woods et al., 2006).

One of the most popular interventions in psychosocial dementia care is Reminiscence Therapy (RT). The therapy involves the telling of life stories by those living with dementia, and is frequently in the form of group sessions, often integrating photographs and mementos, and increasingly including family caregivers. The experience is generally enjoyed by staff and care recipients alike. Thus there is some evidence that it is mood-enhancing for those without dementia, though its efficacy in improving the mood of those with dementia is less clear. Woods et al. (2009) attempted to review previous studies on RT for dementia. Although the studies identified were too diverse to compare scientifically, they found significant increases in the patients' mood and in staff's knowledge of their patients or residents, and a significant decrease in familial caregiver strain. They concluded that further research is required to draw robust conclusions.

The person living with dementia is extremely vulnerable and, with increasing cognitive degeneration, he or she becomes less and less able to articulate needs and demand (human) rights. However, it should be noted that this decline is gradual, and someone with dementia in a mild form may be very capable of expressing needs. Further, a patient-centred approach aims to keep the individual at the hub of decision making for as long as possible. Putting this into practice is not always an easy task. As Hubbard et al. (2003) note, ways to facilitate this include staff showing greater flexibility and time, timely meetings with the affected person, involving formal and informal caregivers and providers in discussions, and research training. Indeed, (not) meeting patients' needs is assessed differently by caregivers than by the patients themselves (Orrell et al., 2008); caregivers may feel they are meeting needs, but in many instances the patients do not.

For those living in residential care, an approach (initiated by Kitwood, 1997) that has emerged since the early 1990s is Dementia Care Mapping (DCM), a training package that has been developed for multidisciplinary teams working with dementia patients. DCM is a tool with which to measure the effects of care given on dimensions such as well-being, ill-being and positive person work (Bradford Dementia Group, 2007). Through multidisciplinary dialogue, the care team is able to assess each patient's response to his or her care package, and action plans can be drawn up to (1) promote the quality of the patient's well-being, (2) organise staff care in a patient-centred way, and (3) inform management with regard to resource allocations and staff training needs.

dementia

73

Finally, the pathway of the person with dementia reaches the severe stage. Downs (n.d.) likens dementia to a series of losses: loss of role, of place, of abilities and control, of family and friends, of who one knew oneself to be. She argues strongly for the necessity of advocacy, from diagnosis to end of life. People living with dementia may come to rely on advocates and advocacy groups increasingly, and without an advocate, they can all too easily lose their value as persons with human rights.

See also: *Advocacy, Biographical Approaches, Care, Gerontology, Quality of Life*

REFERENCES

American Psychiatric Association (1994) *Diagnostic and Statistical Manual of Mental Disorders* (4th edition). Washington, DC: American Psychiatric Association.

Bond, J. and Corner, L. (2001) Researching dementia: are there unique methodological challenges for health service research? *Ageing and Society*, 21: 95–116.

Bradford Dementia Group (2007) *Dementia Care Mapping (DCM): Report on Activity August 2006–2007*. Bradford: University of Bradford.

Department of Health (2001) *National Service Framework for Older People: Executive Summary*. London: Department of Health.

Downs, M. G. (n.d.) *Living with Dementia: Advocacy from Diagnosis to End of Life*. Bradford: University of Bradford, Division of Dementia Studies.

Hubbard, G., Downs, M. G. and Tester, S. (2003) Including older people with dementia in research: challenges and strategies. *Ageing and Mental Health*, 7(5): 351–362.

Kitwood, T. (1997) *Dementia Reconsidered: The Person Comes First*. Buckingham: Open University Press.

NICE (National Institute for Health and Clinical Excellence) (2006) *Dementia: Supporting People with Dementia and their Carers in Health and Social Care*. NICE clinical guideline 42. London: NICE.

Orrell, M., Hancock, G. A., Liyanage, K. C., Woods, B., Challis, D. and Hoe, J. (2008) The needs of people with dementia in care homes: the perspectives of users, staff and family caregivers. *International Psychogeriatrics*, 20(5): 941–951.

Woods, B., Spector, A., Jones, C. A., Orrell, M. and Davies, S. P. (2009) Reminiscence therapy for dementia (review). *The Cochrane Library, Issue 1*.

Woods, B., Thorgrimsen, L., Spector, A., Royan, L. and Orrell, M. (2006) Improved quality of life and cognitive stimulation therapy in dementia. *Ageing and Mental Health*, 10(3): 207–210.

> *A complex phenomenon to define impairments and limitations to older people's activity.*

There are two areas of concern to contend with when discussing disability in the context of social gerontology. First, there is a tendency to view disability from the medical perspective alone, whereas a cogent argument proposes that the individual has impairments and it is society that disables (Oliver, 1996; Shakespeare and Watson, 2002). Secondly, there is a wealth of research on disability and research on older people, but a lack of research on disability in later life (Priestley and Rabiee, 2001).

In the UK, Help the Aged (2004) reports that within the working population in Great Britain in 2003 nearly one in five (6.9 million) people were disabled. There are much higher figures among the older population. For example, in 2001, 60% of this group reported having a longstanding illness and in 2003, 32% experienced hearing difficulties and nearly half of those aged 85 plus experienced eyesight difficulties. Women experience more disability in later life than men. All of these difficulties can affect instrumental activities of daily living (IADLs), such as household chores, shopping and using public transport, and they can also be affected significantly by cognitive impairment (Preston, 2008). Both normal ageing processes (e.g. reduction in bone mass, changes in body composition) and co-morbidities (e.g. Alzheimer's, depression) increase the risk of disability. Many of these factors make it more likely that an older person may fall, which in turn can lead to injury, pain and loss of function.

The traditional model of disability (the medical model) maintains that a disabled person cannot participate fully in society due to their disability, and the goal is to overcome the impairment – which is, of course, not always possible. In other words, disabled individuals need 'to be treated' in some way in order to 'allow' them to live in mainstream society as well as they can. On the other hand, the social model of disability differentiates between *impairment* and *disability*. The impairment may have a long-term effect on the appearance and/or functional capacity of an individual. The

disability

disability is 'the loss or limitation of *opportunities to take part in society* on an equal level with others due to social and environmental barriers' (Office for Disability Issues, n.d.: para. 3, emphasis added).

The social model paradigm, which was initially specific to the UK, has evolved since the 1970s, largely thanks to the activists working within the Union of the Physically Impaired Against Segregation (UPIAS) (Shakespeare and Watson, 2002). At the heart of the model lies the sentiment that, 'if people with impairments are disabled by society, then the priority is to dismantle these disabling barriers' (2002: 4–5). The means to attaining this was through a campaign for civil rights, which led to anti-discrimination legislation, but also through raising awareness amomgst the non-disabled and bringing about a change in societal perceptions of 'the disabled'. A prime example of how this was done is illustrated in Oliver (1996: 34) with a comparison of the medical model, which he refers to as 'the individual model', and the social model. Medical terminology such as 'personal tragedy theory', 'care', 'control' and 'individual adaptation' is replaced respectively in the social model by 'social oppression theory', 'rights', 'choice' and 'social change'.

The social model of disability has since gained universal acceptance. However, as much as the activists' work has contributed to equality of opportunity (the degree of its success being a contentious point), some would argue that this has had little impact on disabled older people. For example, much public debate has focused on disability rights and the workplace, whereby most disabled people are older and retired (Priestley and Rabiee, 2002).

The natural process of ageing brings with it an increasing risk of disability. From the clinical standpoint, the focus is on health promotion and prevention as well as intervention and rehabilitation. At the same time, there are psychosocial implications for the disabled individual, because disability can lower quality of life, and both mental and physical disability can lead to hospitalisation or, indeed, residential care. As the British Geriatrics Society (2005) points out, its goal has been to ensure that older people maintain good health and participate in life for as long as possible. It suggests that, through physical activity, a healthy diet and smoking cessation, disability can be delayed by up to ten years. Further preventative measures can include flu immunisation, opportunistic screening of diseases such as osteoporosis and cancer, and early identification of dementia.

For those older people who are contending with increasing levels of disability, there are an array of interventions that can be implemented.

However, as Preston (2008) emphasises, disability often comprises several elements; a multidisciplinary approach is essential, as is the accurate diagnosis of all factors and co-morbidities. Interventions can include physiotherapy, Tai Chi, occupational therapy, adjustments to the home (thus enabling the older person to remain in place), visual and auditory aids, drug treatments and surgery.

According to Priestley and Rabiee (2002), disabled people's groups have campaigned successfully for changes in legislation (and hence in social policy), for example resulting, in the UK context, in the 1995 Disability Discrimination Act. Simultaneously, organisations such as Age Concern and Help the Aged campaign for greater rights for older people without making reference to disability rights explicitly. Additionally, there are parallels between the two sets of campaigns – for example, the former lobby for 'accessible housing' and the latter for 'housing for life'. However, it is crucial to note that there is no 'one size fits all' solution for establishing the needs of and gaining the rights for younger and older disabled people. For instance, while we see older people's groups objecting to age-based decisions on whether to resuscitate a patient or not (Priestley and Rabiee, 2002), we also see a growing number of individuals (younger and older) lobbying to legalise physician-assisted suicide (e.g. Dyer, 2006).

In summary, while academic interest in ageing has increased significantly, there still appears to be little evidence of significant research interest and innovation linking disability issues with theory, nor of debate within the field (see Oldman, 2002; Priestley and Rabiee, 2001). It would seem, therefore, that the way forward is to evaluate more fully the benefits of a closer cooperation between the two research areas.

An umbrella term of disability includes activity limitations and participation restrictions which can result from psychological attitudes, environments (e.g. clothes, housing shopping design) and social support networks. On the clinical front, a wealth of research has informed policy and practice (to debatable degrees), and due to social and political activism from (self-)advocate groups, disabled individuals are now more likely than ever before to claim *some* of their rights, and this trend is at least moving in the right direction.

When understood and implemented correctly by healthcare professionals, the social model of disability is best practice. However, it is often the case that older people suffer the discrimination associated with the medical model as they become service users (Oldman, 2002).

The disabled older person is disadvantaged on multiple levels: services sometimes discriminate against older people, meaning that older disabled service users are receiving lower quality treatment that younger disabled service users (Department of Health, 2001). Secondly, older disabled people are more likely to be affected by mental health issues and cognitive impairment than younger disabled people. In the UK, as Help the Aged (2004) reports, in 2001, 14% of women and 9% of men aged 60–74 were affected by a neurotic disorder such as panic and anxiety, between 10% and 20% have experienced depression, and over 750,000 were affected by dementia. Thirdly, the disabled older person is, by definition, a member of two stigmatised groups. Shakespeare and Watson (2002) note that the fight for the social model of disability, where self-advocacy played a pivotal role, 'transformed' group self-esteem. While some older people are active members of advocacy groups such as Age Concern and Help the Aged, these are largely driven by younger people. Fourthly, considering the implications of pensioner poverty, irrespective of levels of impairment, in Great Britain, 56% of pensioners live in severe poverty (Help the Aged, 2008). This lack of financial resources is a barrier to social participation and can increase feelings of social isolation and loneliness. Additionally, those living in poverty and with impairments are less likely to be able to purchase services and aids that can improve their quality of life than those, for example, who are still in employment. The reality that some service provision is of such poor standard that some service users opt to self-finance disability aids, medical treatments and care is a document of failure.

See also: *Advocacy, Ageing, Care, Gerontology, Housing, Loneliness, Quality of Life, Social Support*

REFERENCES

Department of Health (2001) *National Service Framework for Older People: Executive Summary*. London: Department of Health.

Office for Disability Issues (n.d.). *The Social and Medical Models of Disability: A Brief Introduction to Viewing Disability*. Available at: www.officefordisability.gov.uk/ resources/ models-of-disability.asp (accessed 20 February 2009).

key concepts in
social gerontology

Elder Mistreatment/Abuse

> *Actions perpetrated by a trusted other, intended or not, that risk harm to a vulnerable older adult.*

Elder abuse is widely used in public discourse to describe the maltreatment of older adults. Conceptual developments in the field of gerontology, however, now recognise that elder abuse represents one specific form of a more encompassing range of mistreatment. The concept of elder mistreatment represents the scientific approach to understanding the potential series of situations in which older adults may experience ill-treatment (Bonnie and Wallace, 2003). It is important to note that this concept excludes elder self-neglect as well as harm perpetrated by a stranger, that is committed by one with whom there is no trust-based relationship.

The complexity of elder mistreatment is easily understood via the work of Hudson and colleagues (1998). They propose a theoretical taxonomy that distinguishes five levels to understanding such behaviour. These levels move from the general to the specific. The general form is broadly termed mistreatment, while specific forms distinguish whether the mistreatment occurs through relationships with personal/informal sources or professional/formal providers. Mistreatment is then further defined as either abuse or neglect, and intentional or unintentional. Finally, the specific forms of destructive behaviour – physical, emotional, psychological and financial – are identified.

The legal foundation for addressing elder mistreatment in the USA first appeared after the Second World War when a renewed energy towards addressing social problems arose. The US government recognised the issue when they developed adult protective services in the 1950s, in tandem with attention being paid to family violence generally. Social service and medical professions began directing their attention to the maltreatment of elders during the 1970s, though formal efforts to address the subject had begun at least two decades beforehand

(Wolf, 2003). Renewed interest emerged in congressional hearings during the late 1970s. The outcome of those hearings involved a decision to raise awareness of the problem and continue support for adult protective services. Elder mistreatment and abuse later became subsumed under the Older Adults Act in the late 1980s, due to the diligence of Congressman Claude Pepper, subsumed under the topic of family violence (Bonnie and Wallace, 2003). As a family violence matter, the constituency broadened to include the medical and criminal justice communities. It should be noted that elder mistreatment was initially approached as a caregiving situation, where a vulnerable elder was cared for by an adult feeling overburdened from stresses due to family and job obligations.

Elder mistreatment and abuse first gained much attention in the UK during the 1960s amid reports of abuse in the formal service sector. In 2004, the House of Commons Health Select Committee commissioned a study addressing the prevalence of elder abuse (McCreadie et al., 2006). This call has been taken up by researchers at King's College and the National Centre for Social Research.

Measures for assessing elder mistreatment first surfaced in the early 1980s in the USA. For instance, Fulmer et al. (1984) developed the Elder Assessment Instrument, which was meant to provide clinicians with evidence of possible elder mistreatment. This instrument involves a 40-item screening tool that takes approximately 12–15 minutes to administer. It taps both subjective and objective manifestations of abuse to aid a clinician in deciding whether to refer an older adult for suspected mistreatment. The limitations of the instrument are that specificity of abuse and mistreatment is weak. The Hwalek–Sengstock Elder Abuse Screening Test (Hwalek and Sengstock, 1986; Neale et al., 1991) provides a bit more specificity. This 15-item assessment screen detects suspected elder abuse and neglect regarding physical, financial, psychological and neglectful situations. It represents three conceptual domains: violation of personal rights, characteristics of vulnerability and potentially abusive situations. McCreadie et al. (2006) convened groups of older adults, caregivers and professionals working with older adults to develop an elder abuse measure and research design aimed to capture reliable and valid data on elder abuse in the UK.

It is now widely recognised that no one theory may fully explain the occurrence of elder mistreatment. Wolf (2003) proposes that what must be taken into account are individual, social and cultural aspects in a given situation. It is increasingly accepted that accounting for factors in several domains may represent the best approach to understanding such a complex construct. For instance, accounting for individual psychopathology, such as alcohol abuse, may not fully explain situations of elder mistreatment. One must also consider the nature of interpersonal relationships, as explained by situational theory (referring to caregiver stress and the overburdened informal caregiver) and exchange theory (referring to dependencies that exist between a victim and a perpetrator), both of which take place in a particular socio-historical time period, as potentially explained by political economic theory (referring to the marginalisation of elders in society). Multiple factors, considered in tandem, may provide the most informed understanding of elder mistreatment.

A fully developed theoretical framework is important in so far as it may provide a consensus on what exactly constitutes elder mistreatment. Prevalence levels may then be accurately gauged as well as providing a framework for understanding why elder mistreatment occurs (i.e. provide a causal sequence). In particular, a focus on the process inherent to mistreatment may provide clues as to the factors which produce or predispose a situation of elder mistreatment, which may then lead to the development of strategies to prevent and/or rid us of its occurrence. Of central significance is understanding the heterogeneity that characterises elder mistreatment, and developing a scientific understanding as opposed to a purely legal classification which tends to vary by locale (Bonnie and Wallace, 2003).

The prevalence of elder abuse is of great concern as such information provides a critical basis upon which to understand its occurrence and antecedents. Recent studies carried out in the USA and the UK address prevalence rates. According to the National Council for Social Research report on elder abuse and neglect (O'Keeffe et al., 2007), the overall prevalence rate reported in the UK was 2.6% of people aged 66 and above. A considerable proportion of people reporting mistreatment were users of services. Four types of abuse (as well as neglect) were studied: financial, physical, sexual and psychological. The most often reported mistreatment involved neglect (1.1%), followed by financial abuse (0.7%). When harmful behaviour by neighbours and acquaintances were included, the estimated prevalence rate was 4%. Finally, only women (no men) reported mistreatment. The authors suggest that under-reporting is highly likely because mistreated elders may be least likely to participate.

A recent US population-based study (Laumann et al., 2008) examined mistreatment defined as verbal, financial or physical mistreatment by a family member. Examining those aged 57 and older, prevalence varied from less than 1% with regard to physical abuse, to 3.5% regarding financial abuse, to 10% regarding verbal abuse. Women were approximately twice as likely to report verbal abuse as men, and the young-old were more likely to report mistreatment of any kind.

In practice, the detection of elder mistreatment may be culturally sensitive. Specifically, it is important to know how a group defines abuse as well as to inquire whether or not the older adult feels abused. For instance, Hudson et al. (1998) found that an expert panel's definition of abuse as occurring with 'sufficient frequency and/or intensity' did not sit well with Native Americans, who felt that if it occurred just once, it was to be termed abuse. It is also important to recognise that norms against elder mistreatment and abuse are generally not sufficient to ensure it does not happen. It is useful to arrange intergenerational dialogues about social and cultural patterns as well as to track the changes in trends that may contribute to incidents of elder abuse.

Images of elder mistreatment include a wide array of situations from institutional to family settings. Policy, programme and research initiatives have often been constructed by paying attention to child and intimate partner abuse.

See also: *Care, Gerontology*

REFERENCES

Bonnie, R. J. and Wallace, R. B. (eds) (2003) *Elder Mistreatment: Abuse, Neglect, and Exploitation in an Ageing America*. Washington, DC: National Academic Press.

Fulmer, T., Street, S. and Carr, K. (1984) Abuse of the elderly: screening and detection. *Journal of Emergency Nursing*, 10(3): 131–140.

Hudson, M. F., Armachain, W. D., Beasley, C. M. and Carlson, J. R. (1998) Elder abuse: two Native American views. *The Gerontologist*, 38(5): 538–548.

Hwalek, M. and Sengstock, M. (1986) Assessing the probability of abuse of the elderly: toward development of a clinical screening instrument. *Journal of Applied Gerontology*, 5(2): 153–173.

Laumann, E. O., Leitsch, S. A. and Waite, L. J. (2008) Elder mistreatment in the United States: prevalence estimates from a nationally representative study. *The Journal of Gerontology*, 63B(4): S248–S254.

McCreadie, C., Tinker, A., Biggs, S., Manthopre, J., O'Keeffe, M., Doyle, M., Hills, A. and Erens, B. (2006) First steps: the UK national prevalence study of the mistreatment and abuse of older people. *The Journal of Adult Protection*, 8(3): 4–11.

Neale, A., Hwalek, M., Scott, R., Sengstock, M. and Stahl, C. (1991) Validation of the Hwalek–Sengstock elder abuse screening test. *Journal of Applied Gerontology*, 10(4): 406–418.

key concepts in
social gerontology

O'Keeffe, M., Hills, A., Doyle, M., McCreadie, C., Scholes, S., Constantine, R., Tinker, A., Manthorpe, J., Biggs, S., Erens, B. et al. (2007) *UK Study of Abuse and Neglect of Older People: Prevalence Survey Report*. London: National Centre for Social Research.

Wolf, R. (2003) Appendix C: Elder abuse and neglect: history and concepts, in R. J. Bonnie and R. B. Wallace (eds), *Elder Mistreatment: Abuse, Neglect, and Exploitation in an Ageing America*. Washington, DC: National Academic Press. pp. 238–248.

Environmental Gerontology

> **The interaction between the older person and their environments.**

Ageing occurs in the context of an environment. Peace et al. (2006) broaden this definition to include different layers of environment: the macro (beyond the familial) and micro (the immediate surroundings of the individual); the social, natural and psychological environment; and the environment as public, private and personal space.

The links between the social and the physical environment, however, have been neglected in empirical and theoretical research, particularly in the UK. Yet, it is important to study both the social and physical environment as they present major resources or constraints for older people's quality of life. Such relationships can also be studied across levels – from the local (home) to the global.

Environmental gerontology has been dominated by American researchers, with the primary influence being the Chicago School of Urban Sociology of the 1920s and 1930s. A further formative role in this branch of gerontology was played by Powell Lawton, who developed the relationship between the environment and ageing or the 'ecology of ageing', as it is sometimes called. One of the most acknowledged theories in this area is that developed by Lawton and Nahemow (1973), called the Press–Competence model. The lower the competency (e.g. mobility,

environmental gerontology

cognitive decline) of the older person and the stronger the 'environmental press' (e.g. poor housing conditions), the more negative the impact on the behaviour and well-being of the older person.

The theoretical understanding of this relationship has developed primarily through the discipline of psychology and it is only relatively recently that social science has played a part in looking at the links between the physical and spatial and the cultural, social and psychological aspects of the environment. Consequently, the model has been modified to recognise the complexity of the relationship – that is, older people can shape their environment in positive ways. The model was also later modified into the Person–Environment Fit model with an emphasis on personal needs rather than competence.

Increasingly, there has been a broadening of research under the badge of environmental gerontology to include: psychological aspects of the environment, such as identity and ageing and the meaning and attachment to place; the physical and material environment through the study of housing in later life; retirement communities; rural ageing; urban ageing; ageing in disadvantaged areas; the social environment of ageing and older people's use of space. Much of this research has applicability in policy and practice development.

The broader focus on these areas is a response to the concern that there should be more attention paid to cultural aspects and the meaning of place, integrating social theory and cultural geography into the equation. Trends within geography have also influenced the development of gerontological approaches through the influence of health geography and the application of the concept to the ageing body, the home and institutional settings.

The environmental press model referred to above has been significant in its application to housing adaptation and design. A focus on research of the living arrangements of older people initially concentrated on the design, architecture and structure of individual buildings, along with residential segregation and long-term care settings. Much of this focused on specialist settings such as residential care (Willcocks et al., 1987) or assisted living. The link between accommodation and care, in particular for those with dementia, has been a fruitful area for research and practice with the debate about whether specialist or general community housing is the most appropriate for safety and privacy.

Understanding the influence of environment in ageing has developed into several other applied areas:

- Older people in deprived areas. Looking at how disadvantaged environments impact on older people has highlighted that designing spaces within urban areas will be of increasing importance in an agenda of inclusion, which doesn't leave older people feeling trapped and vulnerable (Scharf et al., 2002).
- The meaning of home and attachment to place is of increasing significance in social relations and impacts on self-perception and identity (Peace et al., 2006). As people age the immediate environment of the home and neighbourhood may become more important to them.
- 'Ageing in place' is a continuing thread in environmental research and is a policy driver for supporting older people to 'stay put'. The impact of change within an area can have significant effects on people who 'age in place', as change can present a significant risk for older people and service delivery as facilities exit certain neighbourhoods. How older people manage such change is increasingly a focus for gerontology. 'Ageing in place' and a familiarity with the environment can hide a deterioration in cognitive and physical functioning.
- The use of space. As people go through the life course and grow older their use of space changes (Rowles, 1978). Spatial use and mobility may be restricted through disability, dependency and care needs; retirement or movement into institutional care; or expanded through retirement, travel and leisure interests, migration and relocation. Different older people will have a different meaning and use of space depending on their biography and past experiences. The use of space may also change as a result of changes in the environment, for example through physical features of the environment (redevelopment, regeneration, topography and the accessibility of buildings and services in the neighbourhood, such as the increase of out-of-town retailing and leisure facilities or the location of bus routes). Social factors such as population density, crime rate and ethnic mix may also influence people's use and perception of space and their radius of activity (Scharf et al., 2002). Changes in the use and meaning of space can relate both to space within the private space of home and outside in the public environment. Peace et al. (2006) looked at the connection between the environment and well-being in relation to older people living in different domestic and residential settings.

Further areas under environmental gerontology which have had a practical application are in relation to reducing the fear of crime and promoting perceptions of safety through urban design (Liang et al., 1986); decision-making in relation to relocation across the life course; and the impact of technology on the environment through the development of 'smart homes', where wireless and digital systems of communication provide older people with solutions to challenges of daily living.

Increasingly, there has been a focus on more macro global environments. Theoretical approaches have not as yet developed at this macro level, although the critical ecological approach drawing on the work of Bronfenbrenner (1979) has begun to address this in relation to rural ageing (Keating and Phillips, 2008). Globalisation and urbanisation is an expanding subject area at this macro level of environment and ageing. As Chris Phillipson (2006) has argued, cities are undergoing rapid change, through the process of globalisation, which is promoting some cities while creating problems for others. Paradoxically, globalisation produces huge movements of people, but with increasing numbers of older people maintaining a strong sense of attachment to particular places. Thus, proximity, distance and transport become particularly significant when care needs arise (Phillips and Bernard, 2008). On a global level, climate change and the impact on vulnerable older people is an area of further development.

The complexity of the relationship between the person and environment requires numerous perspectives to be applied if we are to understand the contextualisation of ageing (Peace et al., 2007). In summarising the state of environmental gerontology, Windley and Wiseman (2004) note that the applicability of the concept to practice at a neighbourhood and macro scale is limited, with most of the application on the interior environment or the scale of the building. There is therefore scope for the application to be further developed, which, given the new environmental challenges facing future cohorts of older people, such as the use of high-tech care within the home environment, will be of crucial importance.

See also: *Ageing, Ageing in Place, Assisted Living, Care, Cohort, Dementia, Disability, Gerontology, Housing, Long-term Care, Quality of Life, Retirement, Social Relations*

FURTHER READING

Peace, S., Wahl, H.-W., Mollenkopf, H. and Oswald, F. (2007) Environment and ageing, in J. Bond, S. Peace, F. Dittmann-Kohli and G. Westerhof (eds), *Ageing in Society* (3rd edition). London: British Society of Gerontology with Sage. pp. 209–235.

REFERENCES

Peace, S., Holland, C. and Kellaher, L. (2006) *Environment and Identity in Later Life*. Buckingham: Open University Press.

Rowles, G. (1978) *Prisoners of Space? Exploring the Geographic Experience of Older People*. Boulder, CO: Westview Press.

Scharf, T., Phillipson, C., Smith, A. E. and Kingston, P. (2002) *Growing Older in Socially Deprived Areas: Social Exclusion in Later Life*. London: Help the Aged.

Willcocks, D., Peace, S. and Kelleher, L. (1987) *Private Lives in Public Places*. London: Tavistock.

Windley, P. and Wiseman, G. (2004) Environmental gerontology research and practice: the challenge of application, in H.-W. Wahl, R. Scheidt and P. Windley (eds), Ageing in Context: Socio-Physical Environments, in *Annual Review of Gerontology and Geriatrics*, 23: 334–365.

Ethnicity

> *Identification of and membership within a social group based on shared values, beliefs and lifestyles.*

The importance of ethnicity to ageing generally occurs in two forms: the significance of cultural characteristics that differentiate the ageing experience, and the influence of a minority (or dominant) status on the ageing experience that arises with an ethnic affiliation. Cultural approaches to the study of ethnicity often address issues of values and norms, while the minority status approach involves attention to power and resources (Markides, 1983). The importance of ethnicity in the USA and UK has emerged only recently, over the last few decades, as key to understanding the ageing process. The emergence of ethnicity as a significant factor parallels the rise of immigration to both countries, and the associated growth in diversity.

The meaning and experience of ageing are linked to diverse cultural codes and priorities, which occur over the life course. Expectations based on these ethnic characteristics may stem from a number of specific factors, including religion, national origin and immigrant status. Religious orientations that diverge from the dominant practice often include particular rituals and behaviours. For example, religious practices associated with Islam may provide beneficial outcomes in old age. Conversations with older Muslims in the USA suggest multiple health advantages stemming from the practice of Islam. Religious beliefs that guide behaviours and result in these health benefits include the dietary restrictions associated with a prohibition from consuming pork or alcohol, rituals that demand discipline, such as fasting from dawn until sunset during the month of Ramadan, as well as physical activity, including the bowing/prostration involved in the five daily prayers. These and similar activities are often listed as contributing to both the mental and physical well-being of Muslims as they enter their later years (see Ajrouch, 2008).

Cultural codes may also stem from national origins. Wray (2003) suggests that women in various national origin groups are more likely to feel older at younger chronological ages because of cultural life-course differences that stem from particular countries. Bangladeshi women in the UK become mothers, on average, earlier in the life course than white British women. The timing of childbirth and family responsibilities constitute two examples of social roles that inform the identification of one as old. The timing of old age is of particular relevance with regard to ethnicity.

Issues of culture and ethnicity are particularly critical when considering immigration. Immigrant elders are at risk of depressed mood or affect due to the stresses of immigration, acculturation and high rates of family disruption (Aranda and Miranda, 1997; Mui, 1996; Plawecki, 2000; Wilmoth and Chen, 2003). Assumptions related to the tenets of assimilation ideas are less often applied to understand the ageing process (Markides, 1983). When they are, the issues addressed often emphasise the differences between members of an ethnic group and the majority culture. For instance, Akhtar and Choi (2004) argue that immigrants face more complicated difficulties in the realm of psychosocial development during middle and old age. Cultural divides between host country and homeland ways of life lead to more emotional turmoil concerning the experiences of children leaving home, retirement and death. As a result, the authors emphasise the critical role that marital status, and particularly high-quality relationships with a spouse, may play in buffering the vulnerabilities associated with the immigrant experience in ageing.

Language abilities also represent a key issue for understanding the import of ethnicity to ageing. Fluency is salient for immigrant/ethnic groups, providing integration opportunities and promoting cultural understanding

(Barresi, 1987; Lubben and Bacerra, 1987). Research on immigrant well-being, however, suggests that bilingual abilities provide a more productive pathway for well-being, allowing individuals to accommodate the demands of both host and home culture expectations. Not having to forfeit their native cultural ways in order to acquire the skills of their new society helps members of an immigrant/ethnic group to achieve bicultural adaptation which is correlated with good well-being (Cuellar et al., 2004).

The significance of immigrant status to ageing is also important when one considers living arrangements (Wilmoth and Chen, 2003). For example, older individuals in the USA see the letting go of children as an element of the rites of passage moving into adulthood, while older immigrants, especially those who come from less individualistic communities, may have trouble with this phase (Akhtar and Choi, 2004). Immigrants, in particular, may be susceptible to cultural differences in changes regarding daily routines. Arriving in the USA, immigrants often find that daily social activities are organised and scheduled to accommodate work obligations. Visiting with friends and other family members more often occurs on weekends or holidays, whereas in the country of origin visiting may be likely to occur daily and/or during evening hours.

Some cultural approaches to understanding the role of ethnicity in the experience of ageing adopt the tenets of modernisation theory, which posits that older people in an ethnic culture lose status because younger members of the group adopt the values of a modern industrial society. The accumulation of life experiences no longer holds the power and prestige it once did due to the emphasis on technology. The changing role of older adults in ethnic settings, particularly between immigrants and US-born, may therefore be understood as shaped by a move from more agricultural settings where their skill set and knowledge base were highly valuable and shaped future generation well-being, to those that are industrialised and contingent on emerging scientific and technological developments. Yet, the place of older adults within ethnic families and communities may include alternative scenarios. Modernisation theory does not uniformly lead to the disappearance of a cultural background. Markides (1983) suggests that older immigrants do not necessarily forfeit their cultural ways. Moreover, the development of *barrios* and ethnic enclaves often provides a critical coping mechanism for the experience of discrimination, prejudice and marginalisation, which also provide opportunities for cultural retention.

With regard to the minority group effects of ethnicity, Markides (1983) argues that we may need to focus less on traditional indicators of well-being, such as life satisfaction and morale, since these are likely to be sensitive to reference group effects. What may be more meaningful is a direct examination of objective factors such as wealth and political power. For instance, many of the most recent immigrant elders tend to live in urban areas, in poverty (Becker, 2003). Markides (1983) suggests that attention to structural factors, or those objective facts that influence well-being such as economic standing and the political economy of ageing, may provide more insight into how inequalities come to bear on ethnic ageing experiences.

For some ethnic groups, particularly those who are most recently immigrants, the challenges associated with ageing are rarely addressed in open forums. This may be due to the embarrassment that often accompanies a call for help among recent immigrants. Additionally, romanticised cultural ideals about the role of family may constitute a barrier to ethnic communities seriously considering developing programme and policy options that serve the needs of older members. Caring for older adults is often shouldered alone, without the benefit of community resources, support or a public validation of the challenges associated with caregiving situations.

Such findings suggest that basic gerontological concepts developed in the USA and the UK may incur different meanings across various cultures (Wray, 2003). For instance, what it means to be independent may hinge on more social and interdependent processes in non-US or non-UK cultures as opposed to individual processes that characterise life in the USA and the UK. Attention to such cultural assumptions allows for the more refined applicability of current theories of ageing (e.g. what constitutes successful ageing?).

See also: Ageing, Care, Cultural Ideals, Retirement, Successful Ageing

FURTHER READING

Sengstock, M. C. (1996) Care of elderly within Muslim families, in B. C. Aswad and B. Bilge (eds), *Family and Gender among American Muslims*. Philadelphia, PA: Temple University Press. pp. 271–297.

REFERENCES

Ajrouch, K. J. (2008) Muslim faith communities: links with the past, bridges to the future. *Generations*, special issue on Religion, Spirituality, and Meaning edited by C. Kozberg and S. McFadden, 32(2): 47–50.

key concepts in
social gerontology

Akhtar, S. and Choi, L. W. (2004) When evening falls: the immigrants encounter with middle and old age. *American Journal of Psychoanalysis*, 64: 183–191.

Aranda, M. P. and Miranda, M. R. (1997) Hispanic ageing, social support, and mental health: does acculturation make a difference?, in K. Markides and M. R. Miranda (eds), *Minorities, Ageing and Health*. Thousand Oaks, CA: Sage. pp. 271–294.

Barresi, C. M. (1987) Ethnic ageing and the life course, in D. E. Gelfand and C. M. Barresi (eds), *Ethnic Dimensions of Ageing*. New York: Springer. pp. 18–34.

Becker, G. (2003) Meanings of place and displacement in three groups of older immigrants. *Journal of Ageing Studies*, 17: 129–149.

Cuellar, I., Bastida, E. and Braccio, S. M. (2004) Residency in the United States, subjective well-being, and depression in an older Mexican-origin sample. *Journal of Ageing and Health*, 16: 447–466.

Lubben, J. E. and Bacerra, R. M. (1987) Social support among Black, Mexican and Chinese elderly, in D. E. Gelfand and C. M. Barresi (eds), *Ethnic Dimensions of Ageing*. New York: Springer. pp. 130–144.

Markides, K. S. (1983) Ethnicity, ageing and society: theoretical lessons from the United States experience. *Archives of Gerontology and Geriatrics*, 2: 221–228.

Mui, A. C. (1996) Depression among elderly Chinese immigrants: an exploratory study. *Social Work*, 41: 633–645.

Plawecki, H. M. (2000) The elderly immigrant: an isolated experience. *Journal of Gerontological Nursing*, 26: 6–8.

Wilmoth, J. M. and Chen, P. C. (2003) Immigrant status, living arrangements, and depressive symptoms among middle-aged and older adults. *Journal of Gerontology*, 58B: S305–S313.

Wray, S. (2003) Connecting ethnicity, agency and ageing. *Sociological Research Online*, 8(4), www.socresonline.org.uk/8/4/wray.html (accessed 5 March 2009).

euthanasia

Euthanasia

> **The deliberate termination of a person's life, normally upon the wish of the person who dies.**

91

Euthanasia can take active, passive, voluntary and involuntary forms. Active euthanasia denotes some deliberate intervention by another person to bring about someone's death, for example by administering a fatal dose of painkillers. In contrast, passive euthanasia refers to a situation in which an individual's death is brought about through non-action, and occurs because some form of treatment has been withheld or withdrawn, for example turning off a life-support machine so that the individual dies from their condition. Voluntary euthanasia means that an individual requests death themselves, while in situations of involuntary euthanasia, the decision to die is taken on someone's behalf, perhaps because they are unconscious or unable to make the decision themselves for other reasons. Euthanasia is also associated with the concept of assisted suicide, often known as physician-assisted suicide, and refers to a situation in which the person who wishes to die requests help from someone to end their life, the third party actively providing the means to do this or carrying out instructions which can be as simple as enabling the person to consume a lethal drug by putting it within their reach.

Despite its illegal status in most countries, contemporary interest in euthanasia partly reflects the increasing likelihood that choosing how and when to end life has now become a reality because of developments in the medical field. The use of mechanically assisted respiration, for example, now means that it is possible to sustain human life artificially for long periods. However, the controversial questions of how long life should be sustained, whether indeed it should be sustained at all and whether individuals should feel they have any choice in the matter still persist. Such questions are not confined to the contemporary period of the twentieth or twenty-first centuries as historical accounts dating to the Greco-Roman period suggest that a form of euthanasia was used by some physicians to alleviate physical pain and suffering. Such practices were, however, challenged by physicians of the Hippocratic School for whom the administration of deadly drugs or providing advice on such matters was not tolerated.

Stolberg (2007) argues that it was only during the late nineteenth century that the concept of euthanasia in fact appeared in the medical field, but historical evidence would suggest that it was a question of debate before this among intellectuals. Sir Thomas More, for example, in his sixteenth-century literary work *Utopia*, refers to a form of euthanasia used to relieve those suffering unbearably, and during the seventeenth century, Francis Bacon argued for the use of science for purposes of improving health but also for enabling an easier end to life if necessary. Other European writers and philosophers, such as Montesquieu, were to challenge prohibitions against suicide, and during the nineteenth century, with the use of anaesthetics and pain-relieving drugs such as morphine, the issue of euthanasia began to have an increasing impact on medical thinking and practice (Ezekiel, 1994; Stolberg, 2007). Initial recommendations to use anaesthetics and pain-relieving drugs as a means of alleviating pain during the dying process were followed by recommendations that they be used intentionally as a means of ending a patient's life, and subsequently led to intense debate on whether patients should be given the right to end their lives. During the late nineteenth and early twentieth centuries attempts in Britain and the USA to legalise euthanasia failed (despite the creation of the UK's Voluntary Euthanasia Legislation Society), and it was only during the late twentieth century that there was a renewed interest in euthanasia in several countries, sparked in part by the increasing acceptance of the idea that individuals should have the right to self-determination with regard to end of life decisions (Stolberg, 2007). In the twenty-first century, it remains to be seen whether current debates about the social and economic implications of population ageing will lead to a heightened interest in euthanasia, if arguments about the potentially conflicting needs of older and younger age groups who must 'fight' for increasingly scarce resources, such as health care, become more pervasive.

Historical speaking, then, euthanasia has been at the centre of ethical and practical arguments from professional and lay audiences for a long period. At the heart of these debates is the question of what value and meaning is placed on human life, and whether people should have the power to make life and death decisions for others and for themselves. Ezekiel (1994) has suggested that the historical fluctuations in an interest in euthanasia reflect not only advances made in the medical field, but also broader social, cultural, political and economic climates. Euthanasia will become topical during times of economic hardship when social policy makers need to make decisions about the allocation of scarce resources, for example, or when it becomes established medical practice to facilitate the dying process by withdrawing life-sustaining medical interventions. Recent cross-national comparative studies have also shown significant variations in public attitudes towards euthanasia (Cohen et al., 2006) and national case studies serve to illustrate how these attitudes are reflected in legislative measures (Akabayashi, 2002).

Arguments for and against euthanasia are therefore complex and to some extent time-dependent, but can nonetheless be viewed in terms of broad categories of concern. Those who consider active, voluntary and physician-assisted suicide to be justifiable in certain circumstances would argue the need to respect people's need for self-determination and to preserve their independence and dignity, for example in situations of incurable or terminal illness when individuals seek help to end their lives or when palliative care has failed to bring pain relief. From this perspective, increasing support for euthanasia in some developed countries at least, reflects a broader search for providing individuals with the means of exercising greater control and self-direction over the dying process (Seale, 1997; Seale et al., 1997).

Opponents to this position regard euthanasia and physician-assisted suicide as contrary to both the preservation of the sanctity of human life and to the physician's professional duty and commitment to saving lives. Legalising euthanasia, for example, could diminish people's trust in the medical profession, or might encourage a disregard for the eventuality of an incorrect medical diagnosis or prognosis. Others invoke the 'slippery slope' argument, reflecting a concern that legalising euthanasia would result in an abuse of power, paving the way for justifying involuntary euthanasia and the killing of people who are thought 'undesirable' – the cognitively impaired, for example. Critics also highlight the potentially wider cultural, social and economic repercussions of euthanasia: diminishing the value and respect that societies place on human life; placing pressure on patients to request euthanasia so that they are not a 'burden' to family and friends; seeing it as a basis for rationing health expenditure by limiting treatment costs for the terminally ill or reducing the investment in palliative care or curative medicine.

While euthanasia is an issue which is not confined to any particular age group, the propensity for experiencing disability and the increasing likelihood of mortality during later life do mean that it is often associated with older rather than younger people, although empirical evidence from the Netherlands suggests that in practice, proportions of euthanasia and physician-assisted suicides among all deaths are particularly high among people aged between 25 and 44 years and lowest among those aged 80 or more (Onwuteaka-Philipsen et al., 1997). Howse (1998) suggests that the ways in which the passage from life to death is managed for older people do raise specific ethical, medical and legal challenges when compared to other age groups. Of particular difficulty are the circumstances in which age is taken into consideration as a means of allocating scarce healthcare resources, or when 'non-treatment' decisions are made for older people experiencing cognitive impairment. Underpinning these concerns is clearly both a preoccupation with questions of social justice and how decisions about the distribution of welfare resources are made, but equally, a concern that associations between euthanasia and later life belie ageist attitudes and practice. Does denying someone medical care because of their age, for example, reflect ageist attitudes or rather, as Ezekiel (1994) has suggested, an increasing acceptance by the medical profession of passive euthanasia as a normal part of later life?

From a socio-cultural perspective, the social value placed on growing and being old will also influence how euthanasia is perceived. As Meucci (1994) points out, in societies where dominant social attitudes reflect the primacy of self-fulfilment, individualism and choice, the potential for intolerance or even fear of the dependency associated with old age, might well be conducive to the practice of euthanasia in later life.

The subject of euthanasia, then, while not confined to the later stages of the life course, lends itself to debate when the possibilities of dying naturally increase and the medical techniques which we now possess make it increasingly more feasible to prolong the final period of life. Euthanasia, in whatever form, continues, as it has done for several centuries, to provoke criticism and debate from all quarters, raising questions about how to distinguish between preserving the quality rather than the quantity of life, whether artificially maintained life simply represents a biological rather than a 'real' existence and whether disposing of life in its final stages can be justified as a socio-economic policy decision based on rationalised considerations of the economic viability of one age group compared to another.

See also: Care, Independence, Palliative Care, Population Ageing

REFERENCES

Cohen, J., Marcoux, I., Bilsen, J., Deboosere, P. and Van der Wal, G. L. D. (2006) European public acceptance of euthanasia: socio-demographic and cultural factors associated with the acceptance of euthanasia in 33 European countries. *Social Science and Medicine*, 63(3): 743–756.

Ezekiel, J. E. (1994) The history of euthanasia debates in the United States and Britain. *Annals of Internal Medicine*, 121(10): 793–802.

Stolberg, M. (2007) Active euthanasia in pre-modern society, 1500–1800: learned debates and popular practices. *Social History of Medicine*, 20(2): 205–221.

euthanasia

Family Relations

> *Family ties or bonds which have traditionally described connections between people based on relations of blood, marriage or adoption, and which are sustained throughout life.*

It is now well recognised that conceptualising family relations is complex because of their dynamic and changing nature, and because social change means that individuals are now likely to experience more diverse and even multiple types of family relations during the course of their lives. The increasing frequency of divorce, remarriage or re-partnership, for example, means that people in later life are now more likely to find themselves in blended families where relationships are defined neither by blood, marriage or adoption, nor perhaps by shared living arrangements. By making a conscious decision to maintain an intimate relationship without necessarily sharing the same household, for example, a new type of family relationship in later life, referred to as 'living apart together', is now emerging.

Despite this diversity, and in contrast to other types of relationship – with colleagues, friends or neighbours, for example, where links tend to be more transient – familial relationships are nonetheless seen to continue throughout life, even when contact or affection are absent, and in some case, even after someone's death. Likewise, they are governed by social norms, such as feelings of obligation and reciprocity, as well as more functional considerations, such as material and financial needs. Just how these factors will shape family relations will vary depending upon individual characteristics, such as class or gender, and the influence that broader socio-cultural norms have on determining how much autonomy individuals have to pursue their own interests rather than conforming to broader group expectations.

Family theorists now generally concur in the observation that contemporary western society reflects a culture of individualism, with the effect that people are much freer than in the past to make voluntary decisions about how they engage and invest in such relationships. This has not always been the perspective taken by scholars interested in establishing the relationships that older people have maintained with their families

key concepts in social gerontology

(Askham et al., 2007). Until industrialisation it was thought that older people were integral and highly respected members of extended kinship networks where relationships were based on reciprocity, obligation and interdependence. This rather idealistic interpretation was subsequently criticised for ignoring the existence of alternative household and family structures, as well as for overlooking the possibility that older people's relationships with others might not necessarily be based on respect or an expectation of care.

Theorists subsequently postulated that modernisation and industrialisation, in particular the nuclearisation of the family and the development of formalised structures and institutions addressing the welfare needs of older people, were to significantly alter the nature of family relations. From being highly valued members of kinship groups, older people, it was thought, became marginalised, solitary individuals adapting to their new situation by progressively disengageing themselves from traditional kinship relationships and role expectations (Cumming and Henry, 1961). More recently, theorists have moved away from these interpretations to suggest that despite their increasing fluidity and variety, family relations, at least in western contexts, still represent a form of enduring relationship for older people, although they are now determined much less by normative obligation, duty and necessity, and much more by choice and emotional motive.

In the field of ageing studies, family relations in later life have become a prominent area of interest, particularly in the growing area of family gerontology. Part of this interest has been spurned by demographic change, which has altered kinship structures and the duration of intergenerational relationships, with more generations alive concurrently but with fewer members in each. One consequence is that people can now expect to experience a greater variety of family relations, for example enjoying the presence of both grandparents and great-grandparents (Bengtson, 2001), and also of living new types and perhaps more demanding relationships – becoming a step-grandparent as the result of increasing divorce among middle-aged offspring, for example. This has broadened perspectives beyond the focus on parent–child relationships during the 1960s and 1970s to a wider array of family ties, including relationships between grandparents and grandchildren, siblings and couples, as well as intra- and intergenerational bonds, and has also led to the development or refinement of numerous theoretical perspectives, notably theories of the life course, exchange, social support, role attachment or stress and coping theories, systems theory, symbolic

family relations

interactionism, feminist interpretations and family solidarity (Roberto et al., 2006).

As this brief historical overview suggests, there have been diverse approaches to the investigation of later life family relationships over the twentieth century. For social gerontologists, these perspectives have been consolidated in various ways, but at least three broad approaches can be identified: (1) those focusing on the solidity and endurance of family ties within and across generations, the *intergenerational solidarity framework*, (2) those stemming from a developmental perspective, the *family life cycle* and the *life course* frameworks; and (3) the *social network* perspective, which permits an understanding of the multiplicity and complexity of relationships in later life.

The notion of intergenerational solidarity has become a prominent framework in family gerontology, providing a means of establishing the strength and endurance of family relationships at the micro level of interaction. Associated with the pioneering work of Bengtson and colleagues (Bengtson and Roberts, 1991), the framework has gained prominence in the analysis of bonds between older persons and their kin, providing a multifaceted conceptualisation of family relations in terms of the basic dimensions of instrumental support, geographic proximity, affection, contact, consensus or agreement, and sharing values or norms. As well as providing the basis for the *Longitudinal Study of Generations* in the USA, the solidarity paradigm has also been the foundation for several international comparative studies, has been used to examine various types of family relations, including, for example, the elaboration of typologies or classificatory approaches which identify different types of intergenerational relationship (Burholt and Wenger, 1998), and more recently has been expanded to include the notions of ambivalence (Lüscher and Pillemer, 1998). Most of these studies have focused on dyadic relationships, although some research on triadic intergenerational relationships has shown how important the presence of a third, aged generation can be in promoting emotional exchanges (Hillcoat-Nallétamby and Dharmalingam, 2006).

A second perspective taken by scholars working at the intersection of ageing and family studies has been the developmental approaches of the family life cycle and, more latterly, the life course. Family life cycle theory, associated with the work of Glick in the 1940s, conceptualised family life in terms of a series of predictable relationships determined by pre-defined developmental stages which it was thought would be integral to the lives of all individuals. More fluid in its conceptual design, the life-course framework, when applied to family and intergenerational relationships, provides insights into how later life relationships are shaped by previous life histories and experiences, and fashioned by historical and individual time as well as by social processes.

Finally, social network approaches have also captured the variety of family, friend and neighbourhood relationships that stem from individuals belonging to multiple kin and non-kin networks. The multigenerational aspect of networks contributes to the diversity of relationships (e.g. sibling–sibling, adult child–ageing parent, grandparent–grandchild, stepson–stepmother) and it is now well recognised that the degree to which older people are engaged within a social network will contribute significantly to how they experience the ageing process. Indeed, as early as the 1950s and 1960s, the empirical work of family researchers such as Litwak (1960) clearly demonstrated that relationships between kin could extend well beyond the confines of the nuclear family and shared living arrangements to encompass interchanges of assistance as well as affective support. Subsequently, research on the composition of social networks in later life has indicated the primacy of familial over other types of relationship, and their importance as sources of emotional, financial and instrumental support, but also conflict (Antonucci and Akiyama, 1991).

Despite the insights to family relations in later life afforded by these approaches, contemporary researchers will nonetheless face new challenges, as they endeavour to anticipate the impact that unprecedented socio-cultural changes, such as high levels of divorce and remarriage, or legislative changes, such as those governing same-sex partnerships, will have on the way later life family relations evolve in the future. How, for example, might the strength of step-sibling relationships evolve in later life? What might an ageing step-parent expect from their relationships with adult step-children?

In sum, the implications of demographic change, the growing complexity of family 'identities', shifting patterns in the timing of life-course transitions such as retirement, the increasing likelihood that divorce and remarriage will characterise life-course trajectories, and the transformations in societal and individual expectations about family obligations and choices when it comes to which ties we maintain and how we support others – all these factors will shape the nature and dynamics of family relationships in new ways, providing unprecedented conceptual, theoretical and methodological challenges to researchers interested in the field of later life family relations.

See also: Ageing, Ambivalence, Care, Gender, Gerontology, Social Support

FURTHER READING

A detailed account of the international studies which have drawn on the intergenerational solidarity paradigm can be found in Hillcoat-Nallétamby, S. (2006) *The Role of Intergenerational Transactions, Interactions and Relationships in Shaping Wellbeing in Later Life.* Working Paper No. 6, Population Studies Centre, University of Waikato, New Zealand. Also available at: www.ewas.net.nz/Publications/filesEWAS/Role% 20of%20intergenerational%20transactions. pdf
Chambers, P., Allan, G., Phillipson, C. and Ray, R. (2009) *Family Practices in Later Life.* Bristol: The Policy Press.
Connidis, I. A. (2009) *Family Ties and Ageing* (2nd edn). London: Sage.

REFERENCES

Antonucci, T. C. and Akiyama, H. (1991) Convoys of social support: generational issues. *Marriage and Family Review*, 16(1/2): 103–123.
Askham, J., Ferring, D. and Lamura, G. (2007) Personal relationships in later life, in J. Bond, S. Peace, F. Dittmann-Kohli and G. Westerhof (eds), *Ageing in Society* (3rd edition). London: Sage. pp. 186–208.
Bengtson, V. L. and Roberts, R. E. L. (1991) Intergenerational solidarity in ageing families: an example of formal theory construction. *Journal of Marriage and the Family*, 53: 856–870.
Cumming, E. and Henry, W. E. (1961) *Growing Old*. New York: Basic Books.
Glick, P. C. (1947) The family cycle. *American Sociological Review*, 12(2): 164–174.
Hillcoat-Nallétamby, S. and Dharmalingam, A. (2006) Solidarity in New Zealand: parental support for children in a three-generational context, in C. Leccardi and E. Ruspini (eds), *A New Youth? Young People, Generations and Family Life*. Aldershot and Burlington, VT: Ashgate. pp. 125–145.
Litwak, E. (1960) Geographic mobility and extended family cohesion. *American Sociological Review*, 25: 385–394.
Lüscher, K. and Pillemer, K. (1998) Intergenerational ambivalence: a new approach to the study of parent–child relations in later life. *Journal of Marriage and the Family*, 60: 413–425.

key concepts in
social gerontology

Filial Responsibility

> *The expectation that adult children will provide assistance to older parents in times of need, giving priority to their parents' needs over their own.*

One of the closest kinship ties across the life course involves the relationship between a parent and child. The birth of a child signifies a new era in the life of their parent, igniting a period of unyielding responsibility to ensure that the infant develops into, at the very least, a healthy adult. Once an adult, their parents have grown older, and the nature of the parent–child relationship may shift. Where once the child was dependent on their parent(s) for well-being, the parent may begin an era of dependence on their child for well-being. The character of this transition is often gradual, involving both emotional and instrumental components. Relying on a child in times of need, particularly related to finances, living arrangements and personal care, is particularly salient as one grows older (Finch and Mason, 1991). The impact is perhaps felt greatest when a health crisis occurs, such as if a parent suffers a stroke, or requires major surgery, and the older parent suddenly is no longer able to live independently. A major issue arises in such cases as to the responsibility that a child has to care for the parent, and the extent to which the child will sacrifice their needs to ensure the well-being of the parent.

The significance of filial responsibility has attracted wide attention in social gerontology due to enormous economic and demographic transitions happening globally. Increased wealth and larger proportions of older adults within a society signify concerns that value shifts to individualism, accompanied by the sheer practical realties of living in a changing world, preclude an adult child's ability or commitment to care for an older parent in need. The accumulating research, however, suggests that filial responsibility is a dynamic occurrence, often context-specific and contingent on a number of situational factors (Finch and Mason, 1991; Gans and Silverstein, 2006; Lee et al., 1998). Norms of filial responsibility continue to guide the relationship between older parents and their adult children, though explanations for why and how it persists vary.

The motivation behind the norm and practice of filial responsibility is explained by a number of theoretical paradigms. We highlight the following theories that are often invoked to account for filial responsibility: life-stage theory, exchange theory, cohort socialisation, and life-course theory. Also considered is the role of religious teachings.

Life-stage theories partition human development into various periods across the life course and advocate that the move from one period or stage to the next constitutes potential psychological growth. With regard to an adult child assuming responsibility for an older parent, Blenkner (1965) introduced the term 'filial maturity' to describe the transition when a grown child experiences a crisis as they recognise that they may no longer depend on their parents for economic or emotional needs. The crisis is overcome when anxiety develops into maturity. As Murray et al. (1995) explain, the parent–child relationship becomes an adult–adult relationship; the child assumes adult responsibilities towards their parent to provide support from one adult to another during times of need.

Exchange theory highlights the act of reciprocity in human interaction. When applied to caregiving needs in late life, Antonucci's (1985) work on the notion of a support bank provides a useful conceptualisation for understanding exchanges of support as it relates to the parent–child relationship. The support bank advances the idea that in birthing, rearing and caring for children, parents are essentially depositing credits of support as insurance that when they reach old age, they may withdraw support in times of need by relying on the very same child(ren) who benefited from the care and sacrifice given by the parent. Not able to fully reciprocate as children, the investment made by a parent(s) into their child(ren) ensures that assistance will be forthcoming during later years. The support bank idea suggests that parents who invest heavily in their child's development may be assured of assistance in later years; on the other hand, those who do not sacrifice as parents may not be guaranteed that they will receive support from their adult child(ren) in later years.

Cohort socialisation suggests that values change over time, with particular historical periods advocating a greater duty to family (i.e. the Great Depression cohort) than others. As Gans and Silverstein (2006) note, however, this paradigm does not suggest an expected direction or pattern of change with regard to filial responsibility; it simply states that values may shift for various cohorts, so that as one cohort dies off, the norms characterising the next cohort become dominant.

Life-course theory posits a link between personal biography, historical time period and social position. It ambitiously seeks to connect multiple levels of human experience to explain ageing patterns and situations. Perhaps most salient for understanding filial responsibility is the recognition that family interdependence constitutes a core social environment. Gans and Silverstein (2006) summarise the literature on this perspective as it relates to filial responsibility. For instance, historical trends, such as high divorce and remarriage rates, are thought to weaken an adult child's obligation towards an older parent.

Finally, a moral imperative grounded in religious teaching also shapes the practice and attitudes towards filial responsibility. Sung (1998) discusses how each major world religion speaks to a child's responsibility to address the needs of an older parent. The three monotheistic religions of Judaism, Christianity and Islam clearly stress the duty of a child to not only support them, but also to honour, love and respect older parents as well. Interestingly, these religious teachings also stress a benefit for the child in adhering to this mandate – that a child will live long for having fulfilled this obligation. Buddhism and Hinduism also teach similar values. Buddhism, in particular, suggests specifically that a mother is to be honoured, and that even the most filial of children would not be able to reciprocate fully.

Though filial responsibility norms appear to permeate societies and cultures around the world, a growing consensus suggests that the practice may differ by culture, and is negotiated depending on various situational and contextual factors (Hillcoat-Nallétamby, under review). In the USA, Lee et al. (1998) advance that aged black parents view a child's obligation to older parents as more normative than do older white parents. This finding emerges after accounting for socio-economic factors to suggest a cultural difference that exists between blacks and whites. This cultural difference implies that black families may be more collectivist in form, stemming from a legacy of slavery and discrimination. Moreover, the strong adherence to filial responsibility norms does not appear to preclude the use of formal support resources. Lee et al. (1998) demonstrate that blacks access formal support options in greater frequency than do whites.

Cultural values also include basic assumptions about filial responsibility. Finch and Mason (1991) carried out ground-breaking research in Great Britain to illustrate the complexity of norms associated with filial responsibility. Addressing core ideas that shape notions of filial responsibility, they discovered that contrary to the belief that there exists an agreed upon and easily recognisable understanding concerning obligations and responsibilities between adult family members, no consensus emerges to define such obligations. Instead, there appears to be agreement on factors to consider (i.e. procedural processes) in deciding what to do in situations involving help and support exchanges between family members. In other words, the process for evaluating appropriate courses of action prevails above the actual act.

Another aspect of filial responsibility examined by Finch and Mason involved expectations from close family versus distant family (e.g. extended kin). It appears that obligations are stronger between close family members, although they are situationally evaluated and conditional. For instance, Finch and Mason find that a consensus emerges where most agree that an adult child should evaluate the effect of caring for an older parent on their life before making the commitment. Again, an emphasis on procedure arises above the actual act.

The third assumption addressed by Finch and Mason involves gender norms in caring for older parents. Findings suggest that initial sentiments about expectations reference children generally, with no gender condition. Asked to specify, however, sons were mentioned with regard to financial care, and daughters concerning personal care and accommodation. Most significant is that sons were never mentioned as preferred sources of personal care, and daughters never as preferred sources of financial care. A gendered division of filial responsibility prevails.

Filial responsibility is a complex issue, malleable and adaptable to the needs of families and the context in which those families live. Although care of older parents by adult children continues to mark an important aspect of family life, it does not appear to replace or substitute support from government or other formal sources. An adult child represents one very important resource, but the accumulating research suggests that filial responsibility cannot meet each and every need of an older parent. An understanding that there is no universal practice of filial responsibility will help in finding ways to maximise support from an adult child in tandem with other sources.

See also: *Ageing, Care, Cohort, Gender, Gerontology*

REFERENCES

Antonucci, T. C. (1985) Personal characteristics, social support, and social behavior, in R. H. Binstock and E. Shanas (eds), *Handbook of Ageing and the Social Sciences* (2nd edition). New York: Van Nostrand Reinhol. pp. 94–128.

Blenkner, M. (1965) Social work and family relationships in later life with some thoughts on filial maturity, in E. Shanas and G. F. Streib (eds), *Social Structure and the Family: Generational Relations*. Englewood Cliffs, NJ: Prentice-Hall.

Finch, J. and Mason, J. (1991) Obligations of kinship in contemporary Britain: is there normative agreement? *British Journal of Sociology*, 42(3): 345–367.

Gans, D. and Silverstein, M. (2006) Norms of filial responsibility for ageing parents across time and generations. *Journal of Marriage and Family*, 68: 961–976.

Sung, K. (1998) Filial piety: the traditional ideal of parent care in East Asia. *Ageing and Spirituality*, American Society on Ageing. Available at: www.asageing.org/networks/forsa/aands-101.html (accessed 18 January 2009).

Frailty

A physical and psychological condition creating vulnerability.

Frailty can be defined as a state of high vulnerability for adverse health outcomes, including disability, dependency, falls, a need for long-term care and mortality (Fried et al., 2004). Frailty syndrome is defined as a series of multiple coexisting conditions, weakness, immobility and poor tolerance to physiological or psychological stressors (Espinoza and Walston, 2005).

It is acknowledged that there are a range of clinical characteristics that define frailty, and many believe that, although its natural course is progressive and the risk of co-morbidity increases over time, active interventions can slow, or indeed potentially reverse, progression (e.g. see Chan, 2008; Woo et al., 2005). According to the British Geriatrics Society (2005), two or more of the following are markers of frailty in hospitalised older patients: an inability to perform one or more basic activities of daily living (ADL) in the three days prior to admission; a stroke in the past three months; depression; dementia; a history of falls; one or more unplanned admissions in the past three months; difficulty in walking; malnutrition; prolonged bed rest; incontinence.

Our understanding of frailty in older people has emerged from the area of geriatric medicine. As Evans (1997) notes, this particular branch of medicine developed thanks to the work of pioneers such as Dr Marjory Warren, who, while working with many old and infirm workhouse inmates, recognised the need to create geriatrics as a speciality. In 1936 she developed a system of classifying the degrees of infirmity (a process to become known as comprehensive geriatric assessment (CGA)) and matched these to inmates' rehabilitation and equipment needs. Recent years have also seen the emergence of areas that can have a positive impact upon frailty, such as *human factors engineering* and *gerontechnology*.

The lack of consensus on which elements constitute frailty means that there is also a lack of consensus on how to measure the degree of an older person's frailty. Therefore, the British Geriatrics Society (2005) advocates a CGA which measures medical, psychological and functional capabilities. Specifically, the CGA measures the individual's medical (e.g. co-morbid conditions, nutritional status), functioning (e.g. basic ADLs, gait and balance), and psychological (e.g. cognitive testing, mood and depression testing), social (e.g. informal needs and assets, care resource eligibility) and environmental (e.g. home safety, transportation) statuses. Although there is, as yet, no 'gold standard' to identify frailty, it has demonstrated its ability to predict (1) death, health status and functional decline – important from the perspective of the frail older person – and (2) the use of health services – important from the perspective of social policy and NHS funding (Chan, 2008). Frailty, then, carries clinical characteristics that impact upon the individual and family and friends, and it brings with it a host of issues that need to be negotiated by a diverse range of actors (e.g. healthcare professionals, healthcare stakeholders, policy makers).

The central issues are how to identify an at-risk individual, what interventions are appropriate for this at-risk individual and what rehabilitation measures would best serve the frail individual. Several frailty measures are available or are being developed. For example, Rockwood et al's (2002) Frailty Index (FI) comprises 62 items (later extended to 70 items) ranging from objective disease burden, use of drugs and self-esteem to lifestyle factors. The question remains on how best to measure not only frailty, but also its antecedents and its correlates (Watson, 2008). A pragmatic approach would be to consider the purpose behind the various frailty scores and apply the most appropriate one in each case (Martin and Brighton, 2008).

A body of evidence has identified links between the clinical condition and psychological and social aspects. For example, frail (and often oldest old) adults have not only an increased burden of symptoms, but also increased social needs: they are more vulnerable to social isolation and institutionalisation (Espinoza and Walston, 2005). Three aspects are considered here in brief. First, there is a range of *social determinants* of frailty. Correlations have been found between items from Rockwood et al's FI and socio-economic, lifestyle and social support factors (Woo et al., 2005) where gender differences have emerged. For example, in men, links were found between frailty and low socio-economic status, no exercise, few relatives and neighbours and no or little participation in helping others. In women, additional links were found: little contact with relatives (not the *number* of relatives) and too little participation in community/religious activities.

Secondly, it is increasingly acknowledged that *positive affect* is linked to better health and well-being (irrespective of age), and that positive affect can 'undo' negative emotions and thus delay the onset of or reverse some physical characteristics of frailty. For example, and in this context, Ostir et al. (2004) found in a longitudinal study of non-frail older adults that the higher the positive affect, the lower the risk of frailty.

Thirdly, there is evidence to suggest that *spirituality* might be a resource that some could draw upon to counteract the negative effects of frailty. Frailty has a negative impact upon psychological well-being. However, Kirby et al. (2004) propose that these negative effects are moderated by spirituality.

There are many open issues regarding frailty (measures, antecedents, interventions). The scope for research is thus extremely broad. Furthermore, frailty is multidimensional; it subsumes several co-morbidities. In the *clinical setting*, therefore, as well as research into frailty markers such as vascular disease and dementia, current areas of research include endocrinology and genetics (Espinoza and Walston, 2005). It seems too that the shift in *psychology* to examine positive rather than negative emotions may well provide further recommendations on how to meet the needs of the non-frail and frail ageing individual (Ostir et al., 2004). Finally, a relatively new research dimension has emerged, that of *gerontechnology*. Its goal is to create technological environments for older people that enhance independence, social participation, good health, comfort and safety. It is essential that frail individuals who wish to age in place are able to do so for as long as possible, and to this end gerontechnology embraces a collaboration between, for example, designers, engineers, human geographers and health professionals.

In the UK, in the *National Service Framework for Older People* (2001), the Department of Health has pledged its commitment to extending

frailty

access to services, improving the standards of care and developing services to support independence in older people. At the heart of this lies the maxim that 'older people ... receive appropriate and timely packages of care which meet their needs as individuals, *regardless of health and social services boundaries*' (Department of Health, 2001: 8, emphasis added). At face value, this pledge seems to have been written with frail older individuals in mind. Sadly, the treatment that many receive is anything other than 'appropriate and timely'.

Providing appropriate support for frail older people is a difficult challenge for several reasons, four of which are outlined here. First, there could be a whole array of physical conditions that necessitate hospitalisation. This increases the likelihood that the frail person loses their sense of independence and control, both of which are essential coping strategies. Secondly, early identification of at-risk individuals requires a proactive approach on the part of health and social care professionals, and even when an at-risk individual is identified, a good (and perhaps costly) intervention programme can succeed only with the cooperation of that individual. This is less likely when the frail person is, for example, clinically depressed or has impaired cognitive functioning. Thirdly, frailty is progressive. Therefore, in order to maintain independence for as long as possible, it is essential that interventions *do not* provide too much too soon. Finally, the question must be raised regarding staff resources (especially time) and staff training, both in hospitals and in residential care homes. It has been suggested, for example, that residential care home staff may understand the duty to care as a duty to perform tasks that the frail individual may be able to perform alone to some degree, but this 'misplaced' help can actually decrease the resident's sense of autonomy and promote learned helplessness (Foos and Clark, 2003).

It is apparent, therefore, that working with frail individuals involves a complex balancing act. An individual's placement on the frailty continuum must be identified clearly at the outset, for example by employing Fried's initial screening tool, *Phenotype for Frailty*, to identify whether the individual is robust, pre-frail or frail (Fried et al., 2001). The assessment should then help decide upon a model of care. For example, in the case of robust findings, interventions could include an exercise programme and nutritional recommendations. In the case of moderate to severe frailty, other measures are called for. Here the British Geriatric Society (2005) notes that, in the case of hospitalisation, the goal should be early discharge. The CGA serves to this end. Further, the CGA should involve a multidisciplinary team involving specialist doctors and nurses, social workers and therapists. As the Society further notes, the assessment can reduce short-term mortality, increase the chances of returning home and improve cognition, and, ultimately, the quality of life.

See also: Ageing, Care, Dementia, Disability, Independence, Long-term Care, Quality of Life, Social Support

REFERENCES

Department of Health (2001) *National Service Framework for Older People: Executive Summary*. London: Department of Health.

Martin, F. B. and Brighton, P. (2008) Frailty: different tools for different purposes? *Age and Ageing*, 37: 129–131.

Ostir, G. V., Ottenbacher, K. J. and Markides, K. S. (2004) Onset of frailty in older adults and the protective role of positive affect. *Psychology and Ageing*, 19(3): 402–408.

Rockwood, K., Mitniski, A. B. and McKnight, C. (2002) Some mathematical models of frailty and their clinical implications. *Review of Clinical Gerontology* 12: 109–117.

Watson, R. (2008) Research into ageing and older people. *Journal of Nursing Management*, 16: 99–104.

Woo, J., Goggins, W., Sham, A. and Ho, S. C. (2005) Social determinants of frailty. *Gerontology*, 51(6): 402–408.

Gender

gender

Social constructions of masculinity and femininity that distinguish characteristics believed appropriate and core to being a man as well as those specific to being a woman.

109

Gender constitutes a critical social force in the experience of ageing, and is considered a pervasive marker of inequality. Men and women often differ with regard to earlier life-course opportunities and encounters, which then shape situations during later life. On the other hand, some argue that with age, differences which distinguished men and women earlier in life tend to disappear, and therefore inequalities based on gender diminish. Although gender issues may vary depending on the social, cultural and political context in which people grow older, research suggests that areas where older men and older women differ frequently include life expectancy, health, social relations and socio-economic resources.

Life expectancy. In all countries of the world, women have longer life expectancies than men. In the USA, generally men die an average of seven years earlier than women (Barer, 1994; Verbrugge, 1985). In less industrialised nations, the life expectancy gap is not as great, but nevertheless exists (Knodel and Ofstedal, 2003). Social influences on shorter life expectancies among men may stem from culturally sanctioned masculine behaviours, including smoking, drinking, hazardous occupations and serving during times of war. Though shorter life expectancies suggest a disadvantage for men, shorter male life expectancies may also negatively influence older women, who end up being widowed in larger numbers than men, are less likely to remarry, and hence are more socio-economically vulnerable (Knodel and Ofstedal, 2003). Inequalities deriving from gender characteristics produce negative impacts for both men and women.

It is instructive to consider how gender (a social construction) relates to sex (a biological given). It may be that the social construction of gender follows from biological givens such as hormonal and physiological differences, could be completely independent of them, or could act against them. A comparative perspective (comparing cultures and societies) would provide insight into the explanatory power of gender as a social construction versus a biological given. If the extent of gender differences in a certain domain (i.e. life expectancy) co-vary across societies and cultures, with differences in the living situation of men and women (measured, for instance, by the Gender Equality Measure of the United Nations), this would point to the social origin of gender differences. If gender differences do not vary with differences in the living situation of men and women, this could suggest a biological origin of this difference. In sum, the concept of gender does include a biological aspect, although it is by no means completely clear how social constructions and biological givens interact with each other.

Health. Physical health status varies by gender in old age. Older women are more likely to report chronic illness and functional limitations than are older men. Reasons for this discrepancy may include that women have a higher likelihood of visiting the doctor regularly (due to reproductive needs) and hence are more aware of their health status, or women simply may be more willing to talk about health issues than are men, who do not wish to violate masculine norms of strength. Differences among older men and women regarding mental health, on the other hand, appear minimal. For instance, gender gaps in depressive symptoms documented during earlier parts of the life course diminish in old age so that men's and women's experience of depressive symptoms do not vary greatly from one another (Akiyama and Antonucci, 2002). The status of men's and women's health therefore varies depending on the particular health outcome examined.

Social relations. In the USA and the UK, women are known to engage in numerous and more intimate relationships, often serving as the 'kin keeper' of the family (Turner and Troll, 1994). They are also more likely than men to be primary caregivers in their social networks (Bengtson et al., 1995), and perceive there to be a greater amount of social support available than men do (Antonucci and Akiyama, 1987). Other research has suggested that men may benefit more from social relations than do women because they do not suffer negative consequences from relationship conflict, but are equally or more likely to benefit from the positive aspects (House et al., 1988). Social relations among older men and women in countries where family constitutes the sole source of security in old age may differ in that men and women both exhibit qualities were they are equally involved in developing and maintaining social ties (Joseph, 1993).

Socio-economic resources. Older men and women vary in their access to socio-economic resources in later life. Men, for the most part, have acquired higher education levels than women, although this trend is changing across the globe. Such discrepancies have often contributed to inequalities in income-generating occupations, with men historically developing work careers that provide higher incomes and benefits. In most industrialised nations, men tend to benefit in greater proportions from pension and retirement programmes because they are more likely to work outside the home than women, and even when women have worked for wages, their work patterns tend to be intermittent (due to childbearing or other family caregiving obligations) or women have been more likely to work in occupations that provide lower wages and no benefits. In

gender

111

less industrialised nations, government-supported social programmes for older adults are almost non-existent. Instead, the family provides security for older adults. Under such circumstances, women are thought to wield an enormous amount of power, gaining access to resources by influencing or controlling the lives of their children, particularly those of sons and daughters-in-law (Joseph, 1993; Olmsted, 2005).

Currently, men appear to outperform women in the sphere of access to socio-economic resources, yet may suffer from a role discontinuity that comes with exiting the workforce. Women, on the other hand, are more likely to maintain this role continuity in old age due to their primary role in 'kin keeping'. The changing of gender norms, particularly given increased educational opportunities for women, will likely influence the ways that gender shapes ageing in the future.

Negative perceptions associated with growing older also vary by gender. Given that ideal notions of femininity rest on a woman's physical appearance and attractiveness, women often lose status in society when those attributes disappear. On the other hand, many women develop a strong sense of self with age, often reporting a contentment not experienced earlier in the life course (Stoller and Gibson, 1999). Ideal notions of masculinity include success in the workplace and financial prowess, both of which increase with age. As a result, at the same time that women begin to sense a loss of status within society regarding the dissipation of youth, beauty and attractiveness, men discern a status gain through their occupational and economic success. On the other hand, in societies where the patriarchal contract shapes family relations, older women gain an enormous amount of status with age through their socially sanctioned ability to control the lives of younger family members in particular (Joseph, 1993; Olmsted, 2005). As a result, men and women encounter different social pressures and advantages based on ideal notions of masculinity and femininity as they grow older. The manifestation of each varies by culture and country.

See also: Ageing, Care, Family Relations, Retirement, Social Relations, Social Support

REFERENCES

Akiyama, H. and Antonucci, T. C. (2002) Gender differences in depressive symptoms: insights from a life span perspective on life stages and social networks, in J. A. Levy and B. A. Pescosolido (eds), *Social Networks and Health* (Vol 8). London: Elsevier Science. pp. 343–358.

Antonucci, T. C. and Akiyama, H. (1987) An examination of sex differences in social support among older men and women. *Sex Roles*, 17: 737–749.

Barer, B. M. (1994) Men and women ageing differently. *International Journal of Ageing and Human Development*, 38: 29–40.

Bengtson, V. L., Rosenthal, C. J. and Burton, L. M. (1995) Paradoxes of families and ageing, in R. H. Binstock and L. K. George (eds), *Handbook of Ageing and the Social Sciences* (4th edition). San Diego, CA: Academic Press. pp. 253–282.

House, J. S., Landis, K. R. and Umberson, D. (1988) Social relationships and health. *Science*, 241: 540–545.

Joseph, S. (1993) Gender and relationality among Arab families in Lebanon. *Feminist Studies*, 19(3): 465–486.

Knodel, J. and Ofstedal, M. B. (2003) Gender and ageing in the developing world: where are the men? *Population and Development Review*, 29(4): 677–704.

Olmsted, J. C. (2005) Gender, ageing, and the evolving patriarchal contract. *Feminist Economics*, 11(2): 53–78.

Stoller, E. P. and Gibson, R. C. (eds) (1999) *Worlds of Difference* (3rd edition). Thousand Oaks, CA: Sage.

Turner, B. F. and Troll, L. E. (eds) (1994) *Women Growing Older: Psychological Perspectives*. Thousand Oaks, CA: Sage.

Verbrugge, L. M. (1985) Gender and health: an update on hypotheses and evidence. *Journal of Health and Social Behavior*, 26: 56–82.

Generations

A typology that sorts people into time-period cohorts, family role-based and/or life-stage categories.

The concept of generations is widely used in social gerontology to reference multiple situations, although ambiguity surrounds the concept historically as it may refer to a number of situations. It is frequently invoked to identify time-period birth cohorts (i.e. Baby Boomers), but just as often refers to family-based roles and structures (i.e. grandparent, parent, child, grandchild). Less commonly found in the gerontological literature is the meaning applied to immigrant status, though labels such as first- or second-generation immigrant are by no means absent from research on ageing. Generations are also used loosely to refer to various life-stage cycles, such as youth, adult and elder, including, for example, the term 'generation of youth'. Strauss and Howe (1991) argue that in modern industrialised parts of the world, the cohort-based understanding of generations is the most widely used and understood. This is illustrated by the fact that since the early twentieth century cohort groups have come of age with a distinct attempt by society to name that generation. Moreover, there is rarely a confusion of generations with family lineage: 'Four centuries ago, we would have thought that a young person "talkin'" "bout my generation" had a story to share about his grandfather or grandchildren. Today we know otherwise – that he has a story to share about his peers, about how they all came of age and have come to see life' (Strauss and Howe, 1991: 439).

The notion of generations defined in terms of cohorts has emerged over time. Strauss and Howe (1991) suggest that a preoccupation with generations as population cohorts emerged with the development of scientific thought, industrialisation and democracy in the late eighteenth and nineteenth centuries. Great social thinkers of the time, including José Ortega y Gasset and later Karl Mannheim, directly approached the issue by theorising what makes up a generation. The understanding of a cohort generation today accordingly supposes that people born within a specific historical era develop dispositions and personalities commensurate with the experiences of the time period within which they come of age. Social, political, economic and global events that make up the surrounding environment contribute to a particular consciousness and common world view.

It is not just being born within a particular span of time that matters, but the happenings going on during that period that combine to create a particular way of looking a the world. Such generations are thought to comprise a 20-year span. In the USA, a number of generations have been labelled by Strauss and Howe. For instance, the GI generation was born between 1901 and 1924; the Silent generation born between 1925 and 1942; the Boomer generation born between 1943 and 1960, and the 13ER generation between 1961 and 1981. Each generation is thought to have a distinct value system and world view, shaped by the socio-political events of the times. The Boomer generation receives perhaps the most attention today as they comprise an enormous number of people and have been at the forefront of the massive social changes occurring in the mid- and late-twentieth century. This is the cohort generation poised to enter old age in coming decades. More recent generational cohorts are sometimes divided into sub-generations defined according to 10-year spreads (as opposed to the 20-year span) due to rapid technological development and the rise of the information age. Strauss and Howe (1991) suggest that the length of a cohort generation must be likened to the length of a life phase, that is youth, emerging adult, midlife adult, elder. Historically, generations have been defined by larger time spans of around 30 years (Strauss and Howe, 1991). Although confusion as to whether or not generation refers to cohort or family lineage is less prevalent today, the number of years that comprise a cohort generation remains open to negotiation.

The cyclical nature of generations has also been proposed by Strauss and Howe (1991). A four-cycle model, with each cycle consisting of a particular mood and personality type, influences history and is itself influenced by history. This constitutes a feedback loop between generational characteristics and history. Each element of the cycle is termed by Strauss and Howe: the first phase as Idealist, the second as Reactive, the third as Civic, and the fourth as Adaptive. Each type repeats itself every fifth generation, or every 80–90 years, in reaction to the generation before. This understanding of generations in part underpins the strand within gerontology that supposes conflict and competing interests between generation groups. Some advocate that identifying generational cohorts becomes a basis for 'social claim-making' (McDaniel 2004: 30). Each generation (defined by birth cohorts) are presented as having competing interests linked to the way in which society divides and organises appropriate roles according to life stage. More specifically, institutionalisation of policy divides the life course into various periods of education, work and retirement. The notion that older cohorts benefit at the expense of younger cohorts is referred to as generational inequity (Moody, 2000). Older generations seek benefits from the welfare state, which, it is supposed, takes away from resources available to the youngest generation. This pitting of one generation against the other has been criticised as not representative of pragmatic realities. Instead, it is argued that generations are interdependent, and what benefits one generation is sure to benefit the other (Minkler, 1991).

A second prevalent understanding of generation in social gerontology involves family lineage, and a particular focus on intergenerational relations. The family constitutes perhaps the most basic social institution, representing the very first group into which one enters at birth,

generations

and these ties remain primary over the life course. Family provides both history and continuity; generational structure signifies a hierarchy according to family roles. For instance, a three-generation family includes a grandparent, a parent and a child. Common notation to reference this family according to generation includes G1 to represent grandparent, G2 to signify the parent, and G3 to refer to the child. In this framework, generations are seen as social relations with a family context (McDaniel, 2004).

The generational structure of being caught 'in the middle' between parents and children is often presented as a common situation for those occupying the second generation (Soldo, 1996). Women and men who have at least one parent and at least one child may be at risk, 'sandwiched' between two roles, thus potentially resulting in a resource drain from both the generation above and below (Bengtson, 1993; Brody, 1981). Some recent literature, however, suggests that the 'sandwich' generation (i.e. being caught in the middle between competing demands) occurs infrequently (Brody, 1981; Rosenthal et al., 1996). For instance, it is now well documented that most elders tend to have regular contact with their children, are increasingly healthy and more financially secure (in part due to government transfer programmes) (Aldous, 1987). Some studies highlight older people contributing to family functioning, particularly in the role of grandparent (Fuller-Thompson et al., 1997; Troll, 1983). The eldest generation within a family may serve as a resource, providing money in times of need, helping a child to overcome emotional problems and/or chemical dependency, as well as offering support after a divorce (Greenberg and Becker, 1988). Even older people who receive care from an adult child often become needed resources to their caregiver child, for example, aiding with housework and childcare (Ingersoll-Dayton et al., 2001).

Finally, using the concept of generations to refer to the immigrant position will emerge in years to come as significant to understanding the ageing experience. Global trends point to massive emigrations around the world. Economic challenges encourage many to leave their homelands where no jobs exist to go to those where opportunity abounds. In some cases, older parents follow their adult children. In other cases, it is future generations who remain in the newfound country, and grow old in a new culture. Understanding what immigrant generation one occupies holds importance for acculturation, access to resources and overall well-being in old age.

Generations signify a concept with multiple meanings in social geron-tology. Definitions vary depending on the subject of inquiry. At the very least, generations provide a means to understanding social relations between and within groups of people by acknowledging the ways in which age, social role and/or historical time combine to influence social life. Policy directives and government officials may use the generation concept as a starting point for developing programmes and services that best serve all of society over the life course, from birth to death.

See also: *Ageing, Care, Cohort, Gerontology, Retirement, Social Relations*

REFERENCES

Aldous, J. (1987) New views on the family life of the elderly and the near-elderly. *Journal of Marriage and the Family*, 49: 227–234.

Bengtson, V. L. (1993) Is the 'contract across generations' changing? Effects of popu-lation ageing on obligations and expectations across age groups, in V. L. Bengtson and W. A. Achenbaum (eds), *The Changing Contract across Generations*. New York: Aldine de Gruyter. pp. 3–23.

Brody, E. M. (1981) Women in the middle and family help to old people. *The Gerontologist*, 21: 471–480.

Fuller-Thomason, E., Minkler, M. and Driver, D. (1997) A profile of grandparents rais-ing grandchildren in the United States. *The Gerontologist*, 37: 406–411.

Greenberg, J. S. and Becker, M. (1988) Ageing parents as family resources. *The Gerontologist*, 28: 786–791.

Ingersoll-Dayton, B., Neal, M. B. and Hammer, L. B. (2001) Ageing parents helping adult children: the experience of the sandwiched generation. *Family Relations*, 50: 262–271.

McDaniel, S. A. (2004) Generationing gender: justice and the division of welfare. *Journal of Ageing Studies*, 18: 27–44.

Minkler, M. (1991) 'Generation equity' and the new victim blaming, in M. Minkler and C. Estes (eds), *Critical Perspectives on Ageing*. Amityville, NY: Baywood. pp. 67–79.

Moody, H. R. (2000) *Ageing: Concepts and Controversies*. Thousand Oaks, CA: Pine Forge Press.

Rosenthal, C. J., Martin-Matthews, A. and Matthews, S. H. (1996) Caught in the mid-dle? Occupancy in multiple roles and help to parents in a national probability sam-ple of Canadian adults. *Journal of Gerontology: Social Sciences*, 51B: S274–S283.

Soldo, B. J. (1996) Cross pressures on middle-aged adults: a broader view. *Journal of Gerontology: Social Sciences*, 51B: S271–S273.

Strauss, W. and Howe, N. (1991) *Generations*. New York: William Morrow.

Troll, L. E. (1983) Grandparents: the family watchdogs, in T. H. Brubaker (ed.), *Family Relationships in Later Life*. Beverly Hills, CA: Sage. pp. 63–74.

generations

Gerontology

> **Gerontology is broadly defined as the study of ageing from biological, psychological and social perspectives.**

Gerontology is a multidisciplinary subject. Since its conception in 1903, its definition has expanded to include different perspectives on and approaches to ageing, such as critical gerontology, technogerontology and environmental gerontology (Johnson, 2005).

The term is also associated with geriatric medicine, which in the UK is a hospital-based speciality concerned with mental and physical disorders which also includes prevention, diagnosis, care and treatment of older persons through medicine, nursing and the allied health professionals.

Social gerontology concentrates on the study of the social, economic and demographic characteristics of older people and an ageing population. Increasingly, the focus has been on the life-course approach to ageing rather than the study of old age *per se* in gerontology (Johnson, 2005)

The first signs of interest in age as a category to be studied can be dated back to the seventeenth century when the first collection of statistics on mortality and morbidity was recorded (Thane, 2005). By the nineteenth century research on degenerative conditions of old age was underway, with specialist treatment concentrating on older people. For the first time the idea of the 'old' as a separate group emerged, becoming particularly identified in the UK with the first pensions on a large scale in 1909. In 1903, a Russian-born biologist named Elie Metchnikoff first proposed and named gerontology as a new field of study.

Whereas before the Second World War there was a concentration on paediatric care, by the end of the war there had been a greater recognition of the social and medical implications of an ageing population as well as an awareness of the low level of care for older people. The creation of the National Health Service in 1948 in the UK provided financial and administrative support for geriatric medicine.

The study of ageing was advanced through a number of classic texts, such as Howell's *Our Advancing Years* (1953), Exton-Smith's *Medical Problems of Old Age* (1955) and Peter Townsend's *Family Life of Older*

People (1957) and *The Last Refuge* (1962). The latter sociological studies showed the problems older people faced in the community as well as in institutional care. All raised the implications of a growing older population posing problems for society, family and individuals. Policy considerations driven by these studies viewed the elderly population as a 'burden' and ageist assumptions dominated gerontology (Johnson, 2005). Gerontological theory also mirrored this, with the development of 'disengagement' theory and 'activity' theory.

The expansion of gerontology came with the establishment of the associated groups of the British Geriatrics Society, the British Society of Gerontology and the British Society for Research on Ageing in 1945; and journals such as *Ageing in Society* and *Age and Ageing*. In 1948 the International Association of Gerontology held its first meeting when researchers, teachers and practitioners who worked with, or studied, older people and old age were brought together. In Britain, the establishment of the National Old People's Welfare Organisation (now Age Concern) in 1940, the National Corporation for the Care of Old People (now the Centre for Policy on Ageing) in 1947 and, in 1961, Help the Aged were all influential in furthering the study of ageing. This was followed by the growth of gerontology in university settings, for example, university courses in gerontology at King's College, London and Keele. Courses in gerontology expanded along with increasing study on the processes of ageing funded by the major research councils (e.g. the Economic and Social Research Council (ESRC) through the Growing Older and New Dynamics of Ageing programmes).

The late 1980s saw the development of critical perspectives (Estes, 1979; Phillipson, 1982) which recognised that the experience of old age is determined as much by economic and social factors as by biological or individual characteristics. The development of critical approaches (e.g. biographical approaches) which contextualise the ageing process on life histories has subsequently grown, firmly identifying gerontology with a life-course approach. Consequently, there has been a redefinition of the subject's core issues and greater attention on the process of ageing as experienced by individuals.

Other trends within gerontology today include the recognition of diversity within the ageing population, particularly around gender, class and race; a focus on 'non-pathological' ageing; and the expansion in the field of study to encompass the life-course perspective.

gerontology

Ray (1996: 675) defines critical gerontology as: 'a critique of the social influences, philosophical foundations and empirical methodologies on which gerontology as a field has been historically constructed'. Phillipson and Walker (1986: 280) defined critical gerontology as 'a more value-committed approach to social gerontology – a commitment not just to understand the social construction of ageing but to change it'. The emphasis in both of these definitions is on values, change and action.

In relation to older people, critical gerontology has focused on how marginalised and pathologised older people have been in society and how we need to view older people and later life in a different and more positive way, challenging traditional theories in gerontology and the methods by which we study ageing, and giving voice to those people who are often unheard (Holstein and Minkler, 2007). In the UK, the emphasis has been on a critique of the state as the dominant provider of welfare (Phillipson, 1982).

There has been considerable development in relation to the application of critical gerontology. Political economists drew attention to the ways in which our welfare system was effectively transforming ageing into a dependent status (Townsend, 2007) with long-term and community care systems bolstering the power inequities between experts (such as social workers) and lay people, and were creating what Carol Estes (1979) called 'The Ageing Enterprise'. These systems and structures were essentially about controlling and managing people, rather than enabling older people to engage in a full life.

Whereas the UK tradition to critical gerontology has come from an emphasis on the political economy of ageing, Minkler (1996) argued that the other strand of development in critical gerontology stems from more humanistic approaches, stressing a focus on the 'meaning' of old age and growing old, with a greater emphasis (although not exclusively) on individual aspects of ageing. Biographical and narrative perspectives also provide another basis for exploring the social constructions of ageing. Taken together, all three perspectives are seen as empowering older people.

The challenge for gerontology is how to bring the different strands together. The application of the different influences on gerontology for the study of ageing is also a test – how we research and what methods we use will be influenced by our gerontological understanding. Whereas biographical approaches have been favoured under the critical perspective approach, there is a need for a methodological bricolage (Holstein and Minkler, 2007: 22):

Methodological bricolage means not ruling out knowledge that is gained from personal narratives, fiction, poetry, film, qualitative investigations, philosophical inquiries, participatory action research and any other method of inquiry we may discover that yields insights into fundamental questions about how, and why, we experience old age in very particular ways.

Ray et al. (2008: 29) also highlight the challenge of applying this to the ways in which professionals work with older people. Taking the example from social work, they argue that 'a critical gerontology perspective with human rights, empowerment and methodological bricolage at its centre, means that instead of "doing to" older people we need to look at ways of "working with" them, in partnership'.

The history of the concept has illustrated the shift in the 'problematisation' of age to one where solutions across the life course and the positive aspects of ageing are reinforced. Developments in theory and methods have followed with feminist gerontology, critical perspectives and a greater acceptance of qualitative methods in the study of ageing. Older people's voices are increasingly central to understanding the experiences of ageing. Alongside this has been the expansion in the field of gerontology to include ecological and technological aspects of ageing under gerontechnology and environmental gerontology.

See also: *Ageing, Biographical Approaches, Care, Environmental Gerontology, Gender, Life-course Perspective, Pensions, Social Theories of Ageing*

FURTHER READING

Bond, J., Peace, S., Ditmann-Kohli, F. and Westerhof, G. (2007) *Ageing in Society* (3rd edition). London: Sage with the British Society of Gerontology (BSG).

REFERENCES

Holstein, M. and Minkler, M. (2007) Critical gerontology: reflections for the 21st century, in M. Bernard and T. Scharf (eds), *Critical Perspectives on Ageing Societie*. Bristol: The Policy Press.

gerontology

Global Ageing

An unprecedented change in the demographic make up of the world's population marked by a shift towards an increase in both the proportions and number of older people in relation to other age groups.

This change, known as population or demographic ageing, refers to the ongoing shift in the world's population age structure, and which is leading to an increase in both the proportions and numbers of older people. Population ageing is increasingly being referred to as a global phenomenon because most countries in the world are now experiencing this shift in age structure. Such changes are the result of ongoing processes of a global decline in fertility, often referred to as the global fertility transition, and decreasing mortality at older ages (Gavrilov and Heuveline, 2003).

The concept of global ageing describes a new phenomenon in as much as population ageing has, until the last two to three decades, been associated primarily with developed countries. It can best be illustrated when considering the following figures. In 1950, eight out of every 100 people in the world were aged over 60 (a ratio of about one older person to 10 of younger ages). Projections indicate that 100 years later, by 2050, 22 out of every 100 will be 60 years old or more, a shift in ratio to one out of five (United Nations, 2005). Another striking illustration of the concept is the projected increase in the numbers and proportions of the 'oldest old' (normally considered as those aged 80 and above) in the world population. In 2005, this group represented about 1.3% of the world's population and about 88 million people, but projections suggest that by mid-century these figures will have increased to 4.4% and 402 million respectively (United Nations, 2007).

However, it would be incorrect to interpret global ageing as synonymous with the simultaneous ageing of all the world's populations, as there are significant regional variations in both fertility and mortality transitions. Although globally speaking, for example, life expectancy at birth has increased on average by four years for each decade since 1960, this improvement can be attributed primarily to a drop in mortality in Asia (Palacios, 2002). Another example of these variations is that

key concepts in
social gerontology

although the world's projected population will for the first time have more older people aged 60 and beyond (about 22%) than children under the age of 15 (about 20%) by 2050, this transformation of 'demographic maturity' had already occurred by 2000 in 15 European countries, and is projected to occur 40 years hence in Asia, and shortly afterwards in Latin America and the Caribbean. In contrast, Africa's population will remain relatively 'young' until the middle of the century, principally because of higher fertility levels, which do not appear to be declining rapidly, and low life expectancies in sub-Saharan Africa (Haub, 2007). The proportion of those under the age of 15 in sub-Saharan Africa, for example, reaches about 29% in 2050 compared to only approximately 9% for those aged 60 and beyond (United Nations, 2005, 2007; United Nations, Department of Economic and Social Affairs and Populations Division, 2006).

It is difficult to pinpoint precisely when the concept of global ageing began to appear in the literature but already in 1956 the United Nations Population Division had drawn attention to the ageing of populations. By 1978, the United Nations had called for the organisation of a World Assembly on Ageing with the aim of generating international awareness of the need for a programme of action focusing on the economic and social security needs of older persons, and their role in contributing to national development. The Assembly was subsequently held in Vienna in 1982 and although the notion of global ageing does not figure at this stage, the importance of extending the question of population ageing to developing countries and creating international awareness and policy action does reflect the recognition of population ageing as an increasingly worldwide phenomenon. The Vienna International Plan of Action on Ageing, adopted by the Assembly, was to facilitate the development and application of policies at international, regional and national levels to enhance the lives of older people and to counter the negative consequences of population ageing on development. Again, while not referring to the concept of global ageing, the United Nation's political declaration following the Second World Assembly on Ageing in Madrid in 2002 (which led to the adoption of an International Plan of Action on Ageing 2002) refers to the world's population ageing as 'an unprecedented demographic transformation'. At the same time, the World Health Organisation launched a policy framework on Active Ageing which, it was anticipated, would become a global strategy. Prior to this and in response to global ageing, the World Health Organization had launched its Ageing and Health Programme in 1995, incorporating

global ageing

health promotion (active ageing) as well as life-course, socio-economic, cultural, gender, intergenerational, ethical and community-oriented perspectives (Kallache et al., 2005).

It is probably too much of a new field of interest for there to be a lot of critical evaluation at this stage, but the concept of global ageing has nonetheless had a significant impact in the UK, spurning the emergence of a 'new' field of research inquiry (Harper, 2006). This has been clearly marked by the establishment in 2001 of the Oxford Institute of Ageing, which carries out research on the impact of ageing at the global, societal and individual levels, and since 2005, has been completing a global ageing study in 21 countries to investigate attitudes to ageing and longevity. Other initiatives which mark this interest can be found in a new higher education programme in Global Ageing offered for the first time in 2008 by the Institute of Gerontology, King's College, London, and specialist journals dedicated to the theme, such as *Global Ageing: Issues and Action*, produced by the International Federation on Ageing. Other scholars from the European gerontological community have also been arguing for the need to collect robust and comparable data on ageing at an international level in order to monitor global ageing (Robine and Michel, 2004).

If the concept of global ageing has only recently found an application in research and policy agendas, it is essentially because our gaze on population ageing *per se* has generally focused on western nations because of its earlier onset in these countries. Its implications for developed nations are now well established: changing family and household structures, changing patterns of health, welfare, housing and transport consumption needs, transformations in the age-based configuration of the labour market, new financial patterns of savings and consumption sparked by an increasing proportion of individuals with higher levels of disposable income. All these have been met with contrasting reactions and interpretations. They range from the fear of a 'demographic burden', in the form of soaring health and pension costs, to the need for policy makers to question whether population ageing *per se* is at the source of these needs or whether they in fact reflect a political unwillingness or inability to adapt policies and institutions and to respond positively and creatively to the advantages that ageing populations represent (Harper, 2006). These debates have generally evolved in industrialised nations which have a long history of established welfare and public–private infrastructures designed to provide societal responses to social need.

The concept of global ageing forces us to widen the lens and to think of its meaning in the broader context of globalisation itself. What, for example, will be the consequences of demographic ageing in terms of health needs in countries which have yet to master the multiple causes of death during childhood and maternity and which continue to keep infant and maternal mortality rates high, despite declining fertility? How will developing and transitional economies, many of whose existing institutionalised social security and protection provisions are still at a rudimentary level of coverage and efficiency, operating as varied modes or regimes of welfare (Gough et al., 2004), move towards ensuring more comprehensive and sustainable forms of protection and security for their elders when this group is known to be at greater risk of social exclusion and marginalisation than others through inferior education, income levels, possession of assets and marketable skills (HelpAge International, 2002)? How will these nations, if at all, address the debate around the need to ensure an equitable intergenerational redistribution of sometimes scarce economic resources across age groups?

When used in this way, the concept of global ageing enables us to contrast and make relative the implications of population ageing as they are appearing in developing and transitional nations and as they already exist in developed countries. The crucial question that the concept points to is whether, in the latter, there is a political will to shift the focus from population ageing as 'crisis' to 'advantage' and, in the former, to respond quickly enough in the time span available, to incorporate the needs of an ageing population into a broader agenda of development.

See also: Ageing, Gender, Housing, Longevity, Population Ageing, Social Exclusion

REFERENCES

Harper, S. (2006) Addressing the implications of global ageing. *Journal of Population Research*, 23(2): 205–223.

Haub, C. (2007) *Global Ageing and the Demographic Divide*. Available at: www.prb. org/Articles/2008/globalageing.aspx?p=1 (accessed 6 June 2008).

Kallache, A., Barreto, S. M. and Keller, I. (2005) Global ageing: the demographic revolution in all cultures and societies, in M. Johnson in association with V. L. Bengtson, P. G. Coleman and B. L. Kirkwood (eds), *The Cambridge Handbook of Age and Ageing*. Cambridge: Cambridge University Press. pp. 30–46.

Palacios, R. (2002) The future of global ageing. *International Journal of Epidemiology*, 31: 786–791. Also available at: www.ije.oxfordjournals.org/cgi/content/full/31/4/786 (accessed 15 May 2008).

global ageing

Housing

> **A physical structure which accommodates older people's activities of daily living.**

Heywood et al. (2002: 3) define housing as 'a place in which the basic human activities of sleeping, eating, washing, storage of possessions, social contact, recreation, and care within the self-selected household take place. The word may also incorporate the attributes of the structure: its location, size, design, condition, accessibility, affordability, warmth and comfort'. However, even this definition may be contentious as households may form not out of choice but live together by regulation and prescription, such as under the Mental Health Act 1982, or through circumstances such as frailty and disability which require care needs to be met by others, for example living with relatives or in a residential care facility.

Housing is one of the most influential aspects of people's lives, particularly as older people spend more of their time in their home than other groups in society. As the majority of older people live in 'ordinary' housing, then it is appropriate to explore this holistic concept, alongside more specialist concepts, such as 'assisted living'. The concept is also closely related to the 'meaning of home' and 'ageing in place', concepts explored elsewhere in this book. It is also associated with related concepts such as 'independence', 'sense of control' and home as a symbol of self (Heywood et al., 2002).

Since the introduction of the welfare state there has been an increase in older people as owner occupiers, with many older people living alone. Property in both private owner occupied and rented stocks, however, is often in need of repair and overall older people are more likely to experience poorer living conditions, sometimes lacking the basic amenities, than younger people. They are also more likely to face verbal, physical, psychological and financial abuse from landlords.

Heywood et al. (2002: 33) note that although tenure is a powerful component of peoples' housing biography, there is a very limited knowledge of how it is experienced in old age. Indeed, 'tenure, as an indicator of social difference, deserves more attention from the different social gerontological traditions'.

key concepts in
social gerontology

Age-specific housing serves relatively few older people, yet a lack of appropriate housing has led to older people moving into residential care (Phillips, 1992). A response to counter this through the early development of community care led to a number of local authorities developing sheltered housing schemes. Although initially showcased as meeting the needs of older people, this form of provision was criticised for offering inadequate space and poor design. Providing a resident warden made it expensive, and the segregation of older people was also criticised (Bytheway, 1995). Increasingly, local authority sheltered housing became 'difficult to let' (Tinker et al., 1995). Today a mixed economy has led to a variety of providers entering the housing market: local authorities, the voluntary sector, housing associations and large corporations – for profit and not for profit. The sheltered housing concept has also been replaced by the concept of 'extra-care' housing, which in policy terms is often seen as an alternative for residential care, yet marketed for both 'fit' and 'frail' older people. Some commentators (Heywood et al., 2002), however, view special needs housing and schemes as stigmatising, discriminatory and ageist.

Housing conditions are a key dimension of housing. Whereas, in general, housing conditions have improved for older people, the dissatisfaction with the state of housing repair in the rented sector has become an increasingly pressing issue. Forrest and Leather (1998) point to the 'dual ageing' of the homeowner population (the homeowners themselves and the property they occupy) over the next two decades and its policy implications. A population of ageing homeowners living in an ageing housing stock is likely to include increasing numbers of households with limited incomes and with a decreasing physical capacity to carry out their own repair and maintenance work, let alone adaptations. The authors also assert that this process will become more common as the ageing process produces more single-person households. 'Income poor' but 'equity rich' is a growing phenomenon and several schemes seek to realise the potential for older people to release equity to pay for care.

Yet greater disposable income and more affordable lifestyles for older people, coupled with advances in technology in the home, are enabling older people to access a wider range of housing choices (Peace, 2006). Additionally, the requirement for new housing in the UK to conform to 'Lifetime Homes Standards' and the introduction of 'smart technology' where triggers and monitors assisting older people with cognitive or physical impairments become inbuilt into housing stock have the potential to improve the quality of life of everyone, irrespective of age.

For many older people, their housing choices stem from a combination of their life-course circumstances and external barriers. Peace (2006: 180) asserts that where and with whom we chose to live in later life are influenced by our past and present. Housing history will evolve through the interplay of a myriad of factors: family history, gender, marital status, education etc. Housing deprivation in earlier life will also impact on provision in later life (Izuhara and Heywood, 2003).

Life-course events and transitions may also influence moves in later life. 'A Typology of Elderly Migration', by Wiseman and Roseman (1979), asserts that people move at critical points in the life cycle when changes in housing needs and preferences can be seen as stimulating considerations about decisions to move. Not only do such life-cycle events define when people move, but also the passage from one stage to another is often related to the type of move made and the destination chosen. From this theoretical perspective, the authors suggest that abrupt changes in family and personal situations, which occur in the life cycle, would redefine housing needs and preferences. These events are some of the 'triggering mechanisms' which generate high mobility rates for older people during the later stages of life. They include: children leaving home, retirement, spouse's retirement, death of spouse, severe illness, and physical decline to the point of losing independence. With the exception of retirement, these triggering mechanisms do not correspond well with chronological age. After the retirement stage there is a long period of gradually declining migration propensity, followed by increasing rates during the final stage of old age. This last period of increased mobility results from biological decline and the loss of independent residential status (e.g. institutionalisation, 'moving in' with relatives, or relocation to a limited care facility).

The social policy of old age has traditionally ignored housing as a key component of sustained community care. Two strands of policy have shaped the history of housing for older people – the emphasis on 'independence' as a policy goal and the need for special needs provision for older people.

Heywood et al. (2002: 61–67) stress the important contribution of housing and housing organisations in meeting community care objectives. The impact of the Home Improvement Agency and housing associations in raising the profile of housing for older people through

'Care & Repair' schemes placed housing centre stage to the success of community care and the pursuit of 'independence'. A further driver was the emphasis on specialist housing. Sheltered housing was also seen as cheaper than residential care.

Treating older people as a separate group has been criticised as it portrays 'old age' as a problem (Heywood et al., 2002: 41). Rather than being value-free, housing has been imbued with a medical model of old age, focusing on dependency, rather than being seen as a social construction. A much wider debate on the role of housing and the environment is necessary to place policy in a broader framework. Yet the history of housing is characterised by marginalisation in the main debates on the lives of older people (Heywood et al., 2002). As Bernard and Phillips (2000) argue, housing is integral to a social policy of ageing. Linking housing and other concepts, such as 'staying put' and 'Care & Repair', to the debate on independence often constrains older people to remain in their home even if this does not suit their needs. The voice of older people in designing their living environments is also a missing link to policy.

'Housing with care' has become a practical concept that is increasingly being applied to provision for older people. This has been seen as an alternative to residential care and combines both independent living with relatively high levels of care. A UK study in 2006 which looked at such provision found that these schemes could have a positive impact on the health and well-being of residents, yet robust 'quality of life' measures were missing from the studies (Croucher et al., 2006). The evidence on cost-effectiveness is also contradictory and insufficient when forming an opinion on whether such schemes should be a flagship for the future.

Co-housing has also been a concept popular in the European and US contexts. Denmark and the Netherlands have developed this concept, based on a group of people, loosely associated with each other, sharing in a co-housing scheme which has the characteristics of a private dwelling and communal facilities (Brenton, 2001).

Underlying all these approaches is the basic principle that older people living in the twenty-first century have a right to enjoy housing which is comfortable and which suits their individual requirements (Bond and Coleman, 1993: 346–347).

housing

129

See also: *Ageing, Ageing in Place, Care, Disability, Frailty, Gender, Generations, Independence, Quality of Life, Retirement*

FURTHER READING

Heywood, F., Oldman, C. and Means, R. (2002) *Housing and Home in Later Life*. Buckingham: Open University Press.

Mullins, D. and Murie, A. (2006) *Housing Policy in the UK*. Basingstoke: Palgrave Macmillan.

Peace, S. and Holland, C. (eds) (2001) *Inclusive Housing in and Ageing Society*. Bristol: The Policy Press.

Peace, S., Holland, C. and Kellaher, L. (2006) *Environment and Identity in Later Life*. Buckingham: Open University Press.

REFERENCES

Bernard, M. and Phillips, J. (2000) *The Social Policy of Old Age*. London: Centre for Policy on Ageing.

Bond, J. and Coleman, P. (1993) Ageing into the twenty-first century, in J. Bond, P. Coleman and S. Peace (eds), *Ageing in Society: An Introduction to Social Gerontology* (2nd edition). London: Sage. pp. 332–350.

Brenton, M. (2001) Older people's co-housing communities, in S. Peace and C. Holland (eds), *Inclusive Housing in an Ageing Society*. Bristol: The Policy Press.

Bytheway, B. (1995) *Ageism*. London: Open University Press.

Croucher, K., Hicks, L. and Jackson, K. (2006) *Housing with Care in Later Life: A Literature Review*. York: Joseph Rowntree Foundation.

Forrest, R. and Leather, P. (1998) The ageing of the property owning democracy. *Ageing and Society*, 18: 35–63.

Heywood, F., Oldman, C. and Means, R. (2002) *Housing and Home in Later Life*. Buckingham: Open University Press.

Izuhara, M. and Heywood, F. (2003) A life-time of inequality: a structural analysis of housing careers and issues facing older private tenants. *Ageing and Society*, 23: 207–224.

Peace, S. (2006) Housing and future living arrangements, in J. Vincent, C. Phillipson and M. Downs (eds), *The Futures of Old Age*. London: Sage.

Phillips, J. (1992) *Private Residential Care: The Process of Admission*. Aldershot: Ashgate.

Tinker, A., Wright, F. and Zeilig, H. (1995) *Difficult to Let Sheltered Housing*. London: HMSO.

Wiseman, R. and Roseman, C. (1979) A typology of elderly migration based on the decision-making process. *Economic Geography*, 55(4): 324–337.

Independence

> *A sense or state of physical, psychological and spiritual autonomy, self-identity, self-respect, control and degree of functional capacity.*

Since the 1970s, the concept of independence has emerged as an area of interest for academics, policy makers and practitioners alike. Depending upon which perspective is taken, it may mean, at the functional level, being able to complete daily activities unaided, or having a sense of control over life and its resources so that personal aims can be accomplished. In other words, feeling independent in later life reflects a recognition that there is choice in one's lifestyle and the possibility of taking up social, cultural, spiritual and economic opportunities if and when desired.

One reason why it is difficult to define independence more precisely has been the tendency for it to be conceptualised in relation to dependence and not in its own right. Secker et al. (2003), for example, in their review of the literature on the concept of independence, note that one of the few attempts at developing a theoretical model of independence undertaken by Paillat (1976) relied upon a five-level typology, spanning from dependence to complete independence – that is, independence was actually conceptualised only in terms of the relative absence of dependence. This tendency is also reflected in measurements and tools used by researchers and practitioners from various fields to assess older people's needs for support and their ability to maintain independent living. For example, independence is often measured in terms of dependence, and its functional aspects are generally conceptualised in terms of measures of disability rather than ability. These measures are also criticised for failing to capture the individual or person-specific aspects which influence the meaning and experience of independence.

From the field of social gerontology, theorists, many of whom have drawn on Townsend's influential (1981) work on structured dependency, have also been keen to ascertain how dominant social and economic values influence broader social institutions in creating an expectation of dependency in old age (e.g. see some of the earlier works of Walker (1980) and Phillipson (1982)).

Others have suggested a more holistic approach to the concept which links independence with the notions of interdependency and reciprocity (e.g. Fennell, 1986; Finch, 1989). This perspective reflects a recognition that our needs for support and our ability to remain independent vary depending upon life-course context, and that, as social beings, we will always engage in mutually beneficial exchanges with others. Thus, an identity of 'dependence' may also coexist with that of 'independence'. For example, an older person may well be 'dependent' upon a state pension, but may live independently, and may engage in a reciprocal transaction by providing unpaid childcare for those around them in exchange for the socially enriching experience that this provides. Wilson (1993) adopts an interesting perspective to the concept, by distinguishing both positive and negatives connotations of independence. The former could describe a person's ability to act upon their choices without interference or intervention by others, whereas the latter might refer to an unwillingness to accept help or change for fear of a loss of control over their lives, even when acceptance of this change could potentially improve their quality of life. In an attempt to enhance the theoretical conceptualisation of independence, Secker et al. (2003) propose a two-dimensional model which encompasses both high and low levels of independence and dependence. The model considers both the culturally-specific nature of the idea of self-reliance as well as the importance that older people themselves attach to choice and meaningful social roles. Their work is in line with research which seeks to understand how older people themselves interpret and give meaning to the concept of independence. A growing body of research suggests that despite variations in individual biography and socio-cultural context, the meanings attributed to independence by older people nonetheless portray strong and consistent themes. Although by no means exhaustive, these include the importance of being able to look after one self and having a sense of self-reliance (i.e. not depending on others for domestic, physical or personal care); preserving a sense of individuality, self-esteem, self-awareness and identity as an independent person; having the capacity and freedom to make decisions for oneself and remain autonomous (control); not feeling any sense of obligation or debt towards others; engaging in meaningful activities whether these be through reciprocal exchanges or through a recognition of roles by others (e.g. see Ball et al., 2004; Plath, 2008; Secker et al., 2003; Sixsmith, 1986). Leeson et al. (2003), in their review of independent living in later life, also pinpoint numerous individual-level factors which constrain, facilitate and shape perceptions of independence for older people: the importance of living arrangements; people's sense of control and empowerment over their lives; their economic security; involvement and integration in social and familial networks; and issues relating to health and social care. They note, however, that the relative importance of these factors in shaping the experience of independence will vary from individual to individual.

These perceptions of independence have also been situated in relation to broader aspects of everyday living, notably financial independence and independence in the house and home environments. The availability of financial resources, for example, besides their obvious importance in preventing poverty in later life, will be a key determinant of independence improving an older person's ability to assume the costs of maintaining a home or paying for private personal or healthcare. Financial resources may therefore moderate how older people perceive their state of independence, particularly if confronted with increasing physical impairment. Part of the rationale for encourageing 'ageing in place' and independent living has been the recognition that independence is intimately linked to how at ease older people feel with their immediate living environment. Researchers have argued, for example, that the meaning of 'home' often serves as a symbolic representation of the independent self, even when this environment is at times poorly adapted to the functional needs of later life (Heywood et al., 2002).

Not only is the achievement and maintenance of independence valued by older people, but it has also become a key objective of policy makers and practitioners at both national and international levels. In 1991, for example, nine years after its endorsement of the Vienna International Plan of Action on Ageing, the United Nations considered independence as one of its five principles for older persons, defining it in terms of access to the basic resources required for survival (e.g. food, water, shelter); the opportunity to generate an income; to undertake training and education, and to have a choice over retirement options; to live in environments adapted to needs and to remain at home for as long as possible. In many developed countries the promotion of independence for older people is also seen as part of a general move to shift formal or public service provisions away from institutional settings to the local community environment and to facilitate ageing in place. A good illustration of this policy in the European context has been the promotion of the idea of lifetime homes and neighbourhoods, that is adapting or providing living environments designed to cater for the needs of older people (and future generations to come) so that they can live independently for as long as possible even with varying degrees of physical or cognitive difficulties.

Despite the contemporary value placed on independence in later life, critics point to its origins as being deep-rooted within ideologies of self-reliance and autonomy. Whether the pursuit of independence in later life will always bring the positive outcomes anticipated, such as improvements in quality of life and well-being, is also contested. If independence is synonymous with living alone, for example, but along with it comes social isolation and loneliness, and if dependence is living in residential care but always having the possibility for social interaction, how are its outcomes to be evaluated? Further criticisms of the concept have pointed to its ethnocentric focus, which reflects an assumption that independence is a goal shared by all in later life. While this may indeed be the case in contemporary western societies, there is ample evidence to suggest that there are strong cross-cultural differences in the value attached to being independent when old (see Secker et al., 2003). In the Chinese culture, for example, being supported by one's children is highly valued and a mark of esteem, in stark contrast to western cultures where it is often considered as a 'burden of care'.

In sum, independence is a complex and ambiguous concept. From its early focus on individual functional capacity rooted within the dominant perspective of dependency, the focus has since moved to an acknowledgement that wider social structures and individual factors can shape the experience of independence in later life. The question remains, however, whether in promoting independence as a 'social good' for all older people, we are not only ignoring the diversity of individual need and cultural context, but are also perhaps contributing to the elaboration of social expectations about later life which deny the inevitability of dependence for some.

See also: Ageing in Place, Disability, Gerontology, Quality of Life, Retirement

REFERENCES

Finch, J. (1989) *Family Obligations and Social Change.* Cambridge: Polity Press.

Heywood, F., Oldman, C. and Means, R. (2002) *Housing and Home in Later Life.* Buckingham: Open University Press.

Paillat, P. (1976) Criteria of independent (autonomous) life in old age, in J. M. A. Munnichs and J. A. van den Heuval (eds), *Dependency or Interdependency in Old Age.* The Hague: Martinus Nijhoff. pp. 35–44.

Secker, J., Hill, R., Hill, R. and Parkman, S. (2003) Promoting independence: but promoting what and how? *Ageing and Society*, 23: 375–391.

Townsend, P. (1981) The structured dependency of the elderly: the creation of several policy in the twentieth century. *Ageing and Society*, 1(1): 5-28

Wilson, G. (1993) Money and independence in old age, in S. Arber and M. Evandrou (eds), *Ageing, Independence and the Life Course*. London: Jessica Kingsley. pp. 46–64.

Intergenerational Practice

> *Projects which facilitate contact and interaction between older and younger people through their involvement in planned activities.*

Part of the broader intergenerational field, intergenerational practice is designed to enhance relations between and across generations by facilitating contact, interaction and cooperation with the aim of promoting understanding and tolerance and, at the broader levels of community and society, to promote social cohesion. Such activities are also intended to enhance the exchange and sharing of resources and experiences, and to facilitate reciprocal forms of support. Intergenerational practice, then, appears as a mechanism through which to promote social solidarity both at the micro level of individual interaction and at the broader, meso- and macro-social levels of community and society.

In many ways the notion of intergenerational practice refers to longstanding traditions of intergenerational learning, exchange and communication. The step towards conceptualising them under the umbrella of a formalised field of action – 'intergenerational practice' – stems from concerns about the changing nature of modern, industrial societies and the potentially negative consequences that this may have had for relationships between and across generations (Pain, 2005). One such aspect of change has been the impact that increased geographic mobility is thought to have had on the family's capacity to continue sharing

intergenerational practice

135

resources or to provide help and support when needed; another has been a shift from altruistic values and norms to more individualistic aspirations of self-fulfilment. In addition to these social transformations, demographic and epidemiological changes – notably decreasing mortality and improved life expectancies – have not only meant an increasingly larger proportion of older people surviving into later life, but also the increased likelihood of several generations co-surviving and spending more time together than previously possible. This points to the potential for new forms of interaction as well as the issue of meeting the care needs of older family members. Other concerns about the potential volatility of generational relations – often referred to as the 'generational equity debate' – stem from the economic implications that ageing populations may have on public sector spending, particularly with regard to health and social security needs. The crux of this debate is whether younger and older generations will have to 'compete' for increasingly scarce public resources in order to fund their respective life-course needs (Moody, 2006; Vincent, 2003).

Indeed, a key reason why intergenerational programmes emerged in the USA during the 1960s and 1970s was in response to concerns about a growing rift between generations for the reasons noted previously. Further developments in the field during the 1980s and 1990s in North America (including Canada) were to respond to the needs of both younger (e.g. unemployment, substance abuse, school problems) and older generations (e.g. isolation, low self-esteem) and it was during this time that 'Generations United' was established in the USA as the national agency supporting and lobbying for intergenerational initiatives and practice. These programmes were to extend further during the 1990s – the International Consortium for Intergenerational Programmes was created in 1999, for example – but with a broader focus on enhancing and revitalising communities, and were to emerge in the European context in response to problems of social exclusion and as a mechanism to address ageist attitudes and age discrimination.

With a more longstanding history in the USA than in the UK, inter-generational practice in the former context has traditionally focused more on the engagement of older people with other generations, whereas in the UK the focus has been much more on children and youth in school and community settings, with a narrower application to older people (Springate et al., 2008). It was not until 2001 in the UK, for example, that the Beth Johnson Foundation's Centre for

Intergenerational Practice was established and in 2003 that the *Journal of Intergenerational Relationships* was launched. Other initiatives across Europe have also emerged during this period. In 2005, the *Red de Relaciones Intergeneracionales of the Instituto de Mayores y Servicios Sociales* (IMSERSO) was created in Spain, and in 2007, both in the USA and in Wales, at the Universities of Pittsburgh and Lampeter, training courses were established.

The increasing interest taken in intergenerational practice among gerontologists is undoubtedly linked to the significance given by the United Nations to the concept of 'a society for all ages', which became the slogan for the Second World Assembly on Ageing held in Madrid in 2002. The key aspects of the concept had previously been defined in 1995 in the conceptual framework that was to underpin the 1999 International Year of Older People (Sanchez et al., 2007). Integral to this concept is the recognition that multigenerational relations are important, as are principles of reciprocity and equity, and that generations should invest in each other for mutual benefit. Although no explicit reference was made in 2002 to intergenerational practice, the Assembly's report does refer to intergenerational relations in terms of dialogue, interdependence, solidarity and reciprocity (United Nations, 2002).

The development of intergenerational practice has therefore emerged as a mechanism for strengthening generational proximity, improving communication and understanding, and fostering a commitment to reciprocity and shared responsibilities. At a broader societal level, it is seen as a means of enhancing social cohesion through social and community inclusion.

The forms that intergenerational practice take and the activities covered are as varied as the objectives it sets out to achieve; they can involve activities shared by members of one generation or, alternatively, by people from different generations who either work towards a common goal, such as a community activity, or who come together to learn, to provide support or to benefit from mentoring. Bernard (2006) has suggested that intergenerational practices and programmes can be grouped according to the social issues they address: intergenerational learning, which might, for example, aim to improve educational outcomes in young people; care and support initiatives, designed to assist in resolving substance abuse problems or, on a different level, supporting older people with specific physical or mental health needs, such as dementia; and, finally, in the area of community-based initiatives, addressing such issues as environmental regeneration activities or problems of social exclusion. The types of activity involved can be wide-ranging, encompassing performance activities such as theatre and leisure and learning activities. Shared learning activities might involve school children working with older people to develop a local history project or collaborating to address neighbourhood problems. When practice has a mentoring objective, older people may be supportive of young parents and when it is aimed at providing support, it may simply be young volunteers providing services such as shopping for older people. In the UK, much store is placed on intergenerational practice as a means of facilitating neighbourhood regeneration or renewal policies by involving local inhabitants in policy- and decision-making processes, for example with regard to the use of public spaces which accommodate the needs of both younger and older generations (Pain, 2005). It is thought that some of the more obvious outcomes of intergenerational practice for the individuals concerned can be to foster a sense of improved self-esteem, purpose and well-being. When practice involves activities at the community level, these can have the effect of improving relations between different cultural groups, of changing perceptions about such issues as community safety and risks of crime, for example.

Although many positive outcomes are anticipated from intergenerational practice, critiques have drawn attention to several factors which need to be in place before their potential can be fully achieved (Butts, 2007). First, there is a general consensus that the notion of intergenerational practice itself needs more clarification in terms of the age groups considered, whether the activities included are multi- or intergenerational and whether they should encompass family interactions and relationships (Granville, 2002; Springate et al., 2008). From a more applied perspective, some argue that intergenerational programmes may lack adequate funding, and that it may prove difficult to promote an intergenerational focus if those involved represent the interests of distinct age groups. From a strategic perspective, the success of intergenerational practice also depends upon establishing and applying benchmark guidelines which clearly state what it is meant to be, how and what should be measured, monitored and evaluated, and how research and training should be developed in order to consolidate it as a distinct professional field. These requirements are all the more difficult to achieve when recognising that intergenerational practice generally involves small-scale, targeted activities, designed to accommodate the specific cultural, social and other local conditions which characterise the contexts in which they evolve. For this reason, it is difficult to develop generic parameters of what intergenerational practice should be, and to assess their potential relevance to, and impact on, broader groups or communities. In terms of practice, intergenerational activities may be hampered by the conflicting needs of different age groups, such as the health and safety requirements of young children compared to those of older people, or by ageist attitudes which influence just how much older people are considered 'able' enough – either physically or cognitively – to contribute to practice or just how much responsibility youth should be given in projects.

In many respects, therefore, the field of intergenerational practice has yet to be consolidated in terms of its conceptual, strategic and practical dimensions, and before its full potential as a mechanism for strengthening social cohesion between and across generations at both the micro and macro levels of individual and collective interaction and engagement is accomplished.

See also: *Care, Dementia, Generations, Social Exclusion*

FURTHER READING

Izuhara, M. (ed.) (2009) *Ageing and Intergenerational Relations: Family Reciprocity from a Global Perspective* Bristol: The Policy Press.

REFERENCES

Bernard, M. (2006) Research, policy, practice and theory: interrelated dimensions of a developing field. *Journal of Intergenerational Relationships*, 4(1): 5–21.

Granville, G. (2002) *A Review of Intergenerational Practice in the UK*. Stoke-on-Trent: Beth Johnson Foundation Centre for Intergenerational Practice.

Pain, R. (2005) *Intergenerational Relations and Practice in the Development of Sustainable Communities*. Durham: International Centre for Regional Regeneration and Development Studies, Durham University.

Sanchez, M., Butts, D. M., Hatton-Yeo, A., Henkin, N. A., Jarrott, S. E., Kaplan, M. S., et al. (eds) (2007) *Intergenerational Programmes: Towards a Society for All Ages*. Social Studies Collection No. 23. Spain: Obra Social Fundacion la Caixa. Also available at: www.laCaixa.es/ObraSocial (accessed 1 October 2008).

Springate, I., Atkinson, M. and Martin, K. (2008) *Intergenerational Practice: A Review of the Literature*. LGA Research Report F/SR262. Undertaken for the National Foundation for Education Research. Available at: www.nfer.ac.uk/publications/pdfs/downloadable/LIGe report.pdf (accessed 20 July 2009).

intergenerational practice

Life-course Perspective

> *A dynamic and process-based approach to understanding ageing by examining how human lives are socially organised and evolve over time.*

The life-course perspective emerged during the 1960s in response to limitations identified in existing theories about human development, particularly the conceptual and methodological issues associated with ageing. The noteworthy aspect of a life-course perspective involves highlighting the significance of context to human ageing. The personal and biographical level of human experience is examined with simultaneous consideration of timing, social institutions/policies and structural position (i.e. race, class, gender) within a historical time period.

The hallmark study that initiated a life-course perspective was carried out by Glen Elder (1974/1999), who demonstrated in his book, *Children of the Great Depression*, that socio-historical events have lasting effects on individuals, their relationships and their well-being over time. Elder outlined five key principles: the principle that human development and ageing are lifelong processes; the principle of timing which asserts that the developmental antecedents and consequences of life transitions, events and behaviour patterns vary according to their timing in a person's life; the principle of linked lives which states that lives are lived interdependently and social-historical influences are expressed through this network of shared relationships; the principle of historical time and place, which posits that the life-course of individuals is embedded in and shaped by the historical times and places experienced over their lifetime; and the principle of human agency, stating that individuals construct their own life course through the choices and actions they take within the opportunities and constraints of history and social circumstances.

The roots of a life-course perspective may be found in the tenets of multiple disciplines. Assumptions within the fields of psychology, sociology and history each contribute to combine the individual experiences within the context of changing historical and social conditions. A life-course perspective combines multiple sets of assumptions from each discipline to provide an all-encompassing interdisciplinary framework for understanding human ageing. The focus on lifetime accumulations of advantage and/or disadvantage is also one key element to a life-course perspective. Dannefer (2003) elucidates the links between cumulative advantage/disadvantage and age to suggest multilevel social processes. Links between macro and micro levels of social life interact to produce differences within cohorts, particularly those related to inequalities concerning health, resource access and mortality. Advantages and disadvantages accrue from these social processes over time to influence variation in later life.

The concept of the life course is differentiated from that of the life span. Such distinctions are discussed at some length by Settersten (1999). Life course connotes an approach to understanding and studying human development within socio-cultural and historical contexts. Social institutions and policies shape life experiences over time, influencing social roles, positions and statuses as well as providing meaning to such experiences. Moreover, attention to general patterns between and within birth cohorts is key to applying a life-course perspective. Life-span approaches, on the other hand, assume that human development is lifelong, but occurs in stages, and is unidirectional. Life-span psychology takes as the unit of analysis individual behaviour, emphasising plasticity and malleability over and above social structural factors that impinge on human experience.

A political-economic perspective of the life course points to the development by which chronological age became meaningful (Dewilde, 2003). Government-defined roles and statuses have shaped life-course experiences by dictating the ages at which it may be acceptable to engage in activities such as education, marriage, work and retirement. The analytic perspective that the state shapes life-course trajectories also includes attention to policies that influence childhood experiences, military service and wars, retirement and old age (Mayer and Schoepflin, 1989).

Methods for carrying out research informed by a life-course perspective generally refrain from using cross-sectional data on different cohorts to assess change within individuals, or at least interpret findings that come from such sources with caution. Preferred methods in life-course research include those that provide the potential for examining development over time among the same study participants as well as those that allow for an accounting of the bi-directional influence of individuals and contexts upon one another (Elder and Ziele, 1998). Yet, the actual implementation of such methods such as long-term longitudinal studies, cohort-sequential designs and the comparative study of cohort subgroups requires an abundance of resources, and hence is challenging to achieve. Approaches to incorporating a life-course perspective attend to multiple, linking domains, including family, work/retirement and health/well-being. According to the life-course perspective, life events (e.g. marriage) and life phases (e.g. old age) must be studied in tandem, at multiple levels of analysis, and within the context of previous life experiences.

Family. Life-course research on marriage often considers age and time as key variables of analysis. For instance, Umberson et al. (2005) examine marital quality as a trajectory and find that the age at which one marries, along with the age at which various family life-cycle events occur, such as becoming a parent, produce complex effects on martial quality. In particular, they discover that parenting negatively influences the marital quality of young people, has minimal effect during middle age, and more positively effects marital quality in late life. A life-course perspective also sheds light on how marital transitions uniquely influence well-being for men and women at different life stages. The amount of time that has passed since a particular transition is also found to significantly influence how and whether the transition influences well-being. For example, marital dissolution, whether through divorce or widowhood, negatively influences men's health in later life, yet is associated with better health among young and middle-aged men (Williams and Umberson, 2004). On the other hand, if the widowhood status lingers among younger men, it tends to negatively influence their well-being, at least when compared to consistently married men. Moreover, the transition to divorce or widowhood does not significantly influence women's health at any point in the life course.

Work, retirement and leisure. Whether transitions in later adulthood from work to retirement and leisure involve positive/negative experiences or occur at all is often best understood by the tenets of a life-course perspective. The socio-historical period in which one works and potential opportunities for and after retirement are important. For instance, a pessimistic view of retirement among a current cohort of Israeli men is thought to stem from trauma experienced in earlier life stages, the ideology of work/masculinity as well as forced retirement policies with little opportunity for post-retirement employment (Nuttman-Shwartz, 2004).

Health and illness. Applying a life-course perspective to health, illness and well-being involves attention to early life exposures and behaviours. Experiences during early years influence health and functioning during later years. In particular, health is seen 'as the product of risk behaviors, protective factors, and environmental agents that are encountered throughout life and that have cumulative, additive, and even multiplicative impacts on specific outcomes' (Yu, 2006: 768). For instance, Elder and Liker (1982) found that middle-class women who did not experience hardship during the Great Depression when they were young report worse health in later years than middle-class women who did report hardship or than working-class women. This finding is attributed to the notion that the age at which hardship is experienced, along with the resources available to weather such hardship, influence well-being in later life. The life-course perspective also provides a meaningful paradigm for examining and addressing health disparities. Systematically pursuing this approach could inform programme and policy development to potentially reduce the heavy human and economic costs precipitated by inequities between vulnerable and well-off populations.

In conclusion, a life-course perspective provides a useful analytic lens through which to understand human development and ageing. This perspective attends to multiple factors simultaneously, and therefore is seen as an improvement over the stage theories that once dominated the field of ageing. Attention to the extensive array of factors this perspective includes sometimes makes it challenging to utilise fully, but its value is widely acknowledged.

See also: *Ageing, Cohort, Gender, Retirement*

REFERENCES

Dannefer, D. (2003) Cumulative advantage/disadvantage and the life course: cross-fertilizing age and social science theory. *Journal of Gerontology*, 58(6): S327–S337.
Dewilde, C. (2003) A life-course perspective on social exclusion and poverty. *British Journal of Sociology*, 54(1): 109–128.
Elder, G. H. (1974/1999) *Children of the Great Depression: Social Change and Life Experience*. Boulder, CO: Westview Press.
Elder, G. H. Jr. and Liker, J. K. (1982) Hard times in women's lives: historical influences across forty years. *American Journal of Sociology*, 88(2): 241–269.

life-course perspective

143

Elder, G. H. Jr. and Ziele, J. (eds) (1998) *Methods of Life-course Research: Qualitative and Quantitative Approaches*. Thousand Oaks, CA: Sage.

Mayer, K. U. and Schoepfllin, U. (1989) The state and the life course. *Annual Review of Sociology*, 15: 187–209.

Nuttman-Shwatrz, O. (2004) Like a high wave: adjustment to retirement. *The Gerontologist*, 44: 229–236.

Settersten, R. A. (1999) *Lives in Time and Place: The Problems and Promises of Developmental Science*. Amityville, NY: Baywood Publishing Company.

Umberson, D., Williams, K., Powers, D., Checn, M. D., and Campbell, A. M. (2005) As good as it gets? A life course perspective on martial quality. *Social Forces*, 84(1): 493–511.

Williams, K. and Umberson, D. (2004) Marital status, marital transitions and health: a gendered life course perspective. *Journal of Health and Social Behavior*, 45: 81–98.

Yu, S. (2006) The life-course approach to health. *American Journal of Public Health*, 96(5): 768.

Lifelong Learning

A commitment to promoting educational and learning opportunities over the life course.

Lifelong learning (LLL) refers to educational and learning opportunities for adults in general. The focus on LLL for older adults has emerged only recently with the advent of a growing ageing population, as both a policy issue as well as a path to promoting positive well-being in later life. Organised delivery of lifelong learning occurs through Institutes for Learning in Retirement (ILR) in the USA, such as elderhostels, senior centres and community colleges, and most recently universities. The equivalent in the UK and France would be the University of the Third Age. These providers generally acquire funding for educational opportunities through schools, business or community organisations.

Educational and learning opportunities for older adults have historically been absent. Manheimer (1998) chronicles the history of LLL in the USA, suggesting that attention to older adults emerged with the advent of gerontology's influence on public policy. In 1949, the National Education Association established a Committee on Aging, which led to the publication of a book describing the educational needs of older adults (Manheimer, 1998). Nevertheless, two more decades passed before the US government took an interest in promoting educational and learning opportunities for older adults. In the early 1970s, as a result of the White House Conference on Aging, the US government appropriated monies to encourage community colleges to provide educational programming for older adults. Manheimer (1998) chronicles the evolution of LLL for older adults that initially promoted curricula adopting a 'social service' model, geared towards providing information on expected challenges in old age such as role change and retirement adjustment. In other words, ageing was seen as a problem that needed to be overcome, and education constituted one of the solutions to the identified problem.

Today, LLL has burgeoned, with a shift to private (as opposed to public) sources of funding and diverse hosts providing educational and learning opportunities for older adults. The trend of LLL for older adults also developed in Europe and Asia. The French model emerged in the 1970s when universities encouraged their staff to develop tailor-made courses for older segments of the population. The British (or Cambridge) model emerged in the 1980s, emphasising older adults as both teachers and learners (Leung et al., 2005). The Chinese model emanates from the cultural belief that it is a duty to care for oneself in order to spare others from the burden of attending to one's needs. Continued education over the life course, or LLL, represents one such avenue to fulfilling this duty. Continuing education and learning is one way to remain productive and engaged with wider society. Manheimer (1998) elucidates the approach taken in China where learning at every age is perceived as a duty, and where personal fulfilment is seen as one mechanism to achieving communal belonging.

The form lifelong learning takes varies from formal to non-formal (Leung et al., 2005) and informal (Hamil-Luker and Uhlenberg, 2002). Formal types of lifelong learning are best exemplified by schooling that takes place from pre-school to university, and are found in programmes where evaluation of learning is central to the process. Non-formal types are structured learning opportunities, organised with intentional goals and topics, which occur outside traditional educational institutions and do not include an evaluation component to the activity. Informal types come about from simply living and happen in the course of daily activities.

lifelong learning

145

Many older adults do not necessarily gravitate towards structured learning environments to participate in lifelong learning. March et al. (1977) found that two-thirds of older adults were not interested in attending a free audit programme at a university. Those who were potentially interested were younger in age. Although many now advocate the need for education and learning over the life course, it is becoming increasingly clear that the attitudes of older citizens towards lifelong learning are key to developing such opportunities. Formal programming and education is one pathway for lifelong learning, but not necessary the only approach.

Two intentions for pursuing lifelong learning appear to motivate older adults to seek educational and learning opportunities: instrumental ambitions and expressive aspirations. The former relates to career advancement and skill-building; the latter to personal fulfilment and social engagement. At the same time, educational activities may be viewed simultaneously as instrumental and expressive (Manheimer, 1998). They are not mutually exclusive. For instance, an older woman may decide to learn Spanish to fulfil a lifelong dream, but at the same time learning that language may also prove useful when she vacations in Mexico. Reasons that older adults pursue lifelong learning vary widely, making it difficult to design programmes that meet everyone's needs (Manheimer, 1998; March et al., 1977).

Opportunities for education and learning geared towards older adults have been increasing. Wider prospects became available to US citizens after the Second World War with the advent of the G.I. Bill, developed to financially support those who had served in the war to seek higher education. Manheimer (1998) suggests that this generation pushed forward the idea of continued learning in later life. Others credit the generation born after the Second World War, often referred to as the 'Babyboomers', for having instigated educational pursuits at older ages. For instance, Hamil-Luker and Uhlenberg (2002) report that one striking trend in the last decade of the twentieth century involved the increasing number of non-traditional students found in universities across the country. According the National Center for Education Statistics (NCES), by 2000 21% of students in degree-granting institutions reported ages 35 and older, more than double the proportion of 35 and older students reported in 1970. Participation in education increased for all age groups in the USA during the 1990s, but particularly among older adults (Hamil-Luker and Uhlenberg, 2002).

Three possible reasons may explain the increase in older student numbers. First, the demographics of the country have changed. Longer life expectancies and lower fertility rates have led to larger proportions of middle aged and older adults in the US population. Moreover, there are simply larger numbers of older adults than younger ones, in part a result of the baby boom of the 1950s. Secondly, the baby boom generation, as well as the one before it, is more educated than previous cohorts, and high education correlates with higher participation rates in adult education. Finally, the economic shift to technological and service-based industries has increasingly demanded lifelong learning to keep abreast of current developments and new knowledge.

An analysis of educational and learning activities among adults in the 1990s was carried out by Hamil-Luker and Uhlenberg (2002). Findings reveal that although such activities increased throughout the decade, older adults were less likely than younger adults to participate in educational activities organised by business or schools. Two explanations are proposed to explain this trend. The first suggests that business is simply more interested in training and encouraging lifelong learning for younger employees, who are seen as more of an investment for the future of organisations. The second suggests that internalised age norm role expectations inhibit older adults from embarking on such activities. Furthermore, older adults are more likely to participate in community organisations than credit-programmes or job-training. It appears, moreover, that age was a less powerful predictor of educational and learning activities at the end of the 1990s compared to the early 1990s, suggesting that school/work/leisure domains are overlapping and becoming blurred as opposed to a stringent age-graded activity in these realms.

Lifelong learning and education have a role to play in promoting age integration as well as productivity among older age groups. Norms and policies associated with cultural age timetables may shape the life course, yet there does seem to be increasing flexibility in what types of activity are acceptable at different phases and age-defined life stages (Settersten and Hagestad, 1996; Settersten and Lovegreen, 1998). In particular, education constitutes an arena that is less rigid and more flexible with regard to age norms. Echoing the call by social gerontologists (e.g. Hamil-Luker and Uhlenberg, 2002), future consideration should be directed towards cultural values about age and education, not just the matter of removing financial and transportation barriers to participating in educational activities.

See also: Age Integration, Ageing, Care, Cohort, Gerontology, Retirement

lifelong learning

REFERENCES

Hamil-Luker, J. and Uhlenberg, P. (2002) Later life education in the 1990s: increasing involvement and continuing disparity. *The Journals of Gerontology*, 57B(6): S324–S331.

Leung, A., Lui, Y. and Chi, I. (2005) Later life learning experience among Chinese elderly in Hong Kong. *Gerontology and Geriatrics Education*, 26(2): 1–15.

Manheimer, R. J. (1998) The promise and politics of older adult education. *Research on Ageing*, 20(4): 391–414.

March, G. B., Hooper, J. O. and Baum, J. (1977) Life span education and the older adult: living is learning. *Educational Gerontology*, 2(2): 163–172.

Settersten, R. A. and Hagestad, G. O. (1996) What's the latest? Cultural age deadlines for educational and work transition. *The Gerontologist*, 36(5): 602–613.

Settersten, R. A. and Lovegreen, L. D. (1998) Educational experiences throughout adult life: new hopes or no hope for life-course flexibility? *Research on Ageing*, 20(4): 506–538.

Loneliness

> *Undesirable or negative feelings about how individuals perceive their situation in relation to others, particularly with regard to social engagement and interaction.*

In broad terms, loneliness implies that an individual recognises the negative consequences which come from experiencing inadequate relationships, in terms of their quantity and/or quality (De Jong Gierveld, 1998). Feeling lonely therefore suggests a discrepancy between the social engagement individuals would *like* to have with others, compared to what they *actually* have.

There have been numerous efforts to clarify the conceptual meaning and definition of loneliness (De Jong Gierveld et al., 2006). From a cognitive, psychological perspective, it can be viewed as a subjective emotional or affective experience occurring when individuals recognise they lack an intimate relationship with someone (such as a spouse) or feel that their social networks are deficient in some way. Weiss (1973) distinguished

148

key concepts in
social gerontology

two elements to loneliness: emotional loneliness, when someone feels they do not have a close relationship with a particular person (like a partner); and social loneliness, when people lack friends or do not feel they belong to a community. De Jong Gierveld (1998) has demonstrated how loneliness may be conceptualised as a multidimensional construct when considered in terms of how individuals perceive, experience and evaluate their isolation and inadequate communication with others. From this perspective, loneliness is seen in terms of three distinct elements: 'deprivation', that is when people recognise that they have feelings of emptiness or being abandoned; 'time', meaning whether people think loneliness can change or be remedied over time; and its 'emotional aspects', when loneliness involves feelings of sorrow, sadness, shame or guilt, for example.

Researchers have been at pains to point out that feeling or being lonely is not synonymous with being alone. In other words, solitude is not necessarily accompanied by loneliness. This means that it is necessary to distinguishing subjective feelings of loneliness from objective conditions of social isolation, in which the number of social relationships or ties an individual has are small (see Further Reading). Studies that have made this distinction have shown, for example, that individuals can be both lonely and isolated, neither lonely nor isolated, or experience one but not the other (Andersson, 1998). For these reasons, loneliness, being alone, living alone and social isolation have all been conceptualised as interlinked but separate dimensions of social participation in later life. Victor et al. (2005b), for example, distinguish between these concepts. Whereas being alone refers to spending time by oneself, living alone can simply refer to a particular household arrangement, and social isolation to the ways in which individuals are integrated into their broader social environment, through, for example, the number and frequency of contacts they have with others.

Historically in the UK, interest in loneliness for older people can be traced back to the post-war period and the work of Sheldon (1948), Townsend (1957) and Tunstall (1963). Their localised social survey studies, carried out in Wolverhampton, London and England respectively, provided an empirical investigation of loneliness and social isolation among older people and the risk factors associated with these situations. From an interventionist perspective, their aim was to devise screening tools. Such studies have had a lasting impact on the way in which the prevalence of loneliness has been measured, more frequently through the use of Likert-type scales which rely on older people reporting a self-assessed perception of how they rate their degree of loneliness, for example whether they are never, sometimes or often lonely. Asking older people to respond to questions which explicitly require them to talk about loneliness can lead to under-reporting if there is a tendency to see it as something negative, a state to be denied. As a result, composite or derived measures have been developed which rely on indirect questions to measure loneliness (De Jong Gierveld and Kamphuis, 1985; Wenger, 1983). The difficulties with these types of measure are that they make implicit assumptions about what loneliness means, and generally rely on discovering its significance through indirect questions relating to social engagement (Victor et al., 2005a).

As an integral component to assessing quality of life, but also because of its policy significance, studies of loneliness have frequently taken as their focus the task of establishing its prevalence, searching for explanatory factors, and identifying factors which put individuals 'at risk' of loneliness. More recently, researchers have developed studies from a longitudinal perspective, or within a life-course framework. Victor et al. in the UK have shown that loneliness is not a static experience, but varies across the life course and presents itself for people through different 'pathways'. For some it will be an experience that has characterised their lives for a long time, for others it will start only later in their lives, and for others it will actually decrease (Victor et al., 2005b). Certain events will trigger acute loneliness (the death of a spouse or the transition to retirement, for example), while in other circumstances, loneliness becomes chronic over time. These types of findings are important for policy because they help distinguish between people who have had a long-term tendency to be isolated from those who have not, and for recognising sudden, compared to cumulative, loneliness.

Some of the key factors which have been found to affect loneliness among older people include personal circumstance and characteristics such as age, marital status, ethnicity, gender and health status; characteristics such as the size of mediating structures of kin and non-kin networks which may facilitate contact with others; and the norms and values influencing expectations about roles and relationships in later life (De Jong Gierveld, 1998). The risk factors of loneliness and social isolation in later life have been identified as socio-demographic factors (being female, living alone, never having had a partner, having no living children, being very old), individual health status (poor health, cognitive impairment, having a disability), life events (bereavement, retirement) and material circumstances such as low income and poverty.

One of the criticisms of the concept of loneliness has been its construction as a social 'problem', reflecting assumptions that it is a universal phenomenon, likely to be confined to older age groups, that it will inevitably be severe and prevalent during later life, and that it has increased over time. These assumptions have been challenged empirically by examining, for example, the relationship between older age and loneliness, variations depending upon socio-cultural context, and whether it is possible to identify loneliness as a universal characteristic of all societies (see Further Reading). Existing European empirical evidence not only suggests that levels of loneliness are slightly lower than those found among younger age groups (Walker and Maltby, 1997), but also that, historically speaking, there is little evidence to suggest its increase over recent cohorts of older people (Victor et al., 2002). Recent New Zealand evidence, for example, records slightly higher levels of perceived loneliness among young people aged between 15 and 24 than those aged 65 or beyond, and there are clear ethnic variations to this experience (New Zealand Ministry of Social Development, 2007).

Researchers have therefore drawn attention to the dangers of associating loneliness exclusively with the later phases of the life course, and in so doing, indirectly highlight the ageist tendencies associated with this phenomenon.

See also: Bereavement, Cohort, Disability, Gender, Quality of Life, Retirement, Social Relations

FURTHER READING

For an excellent collection of international works on the conceptual meaning and definition of loneliness and other issues relating to the concept, see the special volume of the *Canadian Journal on Ageing* (2004) 23(2).

REFERENCES

Andersson, L. (1998) Loneliness research and interventions: a review of the literature. *Ageing and Mental Health*, 2(4): 264–274.

De Jong Gierveld, J. (1998) A review of loneliness: concept and definitions, determinants and consequences. *Reviews in Clinical Gerontology*, 8: 73–80.

Victor, C. R., Scambler, S. J., Shah, S., Cook, D. G., Harris, T., Rink, E. and Wilde, S. (2002) Has loneliness amongst older people increased? An investigation into variations between cohorts. *Ageing and Society*, 22: 585–597.

Weiss, R. S. (1973) *Loneliness: The Experience of Emotional and Social Isolation*. Cambridge, MA: MIT Press.

Wenger, C. (1983) Loneliness: a problem of measurement, in D. Jerrome (ed.), *Ageing in Society*. Beckenham: Croom Helm. pp. 145–167.

loneliness

Longevity

The long duration of a person's existence.

The term longevity has its roots in the Latin *longaevitās* reflecting the words *longus* or long and *aevum* or age. People are said to have longevity when they have survived longer than the average person.

Longevity should be understood in relation to the terms of life expectancy and life span. Derived from a life table, the former concept is a statistical measurement representing the expected age at which the average individual will die, given current mortality rates, and is commonly reported in terms of the number of years a person is expected to live from their birth onwards, but can be measured at other ages. The concept of the life span (also known as maximum life potential) refers to a theoretical, biological maximum length of life or the number of years an individual could live in the absence of disease or accident. Most literature currently records the French woman Jeanne Calment, who died at the age of 122 in 1997, as the longest living human.

There has always been a longstanding belief shared by many cultures and civilisations that it is possible to extend the duration of human life. Greek mythology, for example, focused on the immortality of the gods, and in early medieval China alchemists spoke of the golden elixir of immortality. The Spanish explorer Ponce de Leon searched for the fountain of life, and there are many reports of populations, such as those in the Hunza Valley of Pakistan, whom it is thought have extremely long lives. Katz (1995) provides a fascinating account of how western understanding of longevity has evolved through the centuries. From the late Rennaissance to the early nineteenth century, documentation on the subject focused primarily on expounding the existence of centenarians, with writers of medicine and hygiene explaining longevity as governed by the laws of nature and something that could be enhanced through attention to personal discipline, moderation and diet. By the beginning of the 1900s, old age was increasingly viewed as a clinical problem, and by the middle of the century, a clearer distinction was made between the life span and the study of old age in terms of the ageing process. During the early twentieth century, longevity became associated with

key concepts in social gerontology

heredity and environmental conditions, and it was increasingly understood that the life span could be established as a clinical and biological certainty with clear developmental phases, the human body having a fixed period of existence. Bringing us to contemporary times, Katz's depiction of the life span in the postmodern period is one where human life is seen as freed from the constraints of time, and the object of cultural industries which focus on overcoming the effects of ageing and promoting long and healthy lives. The modern era of scientific development, he suggests, has not strayed far from the quest to alter or extend longevity. Developments in the field of biological ageing, dating back to the 1930s, for example, demonstrate how the ageing process, life expectancy and the maximum life span can be modified in living organisms such as mice through environmental interventions (e.g. changing the diet) and genetic experimentation.

Our fascination with longevity over time has been matched with improvements to life expectancy, the average number of years we are able to live having roughly tripled over the course of human history. Since the mid-1800s, when the highest recorded life expectancy for females in Sweden reached 45 years, Japan today leads the way with women on average living until the age of almost 86. Such wide variations in life expectancy reflect the combined effects of personal, genetic and environmental risk factors to disease, as well as levels of socio-economic development, medical advances such as vaccines, and health and public policy provisions. Historically speaking, during the course of the nineteenth and early twentieth centuries rapid improvements to life expectancy were a result of decreasing infant and child mortality, but since then they have been attributed, in industrialised nations at least, to a decline in mortality among the older age groups (Wilmoth, 2000).

Whether the human species has, as so many of us still seem to be asking, reached its maximum life span remains a question of constant debate, but a good marker of change is the number of individuals who survive until the age of 100 and beyond. Jeune and Christensen (2005) note that prior to the 1950s there was little evidence of individuals surviving to become centenarians, but by the beginning of the twenty-first century numbers had doubled every 10 years in low mortality countries. From 1980 to 1997, for example, the maximum life span increased in Europe from 112 to 122 years. Although a paucity of longitudinal data means it is difficult to establish the lived experiences of individuals who survive beyond 100 years, explanations of their survival are that they may have avoided, survived or adapted to major age-related diseases such as pneumonia. Alternatively, they may possess particular psychological traits, such as coping strategies, or have preserved biological mechanisms, such as certain immunologic functions. Some scientists suggest that processes of natural selection have led to the development of genes which enhance longevity (Moody, 2006) and Kirkwood (1998) outlines how, in the future, human longevity may be altered by genetic engineering.

One of the more contentious theories about longevity stems from Fries's influential work on the compression of morbidity (Fries and Capro, 1981) which suggests that medical advances will enable us to displace age-related diseases and decline until the very end of life. Integral to this theory is the concept of the 'rectangularization' of the human survival curve, which is based on the assumption that death rates will remain low until a given age and will then increase significantly so that the majority of deaths will occur during a very short and 'compressed' period of the life span. In simple terms, this means that people would remain healthy during old age, then would rapidly decline and die. Fries and Capro (2006) have again argued that individuals have a maximum biological life span which has not increased for at least 100,000 years. Fries's work has been challenged on several grounds, notably for failing to consider whether the maximum human life span is finite. There is also disagreement about whether the compression of morbidity is actually occurring and, indeed, whether certain conditions, such as Parkinson's disease, can really be delayed or prevented. However, the compression of morbidity debate continues (Murray et al., 2000); if there is an appeal to this theory, it doubtless lies in the promise that life expectancy will increase and quality of life in old age will be enhanced because we shall be able to postpone functional decline until the very end of our ever-increasing life span.

Just as the debates over the likelihood and desirability of extending longevity continue, scholars also point to the consequences that such changes could bring. An important feature of human ageing, for example, is women's greater longevity (Coleman et al., 2000). The ensuing gender imbalance carries with it a number of consequences, particularly in terms of marital status and living arrangements. For instance, fewer women than men remarry following widowhood or divorce and consequently more older women than older men live alone. At the micro level of kinship relationships, Harper (2005) notes that increased longevity may increase the time spent in certain kinship roles, for example grandparenthood. Butler (2005) offers a convincing argument countering the position that the growth in longevity and population ageing only engenders increasing economic costs, notably in terms of public expenditure on health and retirement income. Instead, he points to evidence that older populations potentially accumulate more discretionary wealth and facilitate private intergenerational transfers, and that healthy older people will be more likely to remain engaged in both informal and formal work and voluntary activities as well as being less reliant on health services.

Although increasing life expectancy and the potential for prolonging the life span undoubtedly reflect welcome advances in the socio-economic, health and biomedical fields, both phenomena raise many questions and challenges. The key question is: Will a longer life also be a better life? Fries's conviction that it will become increasingly possible for people to be freed from prolonged years of chronic illness towards the end of their lives leaves him with a pronounced optimism that we will be able to age well, preserving both vitality and vigour while experiencing a minimum of disease. Others are much more sceptical, arguing that chronic disease will in fact be experienced across a longer period of the life course and by more individuals as populations continue to see the numbers of older people increase (see Schneider and Brody, 2006). As Hayflick (2006) notes, even if we are able in the future to stop or slow down the ageing process, to extend longevity and to rid old age of disease and disability, there remains the fact that older people would still become functionally weaker as they age. Olshansky (2006) chides us for continuing the civilisation-old quest for immortality, instead reminding us that it is perhaps better to pursue efforts to improve or preserve mental functioning and physical health.

In sum, then, the potential for increased improvements to life expectancy and the lengthening of the life span bring with them as many challenges as they do hopes.

See also: *Ageing, Disability, Gender, Population Ageing, Quality of Life, Retirement*

FURTHER READING

For a good review of issues relating to the compression of morbidity theory and related debates, see Moody, H. (ed.) (2006) *Ageing: Concepts and Controversies* (5th edition). Thousand Oaks, CA: Pine Forge Press, in particular the section on 'Why do we grow old?'.

longevity

REFERENCES

Fries, J. F. and Capro, L. M. (1981) *Vitality and Ageing: Implications of the Rectangular Curve*. San Francisco, CA: Freeman.

Katz, S. (1995) Imagining the life-span: from premodern miracles to postmodern fantasies, in M. Featherstone and A. Wernick (eds), *Images of Ageing: Cultural Representations of Later Life*. London: Routledge. pp. 61–75.

Kirkwood, T. (1998) Genetics and the future of human longevity, in R. Tallis (ed.), *Increasing Longevity: Medical, Social and Political Implications*. London: Royal College of Physicians. pp. 103–112.

Murray, C., Salomon, J. A. and Mathers, C. (2000) A critical examination of summary measures of population health. *Bulletin of the World Health Organization*, 78(8).

Wilmoth, J. R. (2000) Demography of longevity: past, present, and future trends. *Experimental Gerontology*, 35: 1111–1129.

Long-term Care

> *The help and support provided to individuals over a continuous and generally long period of time because they are unable to carry out the normal, personal care activities of daily living for themselves as a result of a functional disability or chronic medical condition.*

There is no single definition of the concept of long-term care which has a universal application. One reason for this is the difficulty in distinguishing between rehabilitation, primary, acute and long-term care, and another in establishing whether people's needs for care are of a medical or social order (Kane and Kane, 2005; Stone, 2006). In addition, medical advancements are such that they now enable acute care and rehabilitation to be provided away from hospitals in people's homes or other nursing environments so that the boundaries between medical and long-term care are blurred even further.

These difficulties notwithstanding, the parameters of long-term care, sometimes referred to as continuous care, can be defined in terms of the profiles of service users, the aims of long-term care, the types of services it includes, who offers them and in which contexts they are delivered.

People in need of long-term care normally have a chronic medical condition and, as a result, are unable to carry out the normal, personal care activities of daily living (ADLs), such as eating, bathing or taking medication. Assessment of need is often based on establishing functional ability in ADL. The broad aims of long-term care services are therefore to help individuals function in their daily lives, so that they maintain as normal and integrated a lifestyle as possible. This will involve helping them to cope with or compensate for a change of situation and loss of physical or mental ability, or working towards a goal of rehabilitation (Stone, 2006). Long-term care services may include a variety of medical, nursing, social and community provisions and supports designed to meet a wide range of personal care, social and health needs, which are normally provided over a sustained period of time. For example, in the context of intermediate care when someone has been hospitalised but has returned home to live independently, they may receive a combination of services including nursing and occupational therapy, accompanied by assistance with daily living activities and more instrumental tasks involving meal preparation and transportation. Remote communication systems, such as an emergency telephone line or monitoring system, may also be installed, and discharge from a medical setting may be contingent upon some adaptation being made to the home environment (a grab rail, for example). These services do not therefore necessarily take the form of assistance provided by other people, and may primarily comprise a combination of technological supports and adaptations to the home environment. More often than not, however, long-term care will involve a combination of personal, social and health services which will be provided by unpaid informal carers made up of family (primarily women, and specifically daughters), friends or volunteers and by paid professional and paraprofessional specialists. Care may be provided in one or a mixture of institutional and non-institutional settings: at the person's home, in purpose-built assisted living environments which generally provide varying forms of personal care and nursing services (like extra-care housing in the UK, for example), in the community setting (e.g. in adult day-centre facilities or adult foster homes), and in institutional contexts of residential and nursing homes.

Although the need for long-term care can exist at any age, the focus has been primarily on the needs of older people, notably because, compared to other age groups, they tend to represent the biggest consumers of health and social care services. Country-specific projections of the costs related to long-term care provisions indicate significant increases over the next 50 years (Comas-Herrera et al., 2003), a trend that will doubtless be common to nations whose populations are ageing and who have formalised welfare systems.

How long-term care is managed and financed, how eligibility criteria are established, where and by whom it will be delivered are all contingent upon the historical period, country context and the types of welfare model in operation. Historically speaking, until the post-war consolidation of modern welfare states, any institutional provision of care in western nations undoubtedly reflected the influence of the nursing home environment, almshouses and, earlier still, the workhouse context. Following the post-war period, a combination of factors, including a growing awareness of the costs associated with population ageing, concern about the quality of life and the treatment of older people in institutional settings (Kane, 2001) as well as the cost and effectiveness of such services, gradually emerged. These considerations contributed to what has generally been recognised as a process of 'deinstitutionalisation' of long-term care, characterised primarily by a shift from institutional (hospitals, nursing and residential homes) to community and domiciliary-based services (Quadagno et al., 2005). Tracing these developments from the 1980s onwards, Glendinning (1998) argues that changing political and economic ideologies, notably the progressive introduction of quasi-markets into welfare services, coupled with a move away from a top-down, centralised, state-driven welfare structure towards more devolved, local level provisions have been the driving force behind reforms to the provision of long-term care. In the UK, for example, prior to the 1980s, care would have been provided primarily by local social services and hospitals, and managed by social services or geriatricians (Kane and Kane, 2005). Today, as in other contexts such as Canada, Australia and additional European countries, the picture is one of a far more diversified set of care provisions, focused primarily around the home and community contexts rather than the institutional setting.

These changes to long-term care provisions, welcomed as they may have been by some, nonetheless raise many challenges and issues. First, there is what Glendinning (1998) refers to as a general process of the blurring of boundaries, as the distinctions between social and nursing care, medical and social needs, institutional and professional responsibilities between the health and social service sectors, and distinctions between public, private, formal and informal service providers are lost (Glasby and Littlechild, 2004).

Integral to these blurred boundaries is the ongoing issue about how long-term care should be financed in the future and how an appropriate balance between collective and individual financial responsibilities or a mixture of both can be achieved (Kane and Kane, 2005). In response to the debate over whether long-term care is primarily a medical or social service, critics argue that the focus of concern should rest much more with ensuring the quality of service provision and enhancing older people's consumer or citizenship rights to long-term care (Chen, 2007; Kane and Kane, 2005; Stone, 2006). Linked to these issues are the specific workforce problems associated with long-term care systems, notably difficulties of recruitment, retention, training and low pay. The recent proliferation of assisted living environments as contexts adapted to long-term care needs illustrates many of these concerns. This development has grown from the policy emphasis on facilitating independent living in later life (also referred to as 'ageing in place'), to concerns that the physical and social environments of traditional nursing and residential home settings do not enhance quality of life for older people (Stone, 2006). Assisted living environments are often marketed in terms of the potential for autonomous and normal living that they provide to older people. However, with increasing demand, there has been a proliferation of models of assisted living settings but a lack of standardised provisions services, poor regulatory frameworks and often no formal training requirements for staff. These failings are problematic for the older consumer when confronted with an array of assisted living options (Grant, 2006; Kane and Kane, 2005).

Given the significant role played by informal carers, notably family members, in ensuring long-term care, another key debate is how much support they should expect in return for the caring work they undertake. Indeed, there is evidence to suggest that the shift from institution-to community-based provisions of long-term care for older people has effectively increased the amount of care undertaken by the family (Sundstrom et al., 2002). Issues therefore revolve around the provision of respite programmes, remuneration (whether in the form of a salary or tax exemption, for example), pension provisions and the need for specialised training. Linked to this is also a growing awareness that the availability of female carers is set to diminish as women become increasingly engaged in the formal, paid labour market, and are hence confronted, more so than previous generations of women, with the multiple roles of carer and employee (Hillcoat-Nallétamby and Dharmalingam, 2003).

In many ways, Stone's (2006) use of the term the 'triple knot' to describe the three domains of long-term care sums up these issues

long-term care

nicely. The 'knot' consists of the financing, delivery and workforce implications of both current and future long-term care provisions for older people. However, as the author points out, all these factors will be influenced by broader, societal influences, such as the value placed on caring work, or on other more temporal factors such as immigration policies which control the flow of labour into countries or labour market fluctuations.

In conclusion, demographic change, notably population ageing, has posed new challenges to health and social welfare services in terms of their ability to adapt to the unprecedented need for long-term care. The shift from experiencing these care needs within the confines of institutional settings to living them in familiar home and community environments should, in theory, be welcomed. However, it appears that such changes bring as many challenges as they do benefits, in terms of how they should be financed, managed, coordinated and diversified to meet the needs of older people. The promise of integrated services, based on collaborative partnerships and shared resources, and where the needs of the older person take centre stage may therefore be some way off.

See also: Ageing, Ageing in Place, Assisted Living, Care, Housing, Population Ageing, Quality of Life

FURTHER READING

Victor, C. R. (2009) *Ageing, Health and Care*. Bristol: The Policy Press.

REFERENCES

Glasby, J. and Littlechild, R. (2004) *The Health and Social Care Divide: The Experiences of Older People* (2nd edition). Bristol: The Policy Press.
Glendinning, C. (ed.) (1998) *Rights and Realities: Comparing New Developments in Long-term Care for Older People*. Bristol: The Policy Press.
Kane, R. L. and Kane, R. A. (2005) Long-term care, in M. Johnson (ed.), *The Cambridge Handbook of Age and Ageing*. Cambridge: Cambridge University Press. pp. 638–646.
Quadagno, J. Reid Keene, J. and Street, D. (2005) Health policy and old age: an international review, in M. Johnson (ed.), *The Cambridge Handbook of Age and Ageing*. Cambridge: Cambridge University Press. p. 605.
Stone, R. I. (2006) Emerging issues in long-term care, in R. H. Binstock and L. K. George (eds), *Handbook of Ageing and the Social Sciences*. London: Academic Press. pp. 397–418.

Palliative Care

Care provided at the end of life.

Derived from the Latin concept of *pallium*, which means a cover or cloak, in a broad sense, the concept of palliative care describes a form of care which is offered to individuals whose illness or disease can be relieved but not cured.

In holistic terms, palliative care may be provided in the home, hospice or hospital environment. It will involve not only medical but also psychological support and is designed to recognise the care and support needs of both the patient and their family community. Two dimensions of palliative care are commonly distinguished. *Palliative treatment* involves attention to, and control of, the symptoms and associated pain of the disease. In the case of cancer, for example, this may involve the use of surgery or chemotherapy. *Supportive care* recognises the emotional, spiritual and social needs of those involved, including family and, in particular, carers.

The essential aims of palliative care are to help those suffering from illness to preserve, as much as possible, their quality of life and sense of dignity and independence, to minimise physical discomfort, reduce anxiety and fear, and accompany both the patient and the bereaved through the experience of death and grieving.

In order to fulfil these aims, palliative care involves an interdisciplinary team of support workers (e.g. physicians, nurses, social workers, chaplains, physiotherapists), and it is hoped that the team's efforts may have a positive impact not only upon the patient's overall well-being, but also upon the trajectory of the illness. In the UK context, the British Geriatrics Society (2004) distinguishes between palliative care (as defined by the World Health Organisation (2002)), terminal care (which may be given in the last few days or hours preceding death) and specialist palliative care (e.g. Macmillan nurses, palliative care consultants). As discussed later, the two foci of palliative care in the UK are upon children with life-threatening illnesses and upon adults with cancer.

palliative care

The last century saw enormous progress in the advancement of medicine and diagnostics technology, and, in turn, this progress has significantly improved the survival chances of those presenting with life-threatening illnesses. As worthy as time and resource investment in these areas are, many would argue that the need for formal end-of-life care was a somewhat late development. Two key figures who played a major role in identifying and responding to the needs of the dying are Dame Cicely Saunders, founder of the modern hospice movement, and Elisabeth Kübler-Ross, a psychiatrist.

Saunders (1996) started her medical career as a nurse in 1941, and later worked at one of the new 'homes for terminal care', where the emphasis was on administering pain relief to patients. She then qualified as a doctor, researching and publishing in the area of pharmacopoeia. Over time, Saunders came to see that the dying person came with their own individual life history, and that holistic care must include physical, emotional, social and spiritual support. In 1967 she founded St Christopher's Hospice in London, the beginning of the modern hospice movement. Two charities that play an important role in end-of-life care in the UK are Marie Curie Cancer Care and The Sue Ryder Foundation. Palliative care wards can also be found in some NHS hospitals.

In 1969, Kübler-Ross published her landmark book *On Death and Dying* (Kübler-Ross, 1969/2008). When she first started her work, where she set out to listen to the dying, Kübler-Ross met with great resistance from health professionals, indicating the degree to which death and dying was a taboo topic. Indeed, she often encountered a broad denial that such patients even existed. Health professionals were not trained to deal with dying patients beyond their clinical needs, and were simultaneously having to confront their own mortality. In other words, the emotional and spiritual needs of those who were about to take the solitary step from life to death were being ignored. Based on extensive interviews with end-of-life patients, she identified initially the five stages of grief: denial, anger, bargaining, depression and acceptance. It is thanks to her that we have attained the level of understanding that we possess today when working with the dying and their families, and are thus more able to provide psychosocial and spiritual support.

Palliative and end-of-life care, then, are particularly and increasingly relevant to older age groups, more particularly at present because of population ageing. In the UK, for example, as the National Audit Office (2008) notes, two-thirds of the half a million people who die in England each year are aged 75 and older.

From a practice perspective, the earlier notion that end-of-life care takes place only during the last few weeks of life has been challenged. In recent years an end-of-life care model has emerged, where support-ive measures are offered from the point of diagnosis rather than at the point of decline. This model acknowledges the individuality of each patient, and factors such as the nature of the condition, living arrange-ments, social circumstances, psychological well-being, cultural matters and spiritual beliefs (Department of Health, 2008). In the UK, a distinc-tion is made between three anticipated speeds of decline, which may be rapid, steadily progressive, or slow with a steep decline before death. Irrespective of trajectory, the end-of-life care pathway recommends that six steps are followed: (1) discussion, (2) assessment, care planning and review, (3) coordination of care, (4) service delivery in different settings, (5) care in the last days of life, and (6) care after death. Alongside these measures, carers and families should also receive support and information as well as spiritual care if required (Department of Health, 2008).

As stated earlier, the patient (and family) are entitled to psychologi-cal support (in the form of a professional psychological assessment and intervention), social support (which may be formal or informal, and should be agreed upon by local health and social care services and the voluntary sector), and spiritual support (where qualified, authorised and appointed spiritual caregivers should be available to patients, carers and staff) (National Institute for Clinical Excellence, 2004).

As well as health professionals, caregivers (both family and volun-teers) are crucial to the palliative care system. The caregiver may expe-rience high levels of emotional and physical stress and strain, and it is essential that that they are offered respite, which can range from a few hours to a few days. Whereas hospices provide such opportunities, hos-pitals generally do not.

Palliative care sees an interaction between health professionals, patient and family/caregiver. It sees an interaction between clinical, psychological, social and spiritual dimensions. The patient is central. They are to be given the same respect and standard of treatment as the non-terminally ill patient, to be treated with understanding and compassion, and to be afforded privacy and dignity (General Medical Council, 2006). The care-giver's needs must not be neglected. It is crucial that staff are exceptionally well empowered, enabled, trained and supported in dimensions above and beyond the clinical level (National Institute for Clinical Excellence, 2004).

The degree to which palliative and end-of-life care are research-worthy is unquestionable. However, as Age Concern (2005) in the UK notes, there is very little research into older people's actual needs during the final life stage. Further, the caregiver is often pivotal in the end-of-life process, and their needs are also central. Franks et al's (2000) systematic review of the literature assessing the need for palliative care found only 682 papers published in Europe, North America, Australia or Israel since 1978. They note that the evidence examining actual needs is generally poor and often conflicting, and that those patients who are not palliative care service users are often disregarded in studies.

There are a number of significant practice issues to take into account.

Place of death. The majority of older people die in hospital, and the cause of death can range from heart disease, cancer, stroke, respiratory or neurological diseases to dementia. In broadest terms, cancer patients are more likely to die at home or in a hospice, heart and pulmonary diseased patients in hospital (possible due to the clinical necessity of hospital care), and dementia patients at home or in a care home. In the UK, for example, approximately 75% of people would prefer to die at home, whereas in 2006 only 35% of people were able to do so (National Audit Office, 2008). In England and Wales, place of death for older people is, in descending order, hospital, care home, own home and hospice (Age Concern, 2005). This raises a major concern. The hospice movement caters for cancer patients only (with the exception of children's hospices), and thus the end-of-life care offered to older people is, by definition, limited to those with terminal cancer. Yet it is believed that cancer as the main cause of death accounts for approximately 25% of deaths only (Age Concern, 2005). The hospice, then, is not equipped to treat non-cancer illnesses, and the hospital and care home environments are not necessarily geared towards providing high-quality end-of-life care.

Quality of care. Two issues warrant attention. First, health profession training focuses on curative treatment alone. There is also a dire need for more palliative care training in the care home environment. Secondly, and as it currently stands, ageism in the forms of access to treatment in general and particularly to palliative care is, alarmingly, acknowledged (e.g. Age Concern, 2005; National Audit Office, 2008).

The taboo of dying. It is recognised that palliative care professionals may spend considerable time, if not all their time, working with end-of-life patients, and this poses significant professional and personal challenges. There must be a shift in emphasis where the end of life is seen as an inevitable step rather than a result of a failure of care (Department of Health, 2008). Training must not only be knowledge-based, but also serve to bring about necessary changes to the attitudes and behaviours of staff groups.

The time to die. Palliative care neither speeds up nor postpones the time to die (World Health Organisation, 2002). It is nonetheless understandable that some healthcare professionals are faced with a moral dilemma in decisions on whether to withhold or withdraw life-prolonging treatments. However, the General Medical Council (2006: section 12) stipulates clearly that 'life has a natural end, and ... the point may come ... where death is drawing near. In these circumstances doctors should not strive to prolong the dying process with no regard to the patient's wishes'.

The good death. What constitutes a good death and whether it is possible or desirable is subject to debate, where some aspects are widely accepted (e.g. pain control, dignity, choice of place of death, etc.). Age Concern (2005) suggest 12 principles that facilitate a good death, three key elements of which are open communication, honest prognostication and symptom control.

See also: *Ageism, Care, Death and Dying, Dementia, Population Ageing, Quality of Life, Social Support*

REFERENCES

Age Concern (2005) *Policy and Position Papers: Dying and Death*. London: Age Concern.
British Geriatrics Society (2004) *Palliative and End of Life Care of Older People: Executive Summary* (revised 2006). Available at: www.bgs.org.uk/Publications/Compendium/compend_4–8.htm (accessed 27 January 2009).
Department of Health (2008) *End of Life Care Strategy: Promoting High Quality Care for All Adults at the End of Life*. London: Department of Health.
Franks, P. J., Salisbury, C., Bosanquet, N., Wilkinson, E. K., Kite, S., Naysmith, A. and Higginson, I. J. (2000) The level of need for palliative care: a systematic review of the literature. *Palliative Medicine*, 14: 93–104.
General Medical Council (2006) *Withholding and Withdrawing Life-prolonging Treatments: Good Practice in Decision-making*. London: GMC. Available at: www.gmc-uk.org/guidance/current/library/witholding_lifeprolonging_guidance.asp#End%20of%20natural%20life (accessed 2 February 2009).
Kübler-Ross, E. (1969/2008) *On Death and Dying*. Oxford: Routledge.
National Audit Office (2008) *End of Life Care*. London: HMSO.

palliative care

National Institute for Clinical Excellence (2004) *Guidance on Cancer Services: Improving Supportive and Palliative Care for Adults with Cancer. Executive Summary.* London: NICE.

Saunders, C. (1996) Into the valley of the shadow of death. *British Medical Journal,* 7062/313: 1599–1601.

World Health Organisation (2002) *National Cancer Control Programmes: Policies and Managerial Guidelines* (2nd edition). Geneva: World Health Organisation.

Pensions

> *A financial resource received once people have reached a certain age or have fulfilled other criteria and which provides protection against life's contingencies by addressing the financial needs of people in later life.*

The concept of pensions can best be understood when linked with the broader terminology of social protection systems, benefits and income maintenance, and a distinction made between pensions and benefits. The former is generally underpinned by a principle of entitlement or social right, the latter a financial resource to which there is no automatic entitlement. In a broad sense, pensions represent a financial resource which people can receive once they have reached a certain age or fulfilled other criteria, such as a minimum number of years in paid work. They are designed to provide protection against contingencies such as widowhood, disability and poverty, addressing the financial needs of people as they enter later life.

Although the meaning of pensions varies depending upon the systems of social protection to which they belong, it is possible to identify different pension schemes: *public pensions*, normally considered as basic statutory schemes, financed through direct and indirect tax contributions; *employer schemes*, often known as occupational or defined benefit schemes, organised by employers of major industries and professions, their financial value normally dependent upon the number of years worked and the level of salary achieved; and finally, pensions from *other*

key concepts in social gerontology

providers (notably private pension providers) and *private savings*. The emergence of more varied approaches to pension provisions over the past 20 years partly reflects the influential World Bank document, *Averting the Old Age Crisis* (1994), which made recommendations that in a context of global demographic ageing, nations should move towards diversification of pension products, following a four-pillar model: public pensions, occupational schemes, private pensions and personal savings.

Historically speaking, although the development of pensions tends to be associated with the late nineteenth and early twentieth centuries, and the emergence of a mass, organised workforce, Midwinter (1997) reminds us that the notion of pensions in terms of a payment for services rendered, in fact dates back to the sixteenth century. Financial remuneration, usually from an official state source, would have been designed to maintain individuals *in* work, and it was not until well into the nineteenth century that payment of a pension became associated with the notion of retirement and the ending of a period of paid service. In earlier, agrarian-based societies, without mechanisation and systems of mass production, individuals would have been expected to work until the end of their lives, unless they possessed assets which could be exchanged or 'traded' for a guarantee of support in later life either from family members or third parties (Thane, 2000). Ensuring survival in later life therefore rested either upon family support, remaining active until the end of life, or failing these, turning to charitable or highly selective public sources. An exception to these provisions would have been a very limited number of public pensions, paid primarily in recognition of services rendered, or as a means of allaying the risk of social unrest among certain groups, particularly those in the military services. These earlier public pensions were to foreshadow the later emergence of private or occupational-based pensions.

From a broader comparative perspective, Hill (2007) points to three factors which have contributed to the consolidation of pension provisions in the western context: the emergence of retirement as a distinct period of the life course, symbolising the end of a period in paid employment; an increasingly long period of post-retirement, achieved through improvements to life expectancy; and the development of institutional structures designed to ensure the channelling of financial resources to individuals once employment has ceased. The spread of more formalised, widespread public pension provisions towards the end of the nineteenth century can be linked to several factors: the rise of industrialisation and the need for a competitive, skilled and highly productive workforce, requisites which would already have begun to exclude older workers; the increasing

pensions

likelihood of individuals surviving beyond retirement age and hence in need of financial security which could no longer be guaranteed through paid employment; a recognition that ultimately, despite charitable initiatives and the development of other ventures (such as friendly societies or insurance companies) the state should be galvanised into playing a more significant role in ensuring support in old age (Hill, 2007). Together, these conditions contributed to the progressive acceptance of state regulation of pension provisions, although these were to emerge during the twentieth century under a variety of forms depending on national political and policy contexts, and whether coverage was to be universal or selective (Schulz and Meyers, 1990). From these historical origins, two types of state provision are generally recognized. The first is modelled on the idea of social insurance as a means of collective provision to protect against risk. The second is a more selective, means-tested form of financial support administered by governments to provide older people with regular, albeit minimal, income sources.

Gerontological interest in the field of pensions reflects a broad range of issues, not least its impact in 'defining' or giving social meaning to old age. Age has invariably been used to determine eligibility for pension entitlement, in turn, leading to an association with retirement, and hence to the onset of old age. As research on the historical origins of pensions has shown, there has also been interest in demonstrating how pensions have served as a mechanism for managing labour market requirements (particularly when there is a need to 'shed' older workers) and for reducing labour turnover and avoiding worker unrest.

Other areas of application in ageing research have included, for example, the relationship between income and well-being or quality of life among older people (e.g. Walker, 2005); the risks of poverty and social exclusion associated with a lack of adequate income in later life, particularly for women (e.g. Ginn et al., 2001); the emergence of inequalities in income distribution within the older population itself, explained partly in terms of differences in life-course trajectories and access to sources of pension income (Meyer and Bridgen, 2008); how ethnicity, birth cohort, class or gender act as stratifying factors in these income inequalities (e.g. Midwinter, 1997), and an interest in demonstrating the relative weakness of income security provisions in reducing poverty in later life (Walker, 2005).

From a critical perspective, it is perhaps not so much the concept of pensions itself which has been the object of debate by gerontologists, but rather the influence of increasingly global policy processes which have brought about a shift in minimising the role of the state in providing for income maintenance in later life, instead placing the emphasis upon occupational and private pension provisions. Entwined in the broader discourse of 'risk society', where insecurity and uncertainty are paramount, debate lies in establishing whether this change will exacerbate the existing divisions between older people as 'haves' and 'have nots' when it comes to the resources required to maintain a decent quality of life.

Other debates taken up by gerontologists in relation to the concept of pensions centre around the characterisation of older cohorts as a financial 'burden' for the younger and proportionally smaller cohorts succeeding them, who, it has been argued, will carry the costs of pensions, particularly when they are financed through pay-as-you-go mechanisms. This debate extends into one of the potential for intergenerational conflict as younger and older age groups compete for limited public resources (Preston, 1984). Gerontologists have been quick to point to the limited focus of this concern, instead highlighting the maintenance of other forms of intergenerational support and 'cycles' of reinvestment as resources circulate between generations (Arber and Attias-Donfut, 2000).

Linked to these issues are criticisms of the way in which a type of 'global discourse' of impending financial crisis arising from population ageing has been used to justify shifting responsibility for ensuring secure and adequate pension provisions from the state to individuals (Naegele and Walker, 2007). This particular issue finds resonance in the developing country context, where current debate focuses on whether economic security in later life should be provided through public- or private-funded programmes and whether these countries can afford to plan for universal, non-contributory pension schemes. At the heart of this debate lies the question of establishing whether public provisions should be strengthened to compensate for declining informal, family support for older persons, or whether this will simply encourage families to relinquish these responsibilities more readily (Harper, 2006).

The concept of pensions therefore takes on a diverse and multifaceted meaning, depending upon national political and policy contexts. However, from the late nineteenth century onwards it has been underpinned by issues of labour force and economic regulation and, at the individual level, by issues of equality, security and well-being in later life. Contemporary debates in the field of gerontology highlight the need for continued vigilance in monitoring these issues, and of questioning the impact that global institutions have in shaping national pension provisions. Ultimately, these institutions may well determine whether at the micro level of daily life, older people will encounter later life as an experience of economic impoverishment.

See also: Ageing, Cohort, Disability, Ethnicity, Gender, Generations, Gerontology, Population Ageing, Quality of Life, Retirement

FURTHER READING

Clark, G., Munnell, A. and Orszag, J. (2006) *The Oxford Handbook of Pensions and Retirement Income*. Oxford: Oxford University Press.

REFERENCES

Hill, M. (2007) *Pensions*. Bristol: The Policy Press.
Meyer, T. and Bridgen, P. (2008) Class, gender and chance: the social division of welfare and occupational pensions in the United Kingdom. *Ageing and Society*, 28: 353–381.
Midwinter, E. (1997) *Pensioned Off: Retirement and Income Examined*. Buckingham: Open University Press.
Naegele, G. and Walker, A. (2007) Social protection: incomes, poverty and the reform of pension systems, in J. Bond, S. Peace, F. Dittmann-Kohli and G. Westerhof (eds), *Ageing in Society* (3rd edition). London: Sage.
Schulz, J. and Myles, J. (1990) Old age pensions: a comparative perspective, in R. H. Binstock and L. K. George (eds), *Handbook of Ageing and the Social Sciences*. London: Academic Press.
World Bank (1994) *Averting the Old Age Cisis: Policies to Protect the Old and Promote Growth*. New York: Oxford University Press.

Population Ageing

Changes to the age and sex structure of a population which result in increasingly higher numbers and proportions of older people in relation to other age groups.

Population ageing is studied as part of the broader field of demography, the scientific study of human populations. The demography of ageing focuses in particular on explaining and monitoring the causes and consequences of long-term shifts or transitions in health, mortality and fertility and how, together, these bring about changes to the age and sex composition or structure of a given population. Many societies are now experiencing an age transition, shifting 'from a very young population in which there are slightly more males than females to an older population in which there are more females than males' (Weeks, 2008: 307), a process which eventually leads to population ageing. Although each individual ages and becomes older, population ageing refers more specifically to the aggregate effect of this ageing process, and means that on average people are getting older.

Population ageing is monitored in several ways in terms of: the onset and speed of structural and numerical ageing (changes in the proportions and actual numbers of older people in a given population); increases to the median age of a population; and shifts in age- and gender-based dependency ratios. The population pyramid, a graphic representation of a population's age and sex structure, is often used to represent the impact of this age transition across time (Shryock and Siegel, 2004). Analysis of population ageing usually involves the disaggregation of populations into the functional or chronological age groups of 0–14, 15–64 and 65 years and above, the broad assumption being that those in the middle age group are economically active while the other two groups are not. In developing countries, the upper limit of the middle group is often lower – usually 60 – and has traditionally reflected differences in life expectancies. With extending life expectancy, the oldest age group is sometimes disaggregated even further to distinguish the 'Third' and 'Fourth' ages or the 'young-old' and 'old-old'.

Advanced industrialised countries now have relatively high proportions of older people aged 60 or more, and these are projected to increase significantly. In 2005, for example, just over one-fifth of Europe's population was aged 60 or more and projections indicate that this will increase to over one-third by 2050. By 2050, projections show that at least one out of ten individuals in each region of the world will have reached this age or beyond. Although developed countries currently have the oldest populations in the world, just under two-thirds of those living in 2005 lived in developing countries and this figure is projected to increase to 80% by 2050 (United Nations Population Division, 2007). Those aged 80 or more represent the fastest growing segment of the population (Kinsella and Velkoff, 2001). From 88 million in 2005, the oldest-old are projected to number 402 million by 2050; for Africa,

Asia, Latin America and the Caribbean this number will have increased at least sixfold (United Nations Population Division, 2007: 8).

Population ageing occurs as the result of a complex interaction between health, mortality and fertility transitions, which together change the number of people at each age in a given population (Kinsella and Velkoff, 2001). The impact of these demographic processes occurs over time so that a population will experience different phases to its age transition. For example, when fertility and mortality are high, a population will be quite 'youthful' in its age structure, but by the time mortality and then fertility have declined significantly (so that the population will not 'rejuvenate' quickly by the addition of babies and that more people will be living longer), and the earlier large birth cohorts are reaching old age, the age transition will have led to an 'ageing' population. Declines in mortality and improvements to health therefore eventually lead to increasing numbers of older people; declines in fertility eventually lead to a higher proportion of older people in a population over time. Migration can also influence the age and sex structure of a population. If, for example, young workers migrate in search of work, as emigrants they may 'drain' the population of its youthful structure, but likewise, as immigrants they may help to 'rejuvenate' the population into which they arrive. The impact of international migration is more significant in countries which depend upon foreign labour (e.g. the United Arab Emirates).

Historically speaking, demographers have developed theories to explain how the age structure of societies changes over time. The most well known of them, the demographic transition theory, is often associated with the work of Notestein (1945). Notestein elaborated three patterns of population growth. Stage one represents the potential for high growth because of high birth and death rates. While women may bear many children, those children are also more likely to die due to infectious disease. As a result, few members survive into middle adulthood, and even less into old age. With the advent of antibiotics, improved sanitation and medical technologies, the first transition occurs as mortality rates decrease. Today, Nigeria's population pyramid equates to Stage one of the transition with high fertility and mortality. Its population's age and sex structure resembles a broad-based triangle (reflecting high fertility and a predominantly young age structure) which rapidly tapers to the top (the oldest age groups). In other words, younger members of the society far outnumber those in middle and old age groups.

Stage two of the demographic transition is associated with rapid population growth as death rates drop before fertility begins to decline. Most countries in Latin America, the Caribbean and Asia are currently experiencing this stage of transition, although their populations are expected to age rapidly because their fertility transitions have been rapid (United Nations Population Division, 2007). In the third stage, death rates reach their lowest levels and fertility may continue to decline, with the effect that populations might eventually be unable to replace themselves. Of core importance in consolidating this demographic model of population growth was modernisation theory, which provided explanations for fertility decline in particular, and introduced the possibility that changes to mortality and fertility could be conditioned by broader societal transformations, such as industrialization, and the transformation of societal institutions such as the family.

Demographic transition theory has subsequently been criticised particularly because of the pioneering work achieved by the European Fertility Project during the 1970s, which focused on regional differences in fertility decline, and through Easterlin's relative cohort size hypothesis (Easterlin, 1968). More recently, it has been reformulated to encompass not one, but several interrelated transitions, notably: 'A decline in mortality [will] almost necessarily be followed by a decline in fertility, and by subsequent transitions in migration, urbanization, the age structure and the family and household structure in society' (Weeks, 2008: 104).

Population ageing raises many questions and challenges, but as a concept which can be measured and monitored, it has a wide application in a number of areas, particularly for social welfare and planning at national, regional and global levels. In particular, it is frequently argued that informal support systems, healthcare systems, work opportunities and welfare state commitments represent spheres which are likely to be affected by the needs of an increasingly large older population. For instance, family serves as a traditional source of informal support to older people, and in developing countries constitutes the primary provider of personal care and material support. However, population ageing challenges the foundations of this support system and, in turn, the well-being of older people. With decreasing fertility comes fewer children, and hence a potentially diminishing 'reserve' of informal providers of support. Coupled with this may be the effects of young people's migration to cities or countries as they search for work or improved economic opportunities, with the consequence that older family members (who are increasingly likely to be living longer due to improved life expectancies) are left behind.

For social gerontology, the concept of population ageing as a measurable phenomenon has been vital in highlighting the extent to which the social face of contemporary societies across the globe is experiencing (or will experience) radical transformations because of the increasing presence of older people. This changing demographic profile of the world's population raises innumerable social, economic, cultural, medical, biological and spiritual issues, all of which are the 'stuff' of social gerontology when it is viewed as an interdisciplinary field. A good example of this is the notion of the feminisation of old age, a concept which depicts the demographic reality that it is almost universally the case that women live longer than men, although in various parts of the world this difference is now decreasing. While women may still have 'the edge' over men in terms of the number of years they live, they are more likely to encounter problems of social isolation, poverty, poor health and other forms of deprivation (Arber and Ginn, 2005).

It is in part from the field of social gerontology, however, that a critical discourse which challenges and questions the potential implications of population ageing is located. Social gerontologists, for example, question whether family relations, norms and values have really weakened to the extent that older members will be isolated from this informal source of support. They critically challenge the argument that population ageing implies unprecedented and soaring economic costs to cover the health and welfare needs and retirement incomes of an increasingly large number of older people, and ask us to question whether biomedical progress and research aimed at further extending life and reducing the period over which we encounter chronic illness at the end of the life course should be pursued at any cost.

Finally, and perhaps more importantly, the concept of population ageing refers to characteristics of a group, therefore and has the potential to minimise or mask the importance of the individual ageing experience. Social gerontology, however, not only highlights this potential weakness, but also provides a different but complementary lens – the biographical perspective – through which to consider the disaggregated effect of population ageing.

See also: Ageing, Care, Cohort, Family Relations, Gender, Gerontology, Global Ageing, Longevity, Pensions, Retirement, Third and Fourth Age

FURTHER READING

Weeks (2008), in the tenth edition of his book *Population: An Introduction to Concepts and Issues*, offers a very straightforward and concise explanation of the demographic transition and its various component transitions, including the health, mortality, fertility and migration transitions. The previous, ninth edition of his book did have an entire section devoted to the concept of population ageing.

REFERENCES

Easterlin, R. A. (1968) *Population, Labor Force, and Long Swings in Economic Growth*. New York: National Bureau of Economic Research.

Kinsella, K. and Velkoff, V. A. (2001) *An Ageing World: 2001*. International Population Reports, Series P95/01–1, Washington, DC: US Government Printing Office. Available at: www.census.gov/prod/2001pubs/p95-01-1.pdf (accessed 15 January 2009).

Notestein, F. W. (1945) Population – the long view, in T. W. Schultz (ed.), *Food for the World*. Chicago, IL: Chicago University Press. pp. 37–57.

Shryock, H. S. and Siegel, J. S. (eds) (2004) *The Methods and Materials of Demography: Condensed Edition* (2nd edition). New York: Elsevier Academic Press.

Weeks, J. R. (2008) *Population. An Introduction to Concepts and Issues* (10th edition). Belmont, CA: Wadsworth.

Quality of Life

> *A multidimensional concept embracing subjective and objective appreciation of an older person's life situation in the context of their socio-cultural and economic environment.*

There is a proliferation of definitions, models and measures of quality of life (QoL), with consequent claims that it is difficult to conceptualise and operationalise (Evans, 2009). What is universal is that there is no single, agreed definition or single measurement of the construct. Similarly, there has been a dearth of systematic evaluations of the measure or concept. The utility of the concept has, however, been widespread through all disciplines, including medical and social science disciplines, despite differing interpretations (Beham et al., 2006). A frequently used concept of QoL is that defined by the World Health Organisation (WHO) as 'an individual's perception of their position in life in the context of the culture and value system in which they live and in relation to their goals, expectations, standards, and concerns' (WHOQoL, 1998: 551). Several studies have drawn on the World Health Organisation's definition in comparing QoL across different cultures and political and geographical contexts.

The main debates on QoL focus on the relative importance of subjective versus objective approaches; whether QoL is uni- or multidimensional; the role of values; the place of self-evaluation; the cultural context; and QoL as a relative or absolute concept (Galloway, 2005). Variation from time to time and whether QoL is relatively fixed or changing over the life course, and the purpose and means of measurement are also well debated in the literature (Draper and Thompson, 2001).

Within social gerontology, quality of life has been a key area of investigation based on the aim to promote a more positive view of later life and to view successful ageing from a variety of perspectives (Evans, 2009). Quality of life has also become a priority for public policy, with its aim of enabling people to retain independence. 'Nevertheless, achieving these objectives depends in part upon the ability of services to assess, monitor, support and review the quality of life (QoL) of the person and their carer, as well as on their responsiveness in accommodating changing health and social care needs' (Evans, 2009: 2).

There is international recognition that the term quality of life is difficult to define; it lacks consistency across studies and there is lack of consensus on its meaning. Whatever definition is used, it is usually contingent upon the research area and question to be studied. Bond and Corner (2006: 154) argue that 'the concept of "quality of life" has become increasingly complex and has lost its ability to coherently describe and explain the well-being of individuals and populations. "Quality of life" nowadays is therefore a heuristic concept used by academics, politicians and global institutions to capture the essence of life for the individual citizen'.

Quality of life has increasingly been associated with qualitative, subjective measures and its objective quantitative aspects. It has also concentrated on the balance between individual (personal characteristics, state of mind) and societal aspects (macro-societal and socio-demographic, state of society) and is grounded in older people's self-perceptions of quality of life (Gabriel and Bowling, 2004). However, there is scope to broaden the measure to incorporate more multilevel or multi-domain approaches to QoL.

Such a distinction between the objective and subjective nature of the measures is significant as Bond and Corner (2006: 155) claim that:

> to understand quality of life an important distinction can be made between the objective measures of quality of life on the one hand – health status, standard of living, living arrangements and the number of social contacts – and subjective accounts on the other – the meaning of health to the individual, their expectations about incomes and living arrangements and the quality of contact with others. This distinction is crucial for understanding the paradoxes of ageing, disability, loneliness and social isolation, relative deprivation and poverty.

As a result of the lack of clarity, some authors have attempted a classification of definitions. For example, Farquhar (1995) has four categories: global definitions, component definitions which break QoL down into its constituent parts, focused definitions which explicitly refer to one component, and combination definitions which incorporate both global definitions but specify components. Global definitions encompass all aspects of human life, including material, physical, social, emotional, psychological and spiritual well-being, and multidimensional generic QoL measures. Focused definitions of QoL, such as health-related quality of life (HRQoL) or disease-specific QoL measures, for example, are used in the health service.

Bowling et al. (2003) stress the importance of older people defining QoL themselves as they can incorporate far broader themes than that of traditional approaches of health satisfaction, independence, etc. They argue that in studying QoL more attention should go on enjoyment of one's home, the importance of the community and social capital, and having enough money to meet basic needs, to participate in society, to enjoy life and to retain one's independence and control over life.

No single factor determines quality of life in older age. Factors such as perceived poor financial situation, depression, functional limitation attributable to longstanding illness and limitations in everyday activities can affect quality of life negatively, while those such as residence in an appreciated neighbourhood, having trusted relationships with children, family and friends, and affluence can improve quality of life.

Whereas today it is widely acknowledged that both subjective and objectives measures for QoL are crucial to definition and measurement,

quality of life

in the past the two approaches to quality of life had distinct disciplinary homes: the Scandinavian level of living approach, which focused on objective measures and was derived from the social sciences; and the American QoL approach, which emphasised subjective well-being and was rooted in the psychological organisational literature. Both quantitative and qualitative measures have considerable histories, with the quantitative measures rooted in numerous clinical trials. Despite the tendency to stereotype both approaches, increasingly there has been acknowledgement that both need to be part of the definition of QoL.

Quality of life as a social phenomenon was evident in the studies of poverty in England in the nineteenth century (Draper and Thompson, 2001). However, the European body of research was largely dominated by the negative dependency paradigm that permeated the study of ageing – that QoL was viewed around the dependency and functional ability of older people, with consequent service provision focusing on the care needs of older people. As Draper and Thompson (2001) note, the US development of QoL indicators arose out of social policy initiatives in the 1960s. Here, the emphasis was on the more positive aspects of ageing. The concept became firmly established in the early 1970s when the journal *Social Indicators* was launched, publishing articles on QoL.

Since 1976 the growth in the number of papers on QoL has been exponential (Draper and Thompson, 2001). In the UK, the quality of life of older people received increasing interest in the 1990s with the emergence of the Economic and Social Research Council's 'Growing Older' programme, entitled 'Quality of Life' (Walker and Hennessy, 2004). Increasingly, measures have been made more applicable to older populations and sensitive to the issues that constitute quality of life in later life. Bowling et al's (2003) observation that little research has tapped into the lay views of older people themselves on how they construct their QoL is addressed in the programme. It also highlights, among other things: the inequalities in QoL among older people from different ethnic backgrounds (Moriarty and Butt, 2004); the quality of life of older people in deprived neighbourhoods (Scharf et al., 2004); the quality of life of older people entering residential care (Tester et al., 2004); and the quality of life of men (Davidson and Arber, 2004).

In summing up the progress in developing QoL measures applicable to older populations, Evans (2009: 2) notes that:

key concepts in
social gerontology

Over the past 20 years or more the field of quality of life measurement has become a diverse and specialised field. The growth in the number of measures has been substantial, and many more measures can be expected to be created that relate specifically to older people and to individual life domains. This will provide a considerable range of possible outcomes tools with which to evaluate the efficacy and effectiveness of targeted interventions with older people.

Evans (2009) concludes that most measures of QoL focus on health-related quality of life issues and are primarily used in evaluations of clinical services and treatment interventions. They were not designed specifically for use with older people.

Bond and Corner (2006: 154) assert that:

> in recent years, increasing the quality of life for individuals and populations has become a key strategic goal for the UK government, other member states in the European Union, the World Health Organisation and the United Nations. Quality of life is also part of the rhetoric of organisations like the World Bank and the World Trade Organisation.

The World Health Organisation developed a QoL measure in the early 1990s. It has been widely adopted, yet there has been criticism of the selection of domains chosen for the definition, which are health-oriented. A second influential quantitative approach to QoL is the Quality Adjusted Life Years (QALY). This technique compared the cost-effectiveness of different forms of medical treatment in the context of resource allocation decisions. Increasingly, more subjective domains have been adopted in the measurement of QoL and these have added to an impressive array of tools for practitioners and policy makers. Such generic measures have since been adapted to ensure that they are valid and reliable when used with older people.

The application of QoL measures that apply to older people has extensive utility in practice settings, whether these are in health or social care. As Evans (2009) notes, this can range from using measures to monitor and maintain life quality, 'prevent deterioration of both physical and mental health, and [can] reduce the need for more intensive and expensive forms of care and treatment. At an aggregate level, QoL data [can] be used to compare the life quality of older people in different community, residential or treatment settings in order to understand the relative cost and outcomes benefits of different interventions. Also, since clinical and service interventions can impact upon individual QoL the availability of these types of data [can] be used to inform services developments that promote productive and successful ageing'.

Galloway (2005: 12) believes a common weakness in the use of the concept is the failure of researchers to state exactly their definition of QoL and to move to measurement. Similarly, they note that there is confusion around the outcomes of QoL and a tendency to conflate the concept with other concepts, such as 'happiness, well-being, health status and living conditions'.

UK research on the quality of life in old age has neglected the increasing ethnic diversity of the older population, and although studies of health and income inequalities have highlighted the contribution played by racism, analyses of the factors influencing the quality of life have rarely considered its effects (Moriarty and Butt, 2004).

Bond and Corner (2006) also raise shortcomings in the concept, focusing on the issues of who is best suited to judge older peoples' QoL, given that the standard questionnaire that someone fills in ignores the *meaning* of life to older people or fails to take a life-course approach.

The concept has evolved to be a significant influence in the practice and policy context of social gerontology. It also has significance for future research agendas with diverse groups of older people with different life-course trajectories and experiences.

See also: Ageing, Care, Disability, Gerontology, Independence, Loneliness, Successful Ageing

FURTHER READING

Walker, A. and Hennessy, C. (2004) *Growing Older: Quality of Life in Old Age*. Maidenhead: Open University Press.

REFERENCES

Beham, B., Drobnič, S. and Verwiebe, R. (2006) *Literature Review, Theoretical Concepts and Methodological Approaches to Quality of Life*. Utrecht: Utrecht University.

Bond, J. and Corner, L. (2006) The future of well-being: quality of life of older people in the twenty-first century, in J. Vincent, C. Phillipson and M. Downs (eds), *The Futures of Old Age*. London: Sage. pp. 154–160.

Bowling, A., Fleissig, A., Gabriel, Z., Banister, D., Dykes, J., Dowding, L., Sutton, S. and Evans, O. (2003) Let's ask them: a national survey of definitions of quality of life and its enhancement among people aged 65 and over. *International Journal of Ageing and Human Development*, 56(4): 269–306.

Davidson, K. and Arber, S. (2004) Older men: their health behaviours and partnership status, in A. Walker and C. Hennessey (eds), *Growing Older: Quality of Life in Old Age*. Maidenhead: Open University Press.

Draper, P. and Thompson, D. (2001) The quality of life: a concept for research and practice. *Nursing Times Research*, 6(3): 648–657.

Evans, S. (2009) Quality of life measures in the elderly and later life, in V. R. Preedy and R. R. Watson (eds), *Handbook of Disease Burdens and Quality of Life Measures*. Heidelberg: Springer.

Farquhar, M. (1995) Definitions of quality of life: a taxonomy. *Journal of Advanced Nursing*, 2(3): 502.

Gabriel, Z. and Bowling, A. (2004) Quality of life from the perspectives of older people. *Ageing and Society*, 24: 675–691.

Galloway, S. (2005) *Well-being and Quality of Life: Measuring the Benefits of Culture and Sport. Section 1: A Literature Review*. Edinburgh: Scottish Executive Social Research.

Moriarty, J. and Butt, J. (2004) Inequalities in quality of life among older people from different ethnic groups. *Ageing and Society*, 24: 729–753.

Scharf, T., Phillipson, C. and Smith, A. (2004) Poverty and social exclusion: growing older in deprived urban neighbourhoods, in A. Walker and C. Hennessey (eds), *Growing Older: Quality of Life in Old Age*. Maidenhead: Open University Press.

Tester, S., Hubbard, G., Downes, M., MacDonald, C. and Murphy, J. (2004) Frailty and institutional life, in A. Walker and C. Hennessey (eds), *Growing Older: Quality of Life in Old Age*. Maidenhead: Open University Press.

Walker, A. and Hennessy, C. (eds) (2004) *Growing Older: Quality of Life in Old Age*. Maidenhead: Open University Press.

WHOQOL Group (1998) The World Health Organisation quality of life assessment (WHOQOL): development and general psychometric properties. *Social Science and Medicine*, 46: 1569–1585.

Religion/Spirituality

> **Both religion and spirituality are multidimensional concepts that reference connections to a Higher Power.**

Connection to a Higher Power may signify an important aspect of people's lives, particularly in the later stages of the life course. Some research evidence suggests that academics or those who study ageing are less likely to be religious or spiritual. As a result, matters of religion and spirituality are often not included in gerontological research (Hill et al., 2000). Yet, religion and spirituality remain pervasive and of high importance to a large number of people in the USA and the UK, with established effects on health and well-being across the life course and in old age.

First, it is instructive to elaborate the ways in which the concepts of religion and spirituality are understood. Many suggest that the terms include a range of meanings, and so there is a great deal of difficulty associated with defining these notions in an adequate manner (Traphagan, 2005). The notions of religion and spirituality reference distinct ideas, yet also overlap. Both include the notion of 'the sacred' as a key component, but religion also includes a search for non-sacred goals, including identity and belongingness through adherence to, or belief in, prescribed behaviours as stipulated and identified by a select group of people (Hill et al., 2000). Spirituality specifically involves a search for the meaning of life through transcendence of the human experience, personal transformation, sense of community, search for truth, respect, and understanding of the creation mystery. Religion, on the other hand, may include such facets, but extends to provide a personal and social identity, and stipulates behaviour patterns, rituals and attitudes. In recent times, religion has been viewed more negatively than spirituality because of its emphasis on tradition and restrictions. One may be religious, but not spiritual. Likewise, one may be spiritual, but not religious.

The variety of religious denominations that exist in the world vary with regard to the messages they project about growing older. The Abrahamic, monotheistic religious texts (i.e. Judaism, Christianity and Islam) stress the importance of family in caring for elders, while religions from the Far East (i.e. Buddhism) identify old age as a time for reflection and withdrawal (Idler, 2006). There is more variety in terms of attitudes and beliefs across religions than one finds in actual practice. The old are often protected by religious traditions, but there exists no ceremonial ritual to recognise old age as one often finds in accomplishments or life-stage passages in younger years (i.e. entering adulthood or marriage). Nevertheless, religious beliefs and practices may provide a significant resource for personal and family adjustment in the face of changes (Moberg, 1972). In the end, the role of religion in older people's lives varies – activities that aid spiritual well-being in some may hurt the spiritual well-being of others.

Dimensions of religion identified as key to health and well-being among older populations include organisational aspects such as attending services, non-organisational aspects such as rituals and practices that take place outside a religious institution, and subjective aspects with reference to self-ratings of religiosity/spirituality. These dimensions may operate in unique ways, interacting with one another to influence quality of life in old age.

Role of religious institutions. In a review of studies carried out in the USA on the association between ageing and religious participation, Idler (2006) found that the relationship may be best described as non-linear. Religious participation tends to be most intense in early adulthood and later life. Declines in participation occur in later life due to health issues before death. But subjective religiosity does not diminish.

Religious institutions are uniquely age integrated, and of all social institutions in US society may constitute the one that is able to reach large proportions of elders in the population (Moberg, 1972). Moreover, they have historically been the institution concerned with sponsoring services that address the needs of elders in the community, including housing, leisure activities, volunteer services and health care needs. Indeed, the benefits may be reciprocal, where elders provide a resource to churches through volunteering their services. Churches may benefit from the services offered, as well as providing a pathway for older adults to engage in service opportunities. Such opportunities promote support and solidarity.

Influence on health. Religion has a cumulative effect on health. Idler (2006) suggests from her review of accumulated research that the earlier one practises religion, the more benefit accrues, reducing the risk of disease and increasing social support. Yet, she also cautions that there may be selection effects. In other words, those who are less religious may die before they reach old age, reducing differentiation in old age, and making it seem as if older adults are more religious.

A compelling finding involves the effect of regular service attendance on mortality. For instance, religious attendance at least once a week predicted lower mortality among Mexican Americans aged 65 and older, even accounting for selection factors such as functional health, mobility, cognitive ability and self-rated health (Hill et al., 2005). In a nationally representative US sample, others found that attending services once a month extends the length of life, in particular, the mortality rate decreased by up to 35%. Yet, the effect of service attendance on mortality declined as age increased (Musick et al., 2004). This finding suggests that health effects of service attendance

religion/spirituality

183

are not as pronounced in later life, though it may help in ensuring that adults reach old age.

The influence of religion on health may vary according to cultural norms. For instance, in Japan, religious practice in later life influences men to affectively help others more, which was then associated with better self-health ratings than men who did not engage in religious practice. The finding that religious practice influenced men and not women suggested that religious practice may free men from the constraints imposed by an earlier sex role orientation (Krause et al., 1999). On the other hand, among middle-aged and older Mexican Americans religious attendance was a more powerful predictor of well-being in women than in men (Levin and Markides, 1988). These findings suggest that religious attendance may operate in different ways for men and women depending on the given cultural context.

Religion is thought to provide an effective source of comfort, particularly when faced with loss or hardships. As a result, a growing body of literature suggests that older adults in minority groups are especially likely to benefit from religion. This is particularly evident among older African Americans. For instance, Krause (2003) found in the USA that older blacks enjoy a greater sense of well-being than older whites because they gain a greater sense of meaning from religion. Additionally, the impact of religious meaning on well-being is stronger for older black than older white adults. Similar findings have been found in other societies. In the Lebanon, Chaaya et al. (2007) examined underprivileged communities and found that religious practice influenced depressive symptoms in older adults among Muslims living in Palestinian refugee communities, yet not those living in low-income suburbs. Findings suggest again that such activity provides a coping resource in the age of distress.

Social gerontology most often addresses the role of religiosity and spirituality in old age related to Christian traditions. Still needed are more thorough studies of the multitude of other religions practised by large numbers of the world population. For instance, anecdotal evidence suggests that rituals stemming from the practice of Islam, including the dietary restrictions, fasting and bowing/prostration involved in the five daily prayers, contribute to both the mental and physical well-being of Muslims as they enter later years (Ajrouch, 2008). Additionally, in-depth understandings of spirituality in association with religion, as well as separate from religion, are also needed. Spirituality seems most prominent in the life of older adults when they face life-changing events that directly influence role and identity transitions, such as moving to institutionalised housing, the loss of a loved one, health limitations, and/or facing one's own mortality (Black, 2006). Yet types of spirituality may vary, which then has implications for how an older adult responds to various treatment interventions (see Klemack et al., 2007).

See also: *Ageing, Gerontology, Housing, Quality of Life, Social Support*

REFERENCES

Ajrouch, K. J. (2008) Muslim faith communities: links with the past, bridges to the future. *Generations*, 32(2): 47–5.

Black, H. K. (2006) Questions I now ask: spirituality in the liminal environment of assisted living. *Journal of Ageing Studies*, 20(1): 67–77.

Chaaya, M., Sibai, A. M., Fayad, R. and El-Roueiheb, Z. (2007) Religiosity and depression in older people: evidence from underprivileged refugee and non-refugee communities in Lebanon. *Ageing and Mental Health*, 11(1): 37–44.

Hill, P. C., Pargament, K., Hood, R. W., McCullough, M. E., Swyers, J. P., Larson, D. B. and Zinnbauer, B. J. (2000) Conceputalizing religion and spirituality: points of commonality, points of departure. *Journal for the Theory of Social Behaviour*, 30: 51–77.

Hill, T. C., Angel, J. L., Ellison, C. G. and Angel, R. J. (2005) Religious attendance and mortality: an 8-year follow-up of older Mexican Americans. *Journal of Gerontology*, 60B(2): S102–S109.

Idler, E. (2006) Religion and ageing, in R. H. Binstock and L. K. George (eds), *Handbook of Ageing and the Social Sciences* (6th edition). New York: Elsevier. pp. 277–302.

Klemmack, D. L., Roff, L. L., Parker, M. W., Koenig, H. G., Sawyer, P. and Allman, R. M. (2007) A cluster analysis typology of religiousness/spirituality among older adults. *Research on Ageing*, 29(2): 163–183.

Krause, N. (2003) Religious meaning and subjective meaning in late life. *Journal of Gerontology*, 58B(3): S160–S170.

Krause, N., Ingersoll-Dayton, B., Liang, J. and Sugisawsa, H. (1999) Religion, social support, and health among Japanese elderly. *Journal of Health and Social Behavior*, 40(4): 405–421.

Levin, J. S. and Markides, K. S. (1988) Religious attendance and psychological well-being in middle-aged and older Mexican Americans. *Sociological Analysis*, 49: 66–72.

Moberg, D. O. (1972) Religion and the ageing family. *The Family Coordinator*, 21(1): 47–60.

Musick, M., House, J. and Williams, D. (2004) Attendance at religious services and mortality in a national sample. *Journal of Health and Social Behavior*, 45: 198–213.

Traphagan, J. W. (2005) Multidimensional measurement of religiousness/spirituality for use in health research in cross-cultural perspective. *Research on Ageing*, 27(4): 387–419.

religion/spirituality

185

Retirement

A transition or process signalling a change in status or activity, generally associated with later life and marked by objective lifestyle changes such as receipt of a pension or reduced involvement in labour force activities.

Retirement is a difficult concept to define because its boundaries are fluid. It may represent a transition or process which has no single cut-off point – shifting from full-time to part-time, and then to a complete withdrawal from paid activity, for example. Conversely, it may be marked by a specific event – stopping paid work at a precise and given age and receiving some form of retirement income for the first time. Although, for purposes of measurement, it may be important to establish retirement status in terms of its objective elements (receipt of a pension and reduced activity in the labour force at an older age, for example), it then becomes problematic to know how to apply these parameters if individuals have not been involved in paid work during their lives.

Defining the concept of retirement, then, is challenging as it represents a variety of experiences which do not lend themselves to simple classification. As an individual experience, however, it can be conceptualised as a process involving different pathways and outcomes, defined with reference to a cut-off point or an event occurring at a given age. Alternatively, if retirement forms part of a broader inquiry about how people's social, psychological and economic well-being evolve in later life, then its meaning and definitional boundaries will relate to a broader spectrum of events and transitions occurring across the life course (Künemund and Kolland, 2007). In some senses then, retirement is more a construct than a clearly defined concept and can be used interchangeably to represent different things – a specific ceremony marking the end of a working life, a period of a person's work life history during which they prepare for this departure, a change of social role from worker to retiree. As such, its meaning will be fluid, depending not only upon individual trajectories but also on macro-level influences such as labour market fluctuations or socially prescribed, normative expectations about the life course.

The notion of retirement is a relatively recent social phenomenon, coming into its own as a singular phase or transition in the life course during the mid-twentieth century with the establishment of organised social security systems which provided some form of income security in old age. Prior to this, and with the exception of some military, church or benevolent pension provisions, people did not generally have the opportunity or expectation of withdrawing from the workforce but worked until they were no longer able to do so. One explanation for the emergence of retirement as a social institution is that certain conditions need to be present, such as a system of economic production which is so efficient that it can make a surplus; institutional structures which enable this profit to be redistributed to people who are not economically active; a society which will accept the idea that part of the life course does not have to be dedicated to paid work; and, finally, the possibility of living long enough to be able to take advantage of a period of life without work (Hill, 2007; Midwinter, 1997).

Some gerontologists offer what can be considered as a functionalist explanation for the historical emergence of retirement. As such, retirement is understood as a mechanism which regulates the flow of workers into and out of the labour market, reduces unemployment or creates places in the labour market so that younger people can replace a more costly, older work force. Victor (1994) suggests, for example, that the emergence of retirement at a fixed age in twentieth-century Britain was due not only to the development of pension provisions, but also to demands for labour market changes: an economic recession, reduced demand for certain skills, and pressure for older workers to retire and make way for younger cohorts. Linked to this explanation is the idea that retirement marks a broader process of 'institutionalisation' of the life course. Despite individualised experiences of the retirement process, these nonetheless occur in sequences shaped by the needs of the broader economic and labour force environments of industrialised societies. Retirement thus becomes an anticipated and socially normal phase of the life course, representing a form of social organisation based on age (Kohli, 1986). In the contemporary period, and particularly since the 1970s, an increasing trend towards early exit and early retirement from the labour force, coupled with increasing life expectancy, have consolidated retirement even more as a distinct phase of the life course, although it still remains as a mechanism through which to pursue broader economic objectives. Extending rather than reducing the age of retirement, for example, has now become a prime policy focus in several

retirement

industrialised countries as one means of meeting the costs of pension provisions in a context of population ageing.

In the field of social gerontology, the phenomenon of retirement has become an area of multidisciplinary interest. Post-war gerontological research frequently portrayed retirement as an inevitably difficult and problematic transition, detrimental to social relations and with negative psychological and health implications, brought about through a loss of status and self-esteem and an increased risk of poverty. This perspective was evidenced through the work of prominent gerontologists, geriatricians and sociologists of the time, notably Sheldon (1948) and Townsend (1957), particularly in their work on older people's lives in the UK communities of Wolverhampton and Bethnal Green. As a challenge to this position, other studies emerged which portrayed a more complex picture of the motives for leaving paid work and the outcomes of the transition to retirement. For example, it was found that ill health could be a cause rather than a consequence of retirement, and motivations to retire could also be linked to poor working conditions.

Although emerging gerontological theories during the late 1950s and throughout the following two decades were again influential in reinforcing the representation of retirement as a problematic transition – particularly role and disengagement theories which emphasised the loss of role and reduced social contacts and networks – other theorists were changing this perception. At the individual level, the emergence of continuity theory posited that individuals would supplement one type of activity and role with others, preserving a sense of self-esteem and continued engagement in social relations. The development of critical gerontology during the 1980s and 1990s, in particular the political economy perspective, drew attention to the role of broader, macro-level social, political and economic factors in shaping the retirement experience as a whole, particularly in terms of engendering inequalities between or within groups. Somewhat in contrast, the more recent influence of postmodern theorising has posited retirement as a positive phase of the life course as individuals profit from their power to choose and diversify their lifestyles through increased consumerism.

A distinction is now also being drawn between pre-retirement and post-retirement experiences. Ageing research on the pre-retirement phase has placed an emphasis on understanding the consequences of unemployment and technological innovations in the workplace; the role of pension provisions in retirement decision making, in particular the link between occupational pensions and retirement decisions (Arkani and Gough, 2006); the potentially disempowering nature of the retirement process itself if individuals can do little to alter its timing or inevitability; the increasing diversity of pathways to retirement, which are shaped by experiences of unemployment, redundancy, competing social care responsibilities or options for early retirement; and the different patterns of adjustment to retirement. For the post-retirement phase, there is increasing recognition that retirement may also represent a positive and desired goal in itself and one of an opportunity for engagement in new activities, particularly since more recent cohorts of retirees are generally healthier and wealthier than their predecessors.

These positive connotations notwithstanding, one of the more challenging conclusions to stem from contemporary research on the post-retirement phase is that it will be a product of pre-retirement circumstance, with variations and inequalities across gender, class, occupational status and birth cohort, as well as between retirees and those still active in the labour market. The links between retirement and gender continue to be a major area of interest, notably because of women's markedly different life history and work patterns when compared to those of men, and from socially determined role expectations which have traditionally considered retirement as a more significant life marker for men than for women. More recently, researchers have questioned whether current policy and legislative initiatives to facilitate the retention of older workers will have any impact in changing previous trends of early retirement or withdrawal from the labour force, pointing to the uncertain role of employers in influencing retirement decisions, questioning the real impact that legislation will actually have in practice, and asking whether it will not be more effective to recognise and support alternative pathways from work to retirement (Phillipson, 2004; Vickerstaff, 2006).

Künemund and Kolland (2007) also succinctly point out the significance that retirement will have for individuals, and its potential impact upon society in the future will depend on multiple factors, not least changes to broader economic circumstances which condition provisions for social security benefits; opportunities for early withdrawal from the labour force or the retention of workers in the marketplace; shifts in employer attitudes and workplace conditions; normative expectations and the prevalence of ageist attitudes or assumptions about later life workers; increasing consumerism and its power to offer a choice between work and leisure; and finally, from an individual perspective, the importance that people themselves wish to attribute to work in

retirement

their lives, and the constraints encountered in having to decide between work or retirement for family, health or income reasons.

See also: Ageing, Cohort, Gender, Gerontology, Pension, Population Ageing, Social Relations

REFERENCES

Künemund, H. and Kolland, F. (2007) Work and retirement, in J. Bond, S. Peace, F. Dittmann-Kohli and G. Westerhof (eds), *Ageing in Society* (3rd edition). London: Sage. pp. 167–185.

Midwinter, E. (1997) *Pensioned Off: Retirement and Income Examined.* Buckingham: Open University Press.

Social Exclusion

Feelings or objective situations in which individuals consider themselves progressively cut off or marginalised from mainstream society.

Although the concept of social exclusion has more traditionally been associated with poverty, it is now used to describe a broader range of social issues which are indicative of some form of deprivation, such as unemployment, poor skills, inadequate income, poor health, loneliness or social isolation. Underpinning these forms of deprivation is a concern that they form part of a process which leads to inequalities between people. This broader definition has led to an investigation of exclusion across a variety of domains – education, health, housing, employment, social and leisure activities, communication technologies – and within diverse populations defined, for example, in terms of their age, ethnicity, class, gender or generation.

The concept has been further developed by distinguishing what opportunities or constraints people may encounter when it comes to being able to participate in the labour market, to purchase products, to make informed decisions, to be free to exercise choice when it comes to political activity, and to feel socially included through interactions with communities of family, friends and other groups (Hills et al., 2002). These refinements suggest that social exclusion will occur when social or citizenship rights are not fully recognised or cannot be exercised, either in relation to the labour market, legal systems of representation, the welfare state or the informal institutions of family and community. In short, social exclusion is a multidimensional concept with economic, political and social aspects, and refers not only to what resources individuals may or may not have, but also to what they are able to do or not do.

There has been a longstanding tradition within the field of sociology to associate the concept of social exclusion with a broadly Durkheimian frame of reference where it represents a person's social or normative isolation from wider society. As such, it is related to notions of anomie and concerns regarding the preservation of social cohesion. The application of the concept became more prominent during the last decades of the twentieth century, particularly in the European context, as a reaction against the growing perception that increasing income inequalities were an acceptable outcome of market-driven economies (Room, 1995). Particularly influential in this process was the agreement reached in Lisbon in 2000 among European Union countries to develop common objectives to promote inclusion, eradicate poverty by 2010 and develop policies to combat social exclusion.

In the field of ageing research, the concept of social exclusion has appeared fairly recently. Traditionally, the focus has been more on understanding the risks of poverty and deprivation associated with old age. Since the Second World War research has linked poverty and deprivation in later life to the life course and the cumulative effect of lifelong inequalities, a perspective which was to develop further with the emergence of political economy approaches to ageing (see, for example, the work of scholars such as Estes (1979), Walker (1981) and Phillipson (1982) mentioned elsewhere in this book). Further developments, particularly through the work of Townsend (1981) in the UK, were to emphasise older people's 'engineered' dependency and marginalisation, which were attributed to factors such as an imposed retirement age, restricted social roles and inadequate retirement income (factors which today would be recognised as different facets of social exclusion), exclusion from the labour market, from the social domains of everyday life and from the capacity to exercise economic choice. More recently, social exclusion has been discussed in relation to the effects of increasing income inequalities between older people themselves, particularly when comparing sources and levels of retirement income. Along similar lines, the concept has also been linked to ageist processes which marginalise older people from the labour force through early retirement or redundancy measures, or which favour the recruitment of a younger and less expensive workforce. This form of exclusion may in turn contribute to reduced economic resources prior to retirement, leading to increased risks of poverty or income vulnerability in later life. Finally, researchers interested in the physical environment are now also considering exclusion in relation to older people's abilities or opportunities to access and use neighbourhood and community facilities.

Historically, then, since the post-war focus on poverty and deprivation, contemporary understandings of the notion of social exclusion in later life have come to represent a broad range of issues – exclusion not just from the labour market, but also from relationships of social and physical engagement with people and places as well as impoverished access to material resources.

Taking a broad approach, Scharf et al. (2004) argue that there are specific considerations involved in trying to apply the concept of social exclusion to older people as a specific group. The concept has traditionally been associated with the idea of exclusion from the labour market, a focus which, in itself, generally precludes older people who have withdrawn from economic activity. Furthermore, although other age groups may be able to 'move in and out' of social exclusion, shifting from being homeless to housed or from being poor to economically stable, for example, this flexibility is not as obvious for older people who, with increasing age, will be more likely to experience reduced income and increasing physical impediments. Finally, they argue that the concept needs to be extended to home and neighbourhood environments which, if not adapted to the physical and mobility needs of later life, can become sources of exclusion if they inhibit a physical and social engagement with others. A sense of 'belonging' in later life may also be lost if older people find themselves in community or neighbourhood environments which undergo significant environmental change, such as the closure of local amenities, or significant local population movement so that familiar social and community networks are affected.

Along with attempts to clarify the conceptual meaning of social exclusion and to identify what it means in particular to older people, researchers have also focused on measuring its prevalence, and on identifying the factors which are the most likely to increase older people's chances of experiencing exclusion. For example, research has demonstrated that the likelihood of experiencing multiple forms of social exclusion will be greater for very old people who live alone and have no children, who are tenants with low income and who find it difficult to be mobile and communicate with others because they cannot access transport or a telephone (Barnes et al., 2006). Other contributing factors include the extent of service provision for health, shopping and transport facilities (Kenway et al., 2005).

This work has led not only to an understanding that social exclusion can be attributed to a combination of factors but also to the development of multiple deprivation or multidimensional indicators designed to capture this complexity. In the UK, the English Longitudinal Study of Ageing, for example, has been used to identify seven dimensions of social exclusion. These are exclusion from: social relationships, cultural and civic activities, access to basic services, neighbourhood life and financial and material goods or products (Barnes et al., 2006). Multiple deprivation indicators generally serve the purpose of showing just how much access older people have to material and social resources, and can include the measurement of things such as educational and employment qualifications and experiences, the quality of an individual's housing environment and whether they possess consumer durables (Evandrou, 2000). Multidimensional measurements which are more sensitive to later life circumstances, such as that developed as part of the UK's Growing Older Programme, again reflect the broad range of factors at play. Scharf et al. (2004, 2005), for example, devised a multidimensional measure of social exclusion comprising five axes: exclusion from material resources, social relations (including feelings of loneliness), civic activities, basic services and neighbourhood environments.

Although such applications clearly enhance our understanding of social exclusion in later life, there is still debate about whether individuals in fact create situations of exclusion for themselves or whether they are victims of broader structural factors beyond their control, such as government policies on employment or retirement income. From a policy perspective, keeping the issue of social exclusion on the political agenda has also proved a point of debate (Age Concern, 2008), particularly when such a strong emphasis is given to the positive and, by implication, inclusive nature of the ageing experience. From a cross-national comparative level, a recent study on poverty and the social exclusion of older people in the European context has also indicated that the social exclusion of older people is not recognised as a major issue for several European Union members states, partly because it is viewed as a problem which affects other age groups (Hoff, 2008). In addition, the empirical assessment of social exclusion has come under some scrutiny because of the complexity of measures and indices employed, particularly because they still leave unanswered the question of where the limits to acceptable and unacceptable levels of exclusion should be drawn.

It can therefore be said that although the concept of social exclusion stems from a longstanding tradition of understanding the causes of social and economic marginalisation for people as a whole, it is only more recently that it has found application in the field of ageing research. Recognising that older people's experiences of exclusion stem beyond poverty and material impoverishment to include other dimensions unique to later life has contributed to the advancement of theoretical insights and empirical applications, and is sharpening the focus on social exclusion as an experience to be reckoned with as people age.

See also: *Ageing, Ethnicity, Gender, Housing, Loneliness, Retirement*

FURTHER READING

A useful link for readers on the policy developments and outcomes of the 2000 Lisbon agreement within the European Union relating to social exclusion can be found at www.ec.europa.eu/employment_social/spsi/index_en.htm (accessed 20 October 2008). For further information on the UK's Growing Older Programme, which was funded by the Economic and Social Research Council, readers can access the weblink: www.shef.ac.uk/uni/projects/gop/

REFERENCES

Barnes, M., Blom, A., Cox, K. and Lessof, C. (2006) *The Social Exclusion of Older People: Evidence from the First Wave of the English Longitudinal Study of Ageing (ELSA). Final Report.* Available at: www.communities.gov.uk/documents/corporate/pdf/143564 (accessed 19 March 2008).

Hills, J., Le Grand, J. and Piachaud, D. (eds) (2002) *Understanding Social Exclusion.* Oxford: Oxford University Press.

Room, G. (ed.) (1995) *Beyond the Threshold.* Bristol: The Policy Press.

Scharf, T., Phillipson, C. and Smith, A. (2004) Poverty and social exclusion – growing older in deprived urban neighbourhoods, in A. Walker and C. Hennessy (eds), *Growing Older: Quality of Life in Old Age.* Maidenhead: Open University Press. pp. 81–106.

Social Relations

Social integration processes and mechanisms with distinct, multidimensional aspects, including networks, support types and exchanges, and support quality.

Social relations, at the most basic level, are necessary for an organism to become human. Social integration, a foundational aspect of social relations, is an essential and constitutive element of every human being's personhood and existence. It involves micro processes and mechanisms observed in primary and secondary socialisation (e.g. language learning and the acquisition of perceptions, values, etc.) as well as processes and mechanisms of social control and legitimation (e.g. economic relations that structure opportunities for individuals) at the macro level. Social integration, hence, may be thought of as a universal human act. It constitutes an essential building block upon which development occurs throughout the life course, including old age.

As a key element to human development and personhood, social integration nevertheless may play out in culturally distinct ways. The manifestation of social integration is multidimensional and occurs at multiple levels (micro and macro). Much of the gerontological literature emphasises three elements of social integration in the study of social relations over the life course and in old age: the structure of personal networks, types of support available and quality of relationships. A considerable amount of research has examined the significance of these aspects of social relations for quality of life among older adults.

Network structure. The structure of a social network involves four distinct dimensions: size, composition, contact frequency and geographic proximity. Social networks may be thought of as a key resource over the life course, a form of social capital that potentially serves as a source of help in times of trouble, a source of comfort in times of pain, and a source of information in times of need. Older age is associated with smaller, less frequently seen, and less proximal networks that have a higher proportion of kin (Ajrouch et al., 2001; Mardsen, 1987).

social relations

Older adults seem to have fewer social resources than their younger counterparts. On the other hand, quantity does not guarantee quality, and it may be that older individuals discard the 'draining' aspects that accompany larger networks that are more proximal and more frequently seen. Furthermore, they may derive more satisfaction from relationships with family members than with others, as hypothesised in socio-emotional selectivity theory (Carstensen, 1993), and as suggested in the hierarchical preference finding that older adults choose family members first in situations of need (Cantor et al., 1994). It is also likely to be the case that contact with peers may decline with age due to health problems or moving, and that with age, peers and family members may be lost through death and not replaced (Antonucci and Akiyama, 1987). Thus, ageing well may be threatened on the one hand, as opportunities for contacts and social transactions decrease, yet enhanced on the other hand if older adults focus on those relationships that they find most beneficial.

Types of support exhanges. Social relations also involve various types of support exchanges. Support types include instrumental (e.g. transportation), emotional (e.g. ability to confide), and informational (e.g. advice) (Antonucci, 1985). The types of support available may also be influenced by personal and situational characteristics, and perhaps most significantly affect health and well-being. Each type of support operates in a unique way. According to Cohen and Wills (1985), emotional support provides a buffer to wide-ranging categories of stress while instrumental support is effective when the support provided coincides with the stress experienced (i.e. financial help in the face of poverty). The perception of the support type available is found to be more predictive of well-being than actual, objective support.

As societies around the world face significant demographic changes, improved health and increased life expectancies suggest that older adults may often play an active role in the lives of younger members of society. For instance, increased roles in the family sphere may include grandparents being dynamically involved in their grandchildren's lives, sometimes actually responsible for the daily care and nurturing of their grandchildren. Moreover, older adults may contribute to public life, drawing on their long practice of working out problems and finding solutions. Serving as consultants, mentors and/or advisors, older adults are uniquely positioned to contribute to the needs of all societies, particularly those experiencing crises. Through their lived experience, older adults often have rich resources for recovery. Thus, while social relations often refer to elders as primarily in need of receiving care, older adults may also provide ongoing critical care to others, including family and members of the greater society.

Support quality. Social relations include a quality dimension. Although positive and warm aspects of relations often come to mind when first considering the quality of social relations, negative dimensions are also important. Negative aspects include conflict, irritations and, at the most extreme, abuse. Social relations can be cumulatively negative as well as cumulatively positive. Additionally, positive and negative qualities in social relations are likely to coexist. Among elders, negative social interactions may affect well-being more strongly than do positive relations (Rook, 1984). Some relations may produce a negative effect by supporting or encouraging behaviours detrimental to health and well-being. Such network members are those who encourage health-threatening behaviour, such as drug use, drinking and poor eating habits, or those who discourage exercise. Thus, although social support and social integration are associated with better health in a general sense, the association is likely to be multifaceted and to vary with specific construct indicators.

The nature and influence of social relations are likely to vary across cultural and national contexts. For instance, in societies that are more industrialised and provide high levels of governmental resources to older adults, social relations between older parents and adults children tend to hinge on more emotional aspects of relations, as opposed to obligatory ties (Ajrouch et al., 2007). On the other hand, social relations in Arab-speaking countries between older parents and adult children are traditionally shaped by a patriarchal contract, where family constitutes the sole source of support and security for elders (Olmsted, 2005), emphasising an obligation towards older parents over emotional ties. Within societies social relations may also vary between cultural groups depending on whether the group is part of the dominant culture, or is a minority or immigrant. Norms and ideas about social relations become important on both practical and theoretical grounds. In the realm of practical application, as Daatland and Herlofson (2003) suggest, gathering information about a group's values allows for an understanding of preferred lifestyles and behaviours that contribute to a high quality of life. Additionally, they represent an opportunity to consider where attitudes are changing and where they remain the same.

A final note is necessary about social relations at the societal level with regard to older populations, particularly within advanced industrialised societies. Dannefer (2008) points to the impact that social relations have in the social construction of age. Of particular concern is how social relations structure and organise individuals' perceptions and values to accept ageism, one manifestation of which is the assumption that elders are passive and largely unproductive care recipients. While that is often true, their active role as caregivers, and the increasing trend of providing various kinds of economic or social capital to adult offspring and others, is often disregarded. Similar propositions about larger processes that confer status on groups of people have been discussed concerning the world of work and its effect on individual and personal outcomes such as health status (Kohn and Słomczynski, 1990; Marmot, 2004).

In sum, social relations constitute a basic building block for understanding processes of human development and ageing. Social integration and the multidimensional ways in which social relations at both the macro and micro levels play out have great implications for older adult experiences and well-being.

See also: *Ageing, Ageism, Care, Quality of Life, Social Support*

REFERENCES

Ajrouch, K. J., Akiyama, H. and Antonucci, T. C. (2007) Cohort differences in social relations among the elderly, in H. W. Wahl, C. Tesch-Romer and A. Hoff (eds), *Emergence of New Person–Environment Dynamics in Old Age: A Multidisciplinary Exploration.* Amityville, NY: Baywood Publishing Company. pp. 43–64.

Ajrouch, K. J., Antonucci, T. C. and Janevic, M. R. (2001) Social networks among blacks and whites: the interaction between race and age. *Journal of Gerontology: Social Sciences*, 56B(2): S112–S118.

Antonucci, T. C. (1985) Personal characteristics, social networks and social behaviour, in R. H. Binstock and E. Shanas (eds), *Handbook of Ageing and the Social Sciences.* New York: Van Nostrand Reinhold. pp. 94–128.

Antonucci, T. C. and Akiyama, H. (1987) Social networks in adult life and a preliminary examination of the convoy model. *Journal of Gerontology*, 42(5): 519–527.

Cantor, M. H., Brennan, M. and Sainz, A. (1994) The importance of ethnicity in the social support systems of older New Yorkers: a longitudinal perspective (1970–1990). *Journal of Gerontological Social Work*, 22: 95–128.

Carstensen, L. L. (1993) Motivation for social contact across the life span: a theory of socioemotional selectivity. *Nebraska Symposium on Motivation, Developmental Perspectives on Motivation* (volume 40). Lincoln, NB: University of Nebraska Press.

Cohen, S. and Wills, T. A. (1985) Stress, social support, and the buffering hypothesis. *Psychology Bulletin*, 98: 310–357.

Daatland, S. O. and Herlofsen, K. (2003) Norms and ideals about elder care, in A. Lowenstein and J. Ogg (eds), *OASIS Final Report old Age and Autonomy: The Role of Service Systems and Intergenerational Family Solidarity*. Haifa, Israel: Center for Research and Study of Aging, The University of Haifa, Israel. pp. 127–164.

Dannefer, D. (2008) The waters we swim: everyday social processes, macrostructural realities, and human ageing, in K. W. Schaie and R. P. Abeles (eds), *Social Structures and Ageing Individuals: Continuing Challenges*. New York: Springer. pp. 3–22.

Kohn, M. K. and Słomczynski, K. M. (1990) *Social Structure and Self-direction: A Comparative Analysis of the United States and Poland*. Cambridge: Blackwell.

Mardsen, P. V. (1987) Core discussion networks of Americans. *American Sociological Review*, 52: 122–131.

Marmot, M. (2004) *Status Syndrome: How Your Social Standing Directly Affects Your Health and Life Expectancy*. London: Bloomsbury.

Olmsted, J. C. (2005) Gender, ageing, and the evolving patriarchal contract. *Feminist Economics*, 11(2): 53–78.

Rook, K. S. (1984) The negative side of intimate interaction: impact on psychological well-being. *Journal of Personality and Social Psychology*, 46: 1097–1108.

Social Support

> *The exchange of different types of resources channelled through supportive relationships.*

The discussion of social support is linked to considerations of *social networks*. It is important to distinguish between these concepts. Social networks are vital for social support because social networks are the structural elements of social support (House and Kahn, 1985). Social support refers to the functional content of relationships (the types of help received by individuals – instrumental, emotional or financial, for example). Grey (2009: 6) defines social support as an *outcome* of social capital (an array of social contacts that give access to social, emotional and practical support) rather than an element of it.

The functional components or defining attributes of social support primarily consist of emotional support (provision of care, love and trust);

instrumental support (provision of tangible goods and services); informational support (information provided at times of stress); and appraisal support (the communication of information which is relevant to self-evaluation-affirmational support) (Kahn and Antonucci, 1980).

Early attempts to define social support led to narrow definitions such as 'gratification of a person's needs through environmental supplies of social support' (Kaplan et al., 1977, as quoted in Krause, 2001). Such definitions focused on one or two components of support, such as emotional or practical support. Increasingly, the focus has altered to place emphasis on the operational aspects of the concept and, consequently, different measures of social support. As Krause (2001) illustrates from a study of the literature, it is perceived or subjective support that primarily has a consistent effect on health and well-being. As Krause (2001: 274) goes on to state, it is the anticipated support (the belief that significant others will provide assistance in the future should the need arise) and negative interaction (unpleasant social encounters that are characterised by rejection and a lack of reciprocity) that have a greater influence on health and well-being than received support or indicators of social embeddedness (i.e. the depth and strength of relational ties between people of the network).

Generally, there are commonalities in the definitions used. For example, there is a reciprocal element in the definition. Other common features inherent in a definition of social support are a variety of both structural and functional components, such as network size and density, as well as emotional, practical and perceptual assistance.

Due to differences in the theoretical bases of the construct (e.g. exchange theory, disengagement theory or activity theory), the measurement of social support varies according to the nature of the social support measured. The dimensions used to measure support are inconsistent and few measurements are replicated across cultures and ages. Different measures are often used depending on the emphasis of a particular aspect of the concept.

A considerable body of research has demonstrated the link between social support and 'successful' ageing. Older adults with supportive social networks experience better health, both physically, and psychologically, than those without such support (Ajrouch et al., 2001). Social support is an important factor in coping with hospitalisation and recovery and admission to residential care. Older people who suffer a reduction in their social network through bereavement, redundancies etc., are likely to have reduced social support and consequently poorer health. It is unclear whether the association between health and social support is because social support helps to maintain health or because people who are healthier are also advantaged in other ways (cognitive ability, education, wealth, etc.) and thus have better access to social support. The concept has relevance and applicability in identifying those individuals who are vulnerable to ill health and isolation.

Social network measures have also been used extensively in practice, for example through the tool with social work practitioners in the UK (Wenger and Tucker, 2002). There has been widespread application in epidemiological research, clinical and social assessments and in evaluations of targeted support.

Although social support is discussed in a positive sense, there are also negative aspects to it. Individuals in the social network may provide intense support to the extent that they do not allow autonomy and independence or undermine self-esteem.

Social support is influenced by gender, class and housing tenure (Grey, 2009). Women have larger social networks and tend to receive more support over their life span than men. Social network size and structure appear to increase among women whose life circumstances call for more support (e.g. recent widowhood). Men tend to maintain close, intimate relationships with only a few people, primarily with their spouses. Being married has been found to be more protective for men than for women.

An earlier criticism of the literature was that few studies looked at representative samples across cultures or ethnic groups. Social support is experienced across cultures, and racial and ethnic groups, in similar ways. For example, family are important in providing global support. Yet there are specific instances, such as among African Americans, where kin as well as non-kin and the church are important sources of support. Differences in social support among ethnic groups can be attributed to factors other than ethnicity. For example, wealthy families may chose to buy-in support rather than family members themselves taking care of an older relative.

The decline in social support over generations and solidarity between the generations are continued themes in the gerontological literature (Arber and Attias-Donfut, 2000). Yet research has shown that different types of support may be distributed across different types of relationship and different generations. In a study by Phillipson et al. (2001), 'personal communities' with a reliance on friends rather than kin were a feature, but only in certain respects and functions of social support. The

social support

research sought to assess whom older people identified as 'important' in their lives and the role such people played in the provision and receipt of support. The study found that respondents do not mobilise the whole of their social network when looking for support. Instead, a section of the social network is drawn upon (mainly immediate family) to provide specific kinds of assistance. In addition, locally available friends offer complementary or alternative sources of help. The study also reported clear evidence of older people being active in reciprocal exchanges across their networks, particularly in respect of confiding in and talking to people about health issues, but much less so in relation to instrumental support, such as help with household chores, transport and financial advice. Poor health may limit the extent of reciprocity.

Social support changes across the adult life course, usually with the shrinking of structural support. For example, the size of a social network reduces in later life through widowhood, loss of friends, etc. In relation to the life course, one study (Bourne et al., 2007) found that a person's ability to develop and maintain social support networks is associated with cognitive ability from early life. Further, the lack of relationships with current cognitive ability suggests that change in cognitive ability may not affect social support. Given that lower levels of social support are a risk factor for dementia, it becomes plausible to propose that people with less social support are more vulnerable to cognitive decline. The significance of social support is also evident in the literature on well-being and health, depression, coping behaviour and the recognition of self-worth.

The concept of social support has been described as 'illusive' (Krause, 2001) and in need of a well-articulated conceptual framework. There are a number of critiques in the literature of the concept, measurement and utility of social support. For example:

- The linkages made in a number of studies between social support and social networks have led to ambiguities in each concept being compounded.
- There are few longitudinal studies of social support; most research has been cross-sectional. Mapping social support across time is crucial if a true picture of generational solidarities is to be found. Appraising and reappraising social relationships is a continual activity and hence the types and timings of support may change with time. The timing of support is under-reported in studies. However, there are studies looking at times of stress and types of support

(in relation to bereavement, for example, when practical and emotional support may be necessary simultaneously). The place of support in the sequence of a stressful event is also less reported.

- There is a misconception that social networks become supportive and move to care networks or provide care support. The transformation of social networks into social support at a particular time, however, is not guaranteed (Keating et al., 2003).
- The cultural context of social support in relation to the beliefs and values that people hold about support is increasing in studies, but on the whole the cultural context has been ignored. Most measures were also developed in the USA and are culturally specific. Similarly, many of the early measures were developed with younger people in mind.
- The environmental context in which social support is measured is also a key factor which has been overlooked in the literature. Social support may also include broader dimensions such as the activities to promote independence and reciprocity. Detractors to social support included institutional regimens and routines, dependence and activities that promote isolation.
- Many studies measure global support rather than support at particular times and of particular types.
- The negative aspects of support have been underestimated in the measures of support.

See also: *Ageing, Bereavement, Care, Dementia, Ethnicity, Gender, Generations, Housing, Independence, Social Relations, Social Theories of Ageing*

FURTHER READING

Kahn, R. and Antonucci, T. (1980) Convoys over the lifecourse: attachment roles and social support, in P. Baltes and O. Brim (eds), *Life Span Development and Behavior*, (Volume 3). New York: Academic Press.

Phillipson, C., Bernard, M., Phillips, J. and Ogg, J. (2001) *The Family and Community Life of Older People: Social Networks and Social Support in Three Urban Areas*. London: Routledge.

REFERENCES

Ajrouch, K., Antonucci, T. and Janevic, M. (2001) Social networks among blacks and whites: the interaction between race and age. *Journal of Gerontology: Social Sciences*, 56B(2): S112–SI18.

Arber, S. and Attias-Donfut, C. (2000) *The Myth of Generational Conflict: The Family and State in Ageing Societies*. London: Routledge.

social support

Bourne, V., Fox, H., Starr, J., Deary, I. and Whalley, L. (2007) Social support in later life: examining the roles of childhood and adulthood cognition. *Personality and Individual Differences*, 43: 937–948.

Grey, A. (2009) The social capital of older people. *Ageing and Society*, 29: 5–31.

House, J. and Kahn, R. (1985) Measures and concepts of social support, in S. Cohen and L. Syme (eds), *Social Support and Health*. New York: Academic Press.

Kahn, R. and Antonucci, T. (1980) Convoys over the lifecourse: attachment roles and social support, in P. Baltes and O. Brim (eds), *Life Span Development and Behavior*, (Volume 3). New York: Academic Press.

Keating, N., Otfinowski, P., Wenger, C., Fast, J. and Derksen, L. (2003) Understanding the caring capacity of informal: networks for frail seniors – a case for care networks. *Ageing and Society*, 23(1): 115–127.

Krause, N. (2001) Social support, in R. H. Binstock and L. K. George (eds), *Handbook of Ageing and Social Sciences* (5th edition). New York: Academic Press. pp. 273–290.

Phillipson, C., Bernard, M., Phillips, J. and Ogg, J. (2001) *The Family and Community Life of Older People: Social Networks and Social Support in Three Urban Areas*. London: Routledge.

Wenger, G. C. and Tucker, I. (2002) Using network variation in practice: identification of support network type. *Health and Social Care in the Community*, 10(1): 28–35.

Social Theories of Ageing

Social theories of ageing explain the complexity and diversity of the ageing process in its social context.

No one theory exists to explain the process of ageing yet theory is increasingly important in gerontology. 'Theory is an attempt, an initial step in the process of developing an account of the *how* and the *why* leading to *what* we have observed in our research' (Bengtson et al., 2006: 3). Theories have ranged from those at the micro, individual level, with an emphasis on individual behaviour, to the macro, societal level, such as explaining phenomena relating to social security systems.

In a seminal article, Bengston et al. (1997) highlight the different generations of theories in gerontology. First generation or early theory relied on individual adjustment as a basis, with social factors taken as a given. Many of the approaches developed from social psychology and focused on activity and life satisfaction. As Phillipson and Baars (2007) comment, the first phase of theory development, from the late 1940s to the 1960s, concentrated on ageing as an individual and social problem as the demographic impact of an ageing population was assessed in the western world. The problematisation of old age and its medicalisation contributed to the development of the 'disengagement theory' advocated by Cumming and Henry (1961). Based on a functionalist paradigm, disengagement theory argued that older people withdrew from mainstream social roles as they aged, through retirement and widowhood, for example. This was seen as a natural, normal and universal outcome (Phillipson and Baars, 2007). Alongside this theory lay 'activity theory' (Havighurst, 1957), again based on a functionalist-structuralist paradigm, advocating the necessity of keeping older adults as active as possible within society. Although the latter had wider appeal in its application, both early theories were severely criticised. They did, however, generate a new set of theories which had a powerful impact on the course of gerontology over the years.

One such was modernisation theory (Burgess, 1960), which advocated that the status of the elderly declined with increasing industrialisation, technological advancement and urbanisation. Another was continuity theory (Havighurst, 1968), which argued that as people grow old they are inclined to retain the same habits, personalities and lifestyle they developed in earlier years. New roles are substituted for old roles to maintain ways of adapting to the environment. Such theories consider individuals to have agency over their actions and the capacity to substitute roles. A third was age stratification theory (Riley et al., 1972), which argued that individuals in the same cohort took on similar roles as they progressed through the life course.

As theory developed from the 1970s to the 1990s, the focus was on 'the elderly' as a collective category and on structural circumstances rather than on the individual. Consequently, individuals were seen as active participants in their world. This generation of theory concentrated on bringing the 'social' back into the equation, and its application led to more positive outcomes for older people. Theory in this period comprised social exchange theory, proposed by Dowd (1975), which was premised on the basis that there is a cost–benefit relationship between the individual and society. As the economic, physical and social resources of an individual decrease, then the costs of engaging with the older person become greater than the benefits; the balance can only be restored with an increase in the older person's resources. Another theory in this period was life-course theory (Neugarten and Hagestad, 1976), which remains influential within gerontology. It bridges the micro and macro considerations of ageing. The approach also focuses on ageing rather than old age, and provides a broader definition of ageing from biological, social, psychological and cultural perspectives.

The importance of social structure and a rejection of the 'grand' theories providing a homogeneous view of ageing led to an important set of theories in the 1970s and 1980s. More positive views of ageing emerged and a tranche of studies illustrated that ageing was a diverse experience that could be positive and active. Marxist and feminist perspectives increasingly shaped the development of theory. The political economy of ageing as well as feminist perspectives on ageing (Calasanti, 1999), based on critical theory, used age, race, class and gender to examine power differentials in society. The political economy of age explored the social construction of ageing both in the USA and the UK (Estes, 1979; Phillipson, 1982), the 'problem' and solution of old age being viewed from the perspective of those in power at the time. Such political and economic structures limited opportunities and choices in later life. Subsequently, the political economy perspective became one of a group of theories labelled 'critical gerontology'. Critical gerontology offers a rich framework within which to view and better understand old age, focusing on both the social inequality and the humanistic side of ageing. Humanistic gerontology (Moody, 1993) focuses on the meaning and interpretative dimensions of old age.

The postmodern paradigm in gerontological theory has taken on board past criticisms, making ageing a more positive experience. It also provides a cultural framework for ageing, with an emphasis on the body, consumption and globalisation (Gilleard and Higgs, 2000).

The theoretical hot spots in gerontology have shifted from theory that explains ageing in relation to the nation state to theory that incorporates the actions of global stakeholders and institutions. Globalisation and ageing have become a focus for theorising. Phillipson and Baars (2007) argue that this perspective challenges the development of theory in ageing by challenging the life course as 'normal ageing', which is out of sync on a global basis, with different life events and images as well as cultural meanings associated with old age. Theorising is a reflective activity shaping empirical investigations. It is a way of organising what we think we know about ageing. It is critical activity. Theories are made to explain certain phenomena in ageing (e.g. inequality, social interaction). However, there is also no theory in biology that explains the process of ageing completely.

One of the key challenges in gerontology is to develop a theory that can help us explain the processes of ageing. The lack of research driven by theory is a concern that has been expressed repeatedly. The need for theory in social gerontology is crucial in explaining, linking and interpreting the findings of research, in making sense of how older people experience later life and in providing the bigger picture, yet progress in gerontology has lagged behind other disciplines. Some would suggest that this reluctance to engage in theory has resulted from the vociferous critique of early theoretical developments in the field of gerontology, namely disengagement theory. Early theories were also oversimplified, with little recognition of the differences between people's experiences of ageing. Similarly, most of the funding for gerontological research has centred on the practical application of research rather than the development of theory, yet practice needs theory to connect and make findings applicable. We need to connect the micro and macro in our theoretical advancement and this is a challenge for the twenty-first century (Phillipson and Baars, 2007). Bengtson et al. (1997) also argue that it is essential that developments in knowledge about the social aspects of ageing are cumulative, systematic and incremental.

Putnam (2002) argues that most theories of ageing do not directly address ageing with physical impairment or the cumulative experience of disability over the life course. The debate within disability services around the social model of disability has not been translated into the medically focused nature of social theories of ageing and it is only recently that the paradigms of independence and rights have come under the gerontological gaze.

McMullin (2000: 21) argues that gerontological literature has become dominated by sociological theories of ageing and calls for greater diversity in theorising that 'fully integrates class, age, gender and ethnicity/race as power relations that structure social life'.

Relatively few theories have embraced change and are truly multidisciplinary; for many scholars there is a risk in going down this path.

Hagestad and Dannefer (2001: 6) argue that the individual has been the main focus of theorising in ageing and that macro theory has been abandoned. This trend is a result of 'late modernity's emphasis on individuals and their agency, a medicalisation of old age and strong pressures from professionals and politicians'. The contribution of globalisation and technological change to theory at the macro level has consequently been underplayed. Yet Bengtson et al. (2006) see this focus on the macro perspective as the way forward, promoting a renewed interest in theory building in social gerontology.

See also: *Ageing, Cohort, Disability, Ethnicity, Gender, Generations, Gerontology, Independence, Retirement*

FURTHER READING

Bengtson, V., Burgess, E. and Parrott, T. (1997) Theory, explanation, and a third generation of theoretical development in social gerontology. *Journals of Gerontology Series B: Psychological Sciences and Social Sciences*, 52(2): 72–88.

Estes, C., Biggs, S. and Phillipson, C. (2003) *Social Theory, Social Policy and Ageing*. Buckingham: Open University Press.

REFERENCES

Bengtson, V., Burgess, E. and Parrott, T. (1997) Theory, explanation, and a third generation of theoretical development in social gerontology. *Journals of Gerontology Series B: Psychological Sciences and Social Sciences*, 52(2): 72–88.

Bengtson, V., Putney, N. and Johnson, M. (2006) The problem of theory in gerontology today, in M. Johnson (ed.), *The Cambridge Handbook of Age and Ageing*. Cambridge: Cambridge University Press. pp. 3–20.

Burgess, E. (1960) Ageing in western culture, in E. Burgess (ed.), *Ageing in Western Societies*. Chicago: Chicago University Press. pp. 3–28.

Calasanti, T. (1999) Feminism and gerontology: not just for women. *Hallym International Journal of Ageing*, 1(44): 44–55.

Cumming, E. and Henry, W. (1961) *Growing Old: The Process of Disengagement*. New York: Basic Books.

Dowd, J. (1975) Ageing as exchange: a preface to theory. *Journal of Gerontology*, 30: 584–594.

Estes, C. (1979) *The Ageing Enterprise*. San Francisco, CA: Jossey-Bass.

Gilleard, C. and Higgs, P. (1992) The gerontological imagination: social influences on the development of gerontology. *International Journal of Ageing and Human Development*, 35(1):45–65.

Gilleard, C. and Higgs, P. (2000) *Cultures of Ageing: Self, Citizen and the Body*. Harlow: Prentice-Hall.

Hagestad, G. and Dannefer, D. (2001) Concepts and theories of ageing: beyond microfication in social science approaches, in R. H. Binstock and L. K. George (eds), *Handbook of Ageing and the Social Sciences* (5th edition). London: Academic Press. pp. 3–21.

Havighurst, R. (1957) The leisure activities of the middle-aged. *American Journal of Sociology*, 63: 152–162.

key concepts in
social gerontology

Havighurst, R. (1968) Personality and patterns of ageing. *Gerontologist*, 8: 20–23.

McMullin, J. (2000) Diversity and the state of sociological ageing theory. *The Gerontologist*, 40(5): 517–530.

Moody, H. (ed.) (1993) *Ageing: Concepts and Controversies*. Newbury Park, CA: Pine Forge Press.

Neugarten, B. and Hagestad, G. (1976) Age and the life course in R. H. Binstock and E. Shanas (eds), *Handbook of Ageing and Social Sciences*. New York: Van Norstrand Reinhold. pp. 35–55.

Neugarten, B. and Hagestad, G. (1976) Age and the lifecourse, in R. Binstock and E. Shanas (eds), *Handbook of Ageing and the Social Sciences*. New York: Van Nostrand Reinhold. pp. 35–55.

Phillipson, C. and Baars, J. (2007) Social theory and social ageing, in J. Bond, S. Peace, F. Dittmann-Kohli and G. Westerhof (eds), *Ageing in Society: European Perspectives on Gerontology*. London: Sage.

Phillipson, C. (1982) *Capitalism and the Construction of Old Age*. London: Macmillan.

Putnam, M. (2002) Linking ageing theory and disability models: increasing the potential to explore ageing with physical impairment. *The Gerontologist*, 42: 799–806.

Riley, M., Johnson, M. and Fones, A. (1972) *Ageing and Society. Vol. III: A Sociology of Age Stratification*. New York: Russel Sage Foundation.

Successful Ageing

> *A dynamic, multidimensional process building from earlier life experiences aiming to minimise physical and cognitive functional loss in later years, while maintaining and achieving high social activity.*

The concept of successful ageing has a long history in the field of social gerontology. Today, it is most widely attributed to the seminal work of John Rowe and Robert Kahn (1998) which gained wide academic and public acclaim. The authors proposed a model to challenge the notion that ageing is a period of decline and loss. Instead, ageing is presented in a preventative framework. The concept advocates modifications in individual behaviours as a pathway to success in old age. Successful ageing signifies a time of potential health and well-being, and is measured by objective indicators, including the absence of disease, high physical and cognitive functioning, and active social engagement.

Cultural norms and values, which vary from one society to the next, make a universal definition of successful ageing problematic. As discussed by Willcox et al. (2007), the international gerontological community continues to find it challenging to arrive at an agreed upon common understanding of exactly what it means or even how to define it. As a result, multiple indicators of 'success', are used, such as length of life/mortality, physical and psychological health, cognitive function, life satisfaction and productivity, among others.

Indeed, the successful ageing paradigm has been increasingly critiqued as limited in its applicability. Perhaps the most singularly acknowledged shortcoming of the concept is that it fails to address the fact that a disease-free older age is unrealistic for most people (Bowling and Dieppe, 2005). Major limitations have been identified, including an emphasis on the biomedical model for its definition, a 'western' cultural bias, an assumption of homogeneity among older persons, and limited attention to lay persons' definitions of what is successful ageing. Each of these limitations will be addressed below.

A major tenet underlying notions of achieving successful ageing involves the avoidance of illness. This biomedical definition eschews frailty or disability, propagating a norm of middle age as the ideal to emulate (Holstein and Minkler, 2003). In conjunction, emotional and/or psychological advancements that come with life experience do not surface as legitimated and validated elements of having aged successfully. The gains that come with lived experience are overshadowed by an almost singular focus on health status.

The 'western' cultural bias and assumption of homogeneity among older persons may be most aptly illustrated in the focus on the individual as an agent of change. Interestingly, attaching the term 'successful' to ageing connotes a western, capitalistic, individualism. That is, success is completely attributable to individual action. An equal playing field is assumed, where hard work and determination may produce an outcome deemed to be successful. Success connotes a hierarchy where images of winning surface in a very visible way (i.e. money, trophies, accolades).

Not addressed is that the ability of an individual to respond to life circumstances, and hence the ageing experience, is shaped by social status and social structural factors such as gender, class, race and ethnicity. As Minkler and Holstein (2003) contend, access to resources, including healthy diets, good health care and sufficient income, in great part shape an individual's ability to choose a healthy lifestyle. Ideals of success tend to discount natural processes, threatening to marginalise groups of older adults who already fall outside mainstream ideals. For instance, a woman with thinning hair and a wrinkling face or the wheelchair-bound man who spent his life working as a labourer, each represent situations about which the individual has little control, yet at the same time come to represent failure in the ageing process.

The tenets of successful ageing eschew subjective definitions according to the lay person. In a study undertaken in Great Britain, good health and functioning were most often cited as key to successful ageing, yet these attributes were rarely mentioned alone. Instead, they were often linked with other domains, such the ability to enjoy life, be socially active and have financial security (Bowling and Dieppe, 2005). It appears that older persons also take into account their emotional development and satisfaction with life as key indicators of whether or not they have aged successfully. In other words, classifications based on traditional medical models are too narrow; it is increasingly recognised that the subjective state of the older adult should be considered in any understanding or definition of having aged well.

Though the dominant paradigm for successful ageing proposed by Rowe and Kahn developed from scientifically rigorous studies examining health across the life course, the area of spirituality has been overlooked (Crowther et al., 2002). Not only is the vast body of research illustrating the beneficial effects of religion and spirituality on health omitted, but the notion of spirituality as a construct is also absent. Crowther et al. propose that positive spirituality be included as a fourth major construct to that of absence of disease, physical and cognitive functioning, and social engagement. Positive spirituality is carefully defined by Crowther et al. to omit unquestioning beliefs, restrictive tenants or mandates that discount medical services. They advance a construct that blends community and individualism, is systematic though not formally organised, and is both emotionally and behaviourally directed to positive actions that promote life-enhancing beliefs. Proposing that spirituality is a separate dimension from the other three constructs, and citing the growing body of research linking spirituality to positive health, a case is made to include spirituality in any attempt to develop interventions for successful ageing. For instance, promoting positive health behaviours and/or health information through spiritually-oriented institutions – faith-based or non-faith based – may be a particularly useful avenue.

The policy implications deriving from the concept of successful ageing are great, particularly given that it is influential in many national contexts. Some caution that the concept, with it emphasis on individual responsibility for health and well-being, risks further marginalising individuals and groups of people who do not have access to privileges due to their social locations in society. In particular, Holstein and Minkler (2003) warn that government policies supporting elders financially and materially (i.e. covering the costs of wheelchairs or modifications to homes that better accommodate disability) risk losing support. The tenets of successful ageing also deny realities of sickness and death, which bring with them the need for dependence and interdependence. Yet, these challenges require thoughtful discussion to guide policy directives.

On the other hand, successful ageing is now considered less dependent upon genetic predisposition than previously thought. As a result, potentially positive policy implications include the possibility that the tenets of successful ageing may be used to support people to build up their social activities and networks from a young age. Furthermore, governments may be encouraged to develop and implement programmes designed to enable community facilities that advocate positive healthy behaviours. It is clear that interventions need to target potentially vulnerable groups early on, as research findings based on longitudinal analyses have shown that earlier life experiences predict outcomes in later life. For instance, stressful life events and social class are known to influence health as one grows older.

As a final note, there is little point in developing policy goals if elderly people are not regarded as relevant (Bowling and Dieppe, 2005). Their assessments of what it means to have aged successfully need to be taken into account. Successful ageing is clearly multidimensional. It may be that the concept is most helpful if we follow the advice of Bowling and Dieppe (2005: 1550):

> As an ideal state to be aimed for, and the concept itself should be placed on a continuum of achievement rather than subject to simplistic normative assessments of success or failure. Given the enormous body of ongoing research on the topic, it would be unhelpful to abandon the term altogether; the adoption of a broader perspective will have relevance for elderly people themselves.

See also: *Ageing, Care, Disability, Ethnicity, Frailty, Gender, Gerontology*

REFERENCES

Bowling, A. and Dieppe, P. (2005) What is successful ageing and who should define it? *British Medical Journal*, 331: 1548–1551.

Crowther, M. R., Parker, M. W., Achenbaum, W. A. Larimore, W. L. and Koenig, H. G. (2002) Rowe and Kahn's model of successful ageing revisited: positive spirituality – the forgotten factor. *The Gerontologist*, 42(5): 613–620.

Holstein, M. B and Minkler, M. (2003) Self, society, and the 'new gerontology'. *The Gerontologist*, 43(6): 787–796.

Rowe, J. W. and Kahn, R. L. (1998) *Successful Ageing*. New York, NY: Random House, Inc.

Willcox, D. G., Willcox, B. J., Sokolovsky, J. and Sakihara, S. (2007) The cultural context of 'successful ageing' among older women weavers in a northern Okinawan village: the role of productive activity. *Journal of Cross-Cultural Gerontology*, 22: 137–165.

Third and Fourth Age

> *Biomedical, demographic or sociological terminology describing age groups either in terms of their associated chances of survival to certain ages, or as phases of the life course identified in terms of functions and roles.*

There are generally two approaches to defining the concepts of Third and Fourth Age. The first stems from the biomedical and demographic traditions which refer to them in terms of age groups and associated chances of surviving to certain ages. The second comes from the socio-logical tradition of considering the life course in terms of segments or phases, and relies heavily on defining these in terms of functions and roles. Another conceptualisation draws on both of these approaches to distinguish between stages of life with reference to the chronological terminology of 'young-old', 'old-old' and 'oldest old' (Neugarten, 1974). Neugarten's distinction between the young-old (whom he identified as those aged between 55 and 75) and the old-old was designed to reflect differences between the two groups in terms of individual health and activity status.

There is ongoing debate about exactly when the Third Age begins and gives way to the Fourth Age. From a population-based perspective, the transition from one 'age' to another is more frequently considered to occur during the 75–80 age period, the lower limits of the Third Age encompassing people aged 60 and above. Taking a person-based perspective, however, and estimating an individual's maximum life span, the end of life can occur between a much broader age range, of between 80 and 120 years, making the individual transition from Third to Fourth Age vary considerably. Others have distinguished the two phases in terms of the very significant increasing risk of physical, psychological and social dysfunction (Baltes and Smith, 1999, 2003). Although the life-course perspective has associated the transition to the Third Age with the onset of retirement, here again interpretations are divided, notably because of the shifting nature of social structural factors such as the changing age of retirement (Young and Schuller, 1991).

The conceptualisation of the human life span in terms of discrete age groupings has occurred in different historical and cultural settings and would have involved the subdivision of old age into active, younger-old and decrepit stages. Identifying different 'ages' in later life has also served the purpose of highlighting the heterogeneity of the older population in terms of their characteristics and needs (socio-economic, health, patterns of mortality, morbidity, etc.). Neugarten, for example, saw the 'young-old' group she had identified during the 1970s as having the potential to bring about significant social change in American society, in particular by challenging ageist expectations.

The emergence of interest in the Fourth Age came at a time when the consequences of continued improvement to life expectancy were beginning to be recognised. Fries's influential (1980) model of the compression of morbidity and mortality, based on the assumption that individuals have a maximum biological life span, led him to predict that the future length of the period during which individuals would be likely to die, and by consequence experience disease and disability, would shorten, occurring over a much narrower range of time at the end of the life span. For the Fourth Age this meant it would be of increasingly short duration, culminating at a peak of human life expectancy of about 85 years. Although Fries's work has subsequently been challenged on several grounds, notably because the premise of a fixed maximum life span has not stood the test of time and his predictions ignored the influence of environmental factors on life expectancies, it has still been influential in casting the Fourth Age as a period of ultimate decrepitude, preceded by more years of disability-free time.

In the UK, although one of the earliest recordings of the use of the terms First, Second and Third Ages was in a study of population ageing carried out by the Office of Population Censuses and Surveys, their use is more commonly associated with the work of the historian Peter Laslett (1987, 1989) in his characterisation of the individual life course in terms of four distinct ages. The 'First Age' refers to childhood as a period of dependency and immaturity but also of socialisation and education. It is followed by the 'Second Age' a phase of maturity, independence, responsibility and economic activity. The Third Age is the period for personal achievement and fulfilment, and in stark contrast, Laslett's portrayal of the 'Fourth Age', is as a time of dependence, decrepitude and death. However, Laslett (1996) himself recognises the contribution made by the Carnegie Inquiry (1993) into the promotion of the Third Age concept, but is critical of its usage here strictly in terms of a period of years lived, limited to the ages of 50–74 years.

Although Laslett's contribution to the development of the Third Age concept has been significant in the UK, it was previously used by the French in the early 1970s in the context of the Université du Troisième Age, the same name being subsequently adopted in the UK as Universities of the Third Age. However, Laslett considered his to be the first use of the term as part of the numerical ordering of the different phases of the life course, that is in relation to First, Second and Fourth Ages, conceptualising it as both an individual and population-level attribute, in the latter case observable across time (Laslett, 1987, 1989). He did not consider Neugarten's 'young-old' concept to be synonymous with his own interpretation of Third Age and rejected Pifer and Bronte's (1986) distinction of a 'third quarter of life' (encompassing those aged 50–75) because of its implicit assumption that anyone surviving beyond the age of 75 would necessarily experience the Fourth Age.

For other scholars, the 'Third Age', in particular, has been seen as representing a new life-course stage (Young and Schuller, 1991). Young and Schuller adopt the concept in place of the term 'retirement' in their attempt to distinguish the post-retirement phase of the life course from its association with paid employment. Once the period following departure from paid employment can be disassociated from work, they argue, then a new stage of life with a distinct and potentially positive identity of its own can be identified.

A central criticism of the Third Age concept has been that it portrays a period of 'successful ageing' and one of sustained opportunity, fulfilment and independence. As a consequence, one criticism is that the Fourth Age has been rendered less attractive as a field of investigation in its own right because of its association with declining functionality and death. Portrayal of the 'Third Age' as a period when individuals are finally freed from the influences of the state and work (the constraints of the productive processes) and able to fashion a new and fulfilling life for themselves has also been criticised for its over emphasis on individual agency, that is, assuming that the ability to achieve this fulfilment depends upon individual effort alone. Critics in fact argue that social structures such as gender and class continue to dominate throughout life, compromising individual agency even during the Third Age. The concept has also been challenged in the British context on the grounds of its cultural and historical bias, which endorses a conceptualisation of the Third Age as a period of life when citizenship rights are recognised solely in terms of people achieving a pensioner status, rather than that of consumers with spending power and independence (Gilleard and Higgs, 2002).

A key area of the current application of both concepts has been in the development of research which attempts to establish whether the gains achieved through improved life expectancy in young-older age, that is the Third Age, can be sustained into the Fourth Age. The recent Berlin Ageing Study (Baltes and Mayer, 1999) provides an extensive research agenda on this issue. There is currently debate about whether, in contrast to the Third Age, the Fourth Age is inevitably a period of the life course characterised predominantly by unavoidable frailty, accompanied by increased physical and psychological dysfunction.

In terms of its policy application, the questioning of the 'viability' of the Fourth Age points to such thorny issues as how to sustain human dignity, and how human rights and needs should be addressed when considering the allocation of scarce economic resources across different age groups (Baltes and Smith, 2003). Establishing the Third Age as an opportunity to consolidate learning has also led to the development of learning and training schemes designed to facilitate successful life management (Dittman-Kohli and Jopp, 2007), and the question of whether quality of life and well-being can be sustained from the Third to the Fourth Age has also become an important issue on the research agenda (Wiggins et al., 2004).

See also: *Disability, Frailty, Gender, Independence, Life-course Perspective, Population Ageing, Retirement, Successful Ageing*

key concepts in social gerontology

REFERENCES

Baltes, P. B. and Mayer, K. U. (1999) *The Berlin Ageing Study: Ageing from 70 to 100*. Cambridge/New York: Cambridge University Press.

Gilleard, C. and Higgs, P. (2002) Concept forum: the Third Age age: class, cohort or generation? *Ageing and Society*, 22: 369–382.

Laslett, P. (1989) *A Fresh Map of Life: The Emergence of the Third Age*. London: Weidenfeld & Nicolson.

Neugarten, B. L. (1974) Age groups in American society and the rise of the young-old. *Annals of the American Academy of Politics and Social Sciences*, 9: 187–198.

Young, M. and Schuller, T. (1991) *Life After Work: The Arrival of the Ageless Society*. London: HarperCollins.

Triple Jeopardy

> *A multiple-hierarchy threat positing that stratification based on age, race/ethnicity, gender and/or social class interact with one another to potentially put female minorities in old age at risk of a poor quality of life.*

The premise of triple jeopardy rests on the belief that discrimination emanating from being old, from being a member of a minority racial/ethnic group, and from being female lead to a potentially poor quality of life in old age. The burden of each status builds from numerous social experiences. First, old age is viewed as having low status and little respect, particularly in more industrialised societies. As a result, older adults generally are at risk for poor treatment and minimal access to resources. Secondly, racial/ethnic minorities potentially experience a lifetime of prejudice and discrimination. This occurrence also results in less access to resources than members of the dominant group in society. Finally, the case of women and old age is particularly central to the triple jeopardy hypothesis. The social norms that have traditionally guided women's life trajectories, including marital and employment trajectories, put women at a heightened risk of a poor quality of life in old age. Women, it seems, are far more likely to be living in poverty in old age than are men, particularly older ethnic minority women (Minkler and Stone, 1985). Living in poverty is frequently included as an additional 'jeopardy' (Manthorpe and Hettiaratchy, 1993). Triple jeopardy advances the belief that the additive effects of being old, being a racial/ethnic minority and being a woman combine to produce negative outcomes in old age, including poor health status, inadequate income levels, unsatisfactory housing and lower life expectancies.

Triple jeopardy evolved from the concept of double jeopardy. The notion of double jeopardy was first empirically examined in the late 1970s in the USA. This hypothesis was proposed by the National Urban League in 1964, with a particular concern for health and income status in later years among minorities. In particular, the prediction suggested that racial/ethnic stratification influenced the ageing process, potentially making the situation for older minorities less than ideal. Not only was it predicted that minorities would have worse health than those who comprise the dominant groups in society, but in addition the decline in health and other quality of life characteristics would be greater in old age among minority group members. The counter-thesis to double jeopardy, called the age-as-leveller hypothesis (Kent, 1971), suggested that ageing in and of itself constitutes a universal human problematic experience, and hence supersedes any effects due to social stratification (i.e. racial/ethnic) that may occur earlier in the life course.

Up until the late 1970s, few US gerontological studies included minorities in their samples (Jackson, 1971). Answering an earlier call that too little social gerontological research investigated the situation of being both old and black, Dowd and Bengtson (1978) examined the double jeopardy hypothesis. They examined three different age strata in a cross-sectional sample to test whether older blacks and older Mexican Americans fared worse than younger blacks, younger Mexican Americans, or whites of all ages in family income, health status, social relations and life satisfaction. Double jeopardy did indeed seem to exist with regard to income and health status, but a levelling effect due to age emerged with regard to social relations and life satisfaction. Needless to say, the findings demonstrated differences and similarities depending on the age group, but the study design precluded the ability to conclude whether such findings did indeed arise from ageing *per se*, or whether they demonstrated a cohort effect (i.e. resulted from the historical period in which participants were born and came of age).

Almost 20 years later, a considerable expansion in research on African American and other minority elders emerged in the USA. Advances in data collection and analyses also developed, leading to a re-examination of the double jeopardy hypothesis. Ferraro and Farmer (1996) capitalised on longitudinal data that spanned a 15-year time period, and extended the analysis to test triple jeopardy, hypothesising that older black women would fare worse than older black men or whites. Findings revealed that the health of black Americans at all ages, not just those over age 65, declined more quickly than their white counterparts. Moreover, the steepest decline appeared to be among older black men, not women.

Though Ferraro and Farmer focused exclusively on health outcomes (as opposed to income and/or social relations), such findings prompted them to propose three caveats to the double (triple) jeopardy hypothesis. First is a recognition of an ontogenetic assumption in the jeopardy hypothesis. The ontogenetic fallacy presumes ageing to be a self-contained process as opposed to one shaped by social and contextual factors. For example, the chronological age at which one is considered 'old' must be acknowledged, particularly given that life expectancies vary by racial/ ethnic group. The second caveat involves an assumption of race and age effects due to discrimination. To better specify this effect, it is suggested that discrimination be directly measured. As Ferraro and Farmer point out, the differential health effects may be due to health behaviour differences, variations in efficacy or cultural practices. The final caveat concerns selective mortality. Ferraro and Farmer caution that any exploration of a jeopardy hypothesis must consider not only health but also survival over the life course, hence the need for longitudinal data. In particular, attention must be paid to the racial-mortality crossover effect, illustrating that black men have lower life expectancies than whites, but if they reach age 75, they have a better chance of outliving their white counterparts. Of course, women in general have longer life expectancies than men, though they are more likely to report living with a chronic illness. It is clear that evidence to support the theoretical specifications of either double or triple jeopardy is mixed.

The policy implications of triple jeopardy are many. Whether one chooses to define jeopardy in terms of health (physical or mental), mortality, income, social relations or life satisfaction/happiness, such targets will guide policy directives. Recognising the multidimensional aspects of quality of life is highly important. For instance, Manthorpe and Hettiaratchy (1993) introduce triple jeopardy as a potentially useful framework for understanding older ethnic minorities in the UK, yet caution against assuming that no strengths exist within such subgroups. Informal support from family and community within ethnic communities may be particularly effective for aiding older ethnics with mental health issues. Ferraro and Farmer (1996) echo a similar caution when they suggest that ageing should not be assumed to constitute loss only. The gains made through the ageing process and lived experience may also provide critical and influential resources. Policy development must acknowledge where potential jeopardizes exists, but also where strengths lie within such stratified groups.

Within-group variation is also highly important. Selective mortality realities point to the need for policy initiatives that target risk factors associated with specific quality-of-life indicators early in the life course. It is clear, furthermore, that racial/ethnic differences alone do not sufficiently address the enormous variation found regarding the multiple indicators of well-being among older adults. Stratification is a necessary factor to consider, particularly the multiple ways that such social positions interact with one another to influence situations in old age. Also critical, however, are the contexts that shape and reshape experiences based on where one sits in the hierarchy of social life over the life course.

See also: *Ageing, Cohort, Ethnicity, Gender, Housing, Quality of Life, Social Relations*

REFERENCES

Dowd, J. J. and Bengtson, V. L. (1978) Ageing in minority populations: an examination of the double jeopardy hypothesis. *Journal of Gerontology*, 33(3): 427–436.

Ferraro, K. F. and Farmer, M. M. (1996) Double jeopardy to health hypothesis for African Americans: analysis and critique. *Journal of Health and Social Behavior*, 37: 27–43.

Jackson, J. J. (1971) Negro aged: toward needed research in social gerontology. *The Gerontologist*, 2(2): 52–56.

Kent, D. P. (1971) The elderly in minority groups: variant patterns of ageing. *The Gerontologist*, 11: 26–29.

Manthorpe, J. and Hettiaratchy, P. (1993) Ethnic minority elders in the UK. *International Review of Psychiatry*, 5: 171–178.

Minkler, M. and Stone, R. (1985) The feminization of poverty and older women. *The Gerontologist*, 25(4): 351–357.

bibliography

Akabayashi, A. (2002) Euthanasia, assisted suicide, and cessation of life support: Japan's policy, law, and an analysis of whistle blowing in two recent mercy killing cases. *Social Science and Medicine*, 55(4): 517–527.

Action for Advocacy (2002) *The Advocacy Charter: Defining and Promoting Key Advocacy Principles.* London: Action for Advocacy.

Action For Advocacy (2006) *A Code of Practice For Advocates: Charter in Action.* London: Action For Advocacy.

Action for Advocacy (2008) *Frequently Asked Questions.* Available at: www.actionforadvocacy.org.uk (accessed 3 July 2008)

Adams, J., Bornat, J. and Pickett, M. (1998) Discovering the present in stories about the past, in A. Brechin, J. Walmsley, J. Katz and S. Peace (eds), *Care Matters: Concepts, Practice and Research in Health and Social Care.* London: Sage.

Age Concern (2008) Out of Sight, Out of Mind: Social Exclusion behind Closed Doors. London: Age Concern. Available at: www.ageconcern.org.uk/AgeConcern/Documents/Out_of_sight_out_of_mind_Feb08pdf (accessed 17 March 2008).

Age Concern Cymru (2007) *Advocacy Counts: A Report on Advocacy Provision in Wales.* Cardiff: Age Concern Cymru.

Age Concern England (2002) *End-of-life Issues.* Policy Position Paper. London: Age Concern England.

Andrews, G., Cutchin, M., McCracken, K., Phillips, D. and Wiles, J. (2007) Geographical gerontology: the constitution of a discipline. *Social Science and Medicine*, 65(11): 51–168.

Antonucci, T. C., Lansford, J. E., Schaberg, L., Smith, J., Baltes, M., Akiyama, H., Takahashi, K., Fuhrer, R. and Dartigues, J. (2001) Widowhood and illness: A comparison of social network characteristics in France, Germany, Japan, and the United States. *Psychology and Ageing*, 16(4): 655–665.

Arber, S. and Ginn, J. (2005) Gender dimensions of the age shift, in M. L. Johnson (ed.), *The Cambridge Handbook of Age and Ageing.* Cambridge: Cambridge University Press. pp. 527–538.

Arkani, S. and Gough, O. (2006) The impact of occupational pensions on retirement age. *Journal of Social Policy*, 36(2): 297–318.

Atkinson, D. (1999) *Advocacy: A Review.* Brighton: Pavillion Publishing for the Joseph Rowntree Foundation.

Ball, M. M. Perkins, M. M., Whittington, F. J, Hollingsworth, C., King, S. and Combs, B. L. (2004) Independence in assisted living. *Journal of Ageing Studies*, 18: 467–483.

Baltes, P. B. and Smith, J. (2003) New frontiers in the future of ageing: From successful ageing of the young old to the dilemmas of the Fourth Age. *Gerontology*, 49: 123–135.

Baltes, P. B. and Smith, J. (1999) Multilevel and systemic analyses of old age: Theoretical and empirical evidence for a Fourth Age, in V. L. Bengtson and K. W. Schaie (eds), *Handbook of Theories of Ageing.* New York: Springer. pp. 153–173.

Bengtson, V. L. (2001) Beyond the nuclear family: The increasing importance of multigenerational bonds. *Journal of Marriage and the Family*, 63(1): 7–17.

Bennett, K and Vidalhall, S. (2000) Narratives of death: A qualitative study of widowhood in later life. *Ageing and Society*, 20: 413.

Beth Johnson Foundation website www.centreforip.org.uk/default.aspx?page=808 (accessed 20 July 2009).

Bornat, J. and Walmsley, J. (2008) Biography as empowerment or appropriation: Research and practice issues. *The Innovation Journal: The Public Sector Innovation Journal*, 13(1): 3–16.

Bowlby, J. (1980) *Loss: Sadness and Depression (Attachment and Loss)* (Volume 3) New York: Basic Books.

British Geriatrics Society (2005a) *Comprehensive Assessment for the Older Frail Patient in Hospital*. Available at: www.bgs.org.uk/Publications/Compendium/compend_4-13.htm (accessed 3 February 2009).

British Geriatrics Society (2005b) *Health Promotion and Preventive Care*. Available at: www.bgs.org.uk/Publications/Compendium/compend_4-1.htm.(accessed 19 February, 2005).

Bronfenbrenner, U. (1979) *The Ecology of Human Development: Experiments by Nature and Design*. Cambridge, MA: Harvard University Press.

Burholt, V. and Wenger, C. (1998) Differences over time in older people's relationships with children and siblings. *Ageing and Society*, 18: 537–562.

Butler, R. (2005) Do longevity and health generate wealth?, in M. Johnson (ed.), *The Cambridge Handbook of Age and Ageing*. Cambridge: Cambridge University Press. pp. 546–551.

Butts, D. M. (2007) Intergenerational programmes and social inclusion of the elderly, in M. Sanchez, D. M. Butts, A. Hatton-Yeo, N. A. Henkin, S. E. Jarrott, M. S. Kaplan et al. (eds) *Intergenerational Programmes: Towards a Society for All Ages*. Social Studies Collection No. 23. Spain: Obra Social Fundacion la Caixa. pp. 92–108.

Carnegie Inquiry (1993) *The Carnegie Inquiry into the Third Age, Final Report: Life, Work and Livelihood in the Third Age*. Kent: Bailey Management Services.

Carr, D., Nesse, R. and Wortman, C. (eds) (2006) *Spousal Bereavement in Late Life*. New York: Springer.

Chamberlayne, P., Bornat, J. and Wengraf, T. (2000) *The Turn to Biographical Methods in Social Science: Comparative Issues and Examples*. London: Routledge.

Chan, F. (2008) Frailty in old age. *Medical Bulletin* 13(9).

Chaplin, R. and Dobbskeepel, D. (2001) Ageing in place in assisted living: Philosophy versus policy. *The Gerontologist*, 41: 43–60.

Chappell, N. and Penning, M. (2005) Family caregivers: Increasing demands in the context of 21st century globalization, in M. Johnson (ed.), *The Cambridge Handbook of Age and Ageing*. Cambridge: Cambridge University Press. pp. 455–462

Chen, H. (2007) Power and autonomy of older people in long-term care: Cross-national comparison and learning. *Social Policy Review*, 19: 175–199.

Clarke, A. (2000) Using biography to enhance the nursing care of older people. *British Journal of Nursing*, 9(7): 429–433.

Clarke, A., Hanson, E. J. and Ross, H. (2003) Seeing the person behind the patient: Enhancing the care of older people using a biographical approach. *Journal of Clinical Nursing*, 12: 697–706.

Coleman, P., Bond, J. and Peace, S. (2000) Ageing in the twentieth century, in P. Coleman, J. Bond and S. Peace (eds), *Ageing in Society: An Introduction to Social Gerontology* (2nd edition). London: Sage.

Comas-Herrera, A., Costa-Font, J., Gori, C., de Maio, A., Patxot, C., Pickard, L. et al. (2003) *European Study of Long-term Care Expenditure: Report to the European Commission, Employment and Social Affairs DG*. London: London School of Economics.

Corden, A., Hirst, M. and Nice, K. (2008) *Financial Implications of the Death of a Partner*. Social Policy Research Unit, University of York, York.

Dalley, G. (1988) *Ideologies of Caring: Rethinking Community and Collectivism* (2nd edition). London: Macmillan.

De Jong Gierveld, J. and Kamphuis, F. (1985) The development of a Rasch-type loneliness scale. *Applied Psychological Measurement*, 9: 289–299.

De Jong Gierveld, J., van Tilburg, T. and Dykstra, P. A. (2006) Loneliness and social isolation, in A. L. Vangelisti and D. Perlman (eds), *The Cambridge Handbook of Personal Relationships*. New York: Cambridge University Press. pp. 485–500.

Department for Communities and Local Government, Department of Health and Department for Work and Pensions (2008). *Lifetime Home, Lifetime Neighbourhoods: A National Strategy for Housing an Ageing Society*. London: Department for Communities and Local Government.

Dittmann-Kohli, F. and Jopp, D. (2007) Self and life management: wholesome knowledge for the Third Age, in J. Bond, S. Peace, F. Dittmann-Kohli and G. Westerhof (eds), *Ageing in Society: European Perspectives on Gerontology*. London: Sage. pp. 268–295.

Department of Health (2001) *Health and Social Care Act*. London: The Stationery Office.

Department of Health (2003) *Care Homes for Older People: National Minimum Standards and the Care Homes Regulations* (3rd edition, revised). London: The Stationery Office.

Department of Health (2008) *More Choice, Greater Voice: A Toolkit for Producing a Strategy for Accommodation with Care for Older People*. London: Department of Health.

Dunning, A. (1998) Advocacy, empowerment and older people, in M. Bernard and J. Phillips (eds), *The Social Policy of Old Age*. London: CPA Publications, Ch. 12: 200–221

Dunning, A. (2005) *Information, Advice and advocacy For Older People: Defining and Developing Services*. York: Joseph Rowntree Foundation.

Dyer, C. (2006) UK House of Lords rejects physician assisted suicide. *British Medical Journal*, 332: 1169.

Edelman, P., Guihan, M., Bryant, F. and Munro, D. (2006) Measuring resident and family member determinants of satisfaction with assisted living. *The Gerontologist*, 46: 599–608.

Edgerton, R. B. (1967) *The Cloak of Competence: Stigma in the Lives of the Retarded*. Berkeley, CA: University of California Press.

Elford, H., McKee, K., Wilson, F., Hinschliff, S., Bolton, G., Chung, M.C. and Goudie, F. (2001) Evaluating the impact of reminiscence on the quality of life of older people. *Proceedings of the British Psychological Society Conference*, 9(2): 180.

Espinoza, S. and Walston, J. D. (2005). Frailty in older adults: Insights and interventions. *Cleveland Clinic Journal of Medicine*, 72(12): 1105–1112.

Estes, C., Biggs, S. and Phillipson, C. (2003) *Social Theory, Social Policy and Ageing: A Critical Introduction*. Buckingham: Open University Press.

Evandrou, M. (2000) *Social Inequalities in Later Life: The Socio-economic Position of Older People from Ethnic Minority Groups in Britain*. Available at: www.statistics.gov. uk/downloads/theme_population/PT101bookV3.pdf (accessed 15 October 2008).

Evans, J.G. (1997) Geriatric medicine: A brief history. *British Medical Journal*, 315: 1075–1077.

Exton-Smith, A. (1955) *The Medical Problems of Old Age*. Bristol: John Wright and Sons.

Fennell, G. (1986) Structured dependency revisited, in C. Phillipson,, M. Bernard and P. Strang (eds), *Dependency and Interdependency in Old Age: Theoretical Perspectives and Policy Alternatives*. Beckenham: Croom Helm.

Finch, J. and Groves, D. (eds) (1983) *A Labour of Love*. London: Routledge and Kegan Paul.

Foos, P. W. and Clark, M. C. (2003) *Human Ageing*. New York: Pearson Education.

Fried, L. P., Ferrucci, L., Darer, J., Williamson, J. D. and Anderson, G. (2004) Untangling the concepts of disability, frailty, and comorbidity: implications for improved targeting and care. *Journals of Gerontology Series A: Biological Sciences and Medical Sciences*, 59(3): 255–263.

Fried, L. P, Tangen, C. M, Walston, J.,Newman, A. B, Hirsch, J., Gottdiener, J., Seeman, T., Tracy, R., Kop, W. J., Burke, G. and McBurnie, M. A. (2001) Frailty in older adults: evidence for a phenotype. *The Journals of Gerontology Series A: Biological Sciences and Medical Sciences* 56:M146–M157.

Fries, J. F. (1980) Ageing, natural death, and the compression of morbidity. *New England Medical Journal*, 303: 130–135.

Fries, J. F. and Capro, L. M. (2006) Vitality and ageing: Implications of the rectangular curve, in H. Moody (ed.), *Ageing: Concepts and Controversies* (5th edition). Thousand Oaks, CA: Pine Forge Press. pp. 43–50.

Gallagher, D., Breckenridge, J., Thompson, L. and Peterson, J. (1983) Effects of bereavement on indicators of mental health in elderly widows and widowers. *Journal of Gerontology*, 30: 565–571.

Gavrilov, L. A. and Heuveline, P. (2003) Ageing of population, in P. Demeny and G. McNicoll (eds), *The Encyclopedia of Population*. New York: Macmillan Reference USA. Available at http://longevity-science.org/Population_Ageing.htm (accessed 7 June 2008).

Gaugler, J. and Kane, R. (2007) Families and assisted living, *The Gerontologist*, 47: 83–99.

Gavrilov, L. A. and Heuveline, P. (2003) Ageing of population, in P. Demeny and G. McNicoll (eds), *The Encyclopedia of Population*. New York: Macmillan. Also available at www.longevity-science.org/Population_Ageing.htm (accessed 7 June 2008).

Genevro, J. L. (2004) Report on bereavement and grief research. *Death Studies*, 28(6): 491–575.

Giarrusso, R., Silverstein, M., Gans, D. and Bengtson, V. L. (2005) Ageing parents and adult children: New perspectives on intergenerational relationships, in M. L. Johnson (ed.), *The Cambridge Handbook of Age and Ageing*. Cambridge: Cambridge University Press. pp. 413–421.

Ginn, J., Street, D. and Arber, S. (eds) (2001) *Women, Work and Pensions: International Issues and Prospects*. Buckingham: Open University Press.

Glaser, B. G. and Strauss, A. (1965) *Awareness of Dying*. New York: Aldine Publishing Co.

Gough, I., Wood, G., with Barrientos, A., Bevan, P., Davis, P. and Room, G. (eds) (2004) *Insecurity and Welfare Regimes in Asia, Africa and Latin America: Social Policy in Development Contexts*. Cambridge: Cambridge University Press.

Grant, B. (2006) Retirement villages: An alternative form of housing on an ageing landscape. *Social Policy Journal of New Zealand*, 27: 100–113.

Hammarstrom, G. (2004) The constructs of generation and cohort in sociological studies of ageing: Theoretical conceptualizations and some empirical implications, in B. M. Oberg, A.-N. Narvanen, E. Nasman and E. Olsson (eds), *Changing World and the Ageing Subject: Dimensions in the Study of Ageing and Later Life*. Aldershot: Ashgate. pp. 40–64.

Hanson, J., Wojgani, H., Mayagoitia-Hill, R., Tinker A. and Wright, F. (2006) The essential ingredients of extracare, in *Developing Extracare Housing for Black and Minority Ethnic Elders: An Overview of the Issues, Examples and Challenges*. Housing LIN report, Department of Health/CSIP.

Hardy, M. and Willson, A. E. (2002) Cohort change, in D. J. Ekerdt (ed.), *Encyclopedia of Ageing*. New York: Macmillan Reference USA. pp. 241–244.

Hardy, M. and Waite, L. (1997) Doing time: Reconciling biography with history in the study of social change, in M. A. Hardy (ed.), *Studying Ageing and Social Change: Conceptual and Methodological Issues*. London: Sage. pp. 1–21.

Harper, S. (2005) Grandparenthood, in M. Johnson (ed.), *The Cambridge Handbook of Ageand Ageing*. Cambridge: Cambridge University Press. pp. 422–428.

Harper, S. (2006) *Ageing Societies: Myths, Challenges and Opportunities*. New York: Hodder Arnold/Oxford University Press.

Hayflick, L. (2006) Why do we live as long as we do? in H.R. Moody (ed.), *Ageing: Concepts and Controversies*. Thousand Oaks, CA: Pine Forge Press. pp. 41–43.

HelpAge International, National Academy of Social Insurance, and Initiative for Policy Dialogue. (2002) *Population Ageing and Development – New Strategies for Social Protection. Seminar Report*. Available at: www.helpage.org/Resources/Policyreports#1118138225-0-11 (accessed 10 June 2008).

Help the Aged (2004) *Delivering Equality for Disabled People: The Help the Aged Response*. London: Help the Aged.

Help the Aged (2008) *Lifting Pensioners Out of Poverty: Automatic Payment of Benefits and Iimproving the Basic State Pension*. London: Help the Aged.

Heuman, L. and Boldy, D. (1993) The basic benefits and limitations of an ageing-in-place policy, in L. Heuman and D. Boldy (eds), *Ageing in Place with Dignity: International Solutions Relating to Low-income and Frail Elderly*. Westport, CN: Praeger.

Hill, M. (2007) *Pensions*. Bristol: The Policy Press.

Hillcoat-Nallétamby, S. (under review) Exploring intergenerational relations in a multicultural context: the example of filial responsibility in Mauritius. *Journal of CrossCultural Gerontology*.

Hillcoat-Nallétamby, S. and Dharmalingam, A. (2003) Mid-life parental support for adult children in New Zealand. *Journal of Sociology*, 39(3): 271–290.

bibliography

Hillcoat-Nallétamby, S. and Phillips, J. (2007) Revisiting ambivalence, in *Book of Abstracts: International Association of Gerontology and Geriatrics. VI European Congress* (Vol. 20, p. 250). Saint Petersburg, Russia: Gerontological Society of the Russian Academy of Sciences.

Hoff, A. (2008) *Tackling Poverty and Social Exclusion of Older People: Lessons from Europe.* Working paper 308. Oxford: Oxford Institute of Ageing.

Howell, T. (1953) *Our Advancing Years: An Essay on Modern Problems of Old Age.* London: Phoenix House.

Howse, K. (1998) Health care rationing, non-treatment and euthanasia: ethical dilemmas, in M. Bernard and J. Phillips (eds), *The Social Policy of Old Age: Moving into the 21st Century.* London: Centre for Policy on Ageing. pp. 237–252.

Horder, W. (2008) Care management, in M. Davies (ed.), *The Blackwell Companion to Social Work* (3rd edition). Oxford: Blackwell. pp. 129–139.

James, E. (1994) *Averting the Old Age Crisis: Policies to Protect the Old and Promote Growth.* New York: World Bank and Oxford University Press.

Jamieson, A. (2002) Strategies and methods in researching ageing and later life, in A. Jamieson and C. R. Victor (eds), *Researching Ageing and Later Life.* Buckingham: Open University Press. pp. 21–32.

Jeune, B. and Christensen, K. (2005) Biodemography and epidemiology of longevity, in M. Johnson (ed.), *The Cambridge Handbook of Age and Ageing.* Cambridge: Cambridge University Press. pp. 85–120.

Johnson, M. (ed.) (2005) *The Cambridge Handbook of Age and Ageing.* Cambridge: Cambridge University Press.

Johnson, M. L. (1976) That was your life: A biographical approach to later life, in C. Carver and P. Liddiard (eds), *An Ageing Population.* London: Hodder & Stoughton.

Johnson, M. L., Gearing, B., Carley, M. and Dant, T. (1988) *A Biographically-based Health and Social Diagnostic Technique: A Research Report.* Project Paper No. 4 of the Gloucester Care of Elderly People at Home Project. Milton Keynes: Open University Press.

Jones, J. (2004) *Adding Value Through Advocacy.* Westminster Advocacy Service for Senior Residents (WASSR). Available at: www.wassr.org *Journal of Marriage and Family* (2002) Special issue, 64(3).

Kane, R. A. (2001) Long-term care and a good quality of life. *The Gerontologist,* 41: 293–304.

Keating, N. and Phillips, J. (2008) A critical human ecology perspective on rural ageing, in N. Keating (ed.), *Rural Ageing: A Good Place to Grow Old?* Bristol: The Policy Press.

Kenway, P., Parsons, N., Carr, J. and Palmer, G. (2005) *Monitoring Poverty and Social Exclusion in Wales 2005.* York: Joseph Rowntree Foundation.

Kirby, S. E., Coleman, P. G. and Daley, D. (2004) Spirituality and wellbeing in frail and non-frail older adults. *The Journals of Gerontology Series B: Psychological Sciences and Social Sciences,* 59B(3): 123–129.

Kohli, M. (1986) The world we forgot: A historical review of the life course, in V. Marshall (ed.), *Later Life: The Social Psychology of Ageing.* Beverly Hills, CA: Sage. pp. 271–303.

Laslett, P. (1987) The emergence of the Third Age. *Ageing and Society,* 7: 133–160.

Laslett, P. (1996) *A Fresh Map of Life: The Emergence of the Third Age* (2nd edition). Cambridge, MA: Harvard University Press.

Lawson, S., Nutter, D. and Wilson, P. (2007) Design of interactive technology for ageing-in-place, in J. Bond, S. Peace, F. Dittmann-Kohli and G. Westerhof (eds), *Ageing in Society* (3rd edition). London: Sage.

Lawton, M. P. (1977) The impact of the environment on ageing and behavior, in J. Birren and K. Schaie (eds), *Handbook of The Psychology of Ageing*. New York: Van Nostrand. pp. 276–301.

Lawton, M. P. (1989) Environmental proactivity in older people, in V. Bengston and K. Schaie (eds), *The Course of Later Life*. New York: Springer. pp. 15–23.

Lawton, M. P. and Nahemow, L. (1973) Ecology and the ageing process, in C. Eisdorfer and M. P. Lawton (eds), *The Psychology of Adult Development and Ageing*. Washington, DC: American Psychological Society. pp. 619–674.

Lee, G. R., Peek, C. W. and Coward, R. T. (1998) Race differences in filial responsibility expectations among older parents. *Journal of Marriage and Family*, 60: 404–412.

Leeson, G., Harper, S. C. and Levin, S. (2003) *Independent Living in Later Life: Literature Review*. A report of research carried out by the Oxford Institute of Ageing, University of Oxford on behalf of the Department for Work and Pensions.

Liang, J., Sengstock, M. and Hwalek, M. (1986) Environment and criminal victimisation of the aged, in R. Newcomer, M. P. Lawton and T. Byerts (eds), *Housing an Ageing Society: Issues, Alternatives and Policy*. New York: Van Nostrand Reinhold. pp. 141–50.

Lorenz-Meyer, D. (2004) The ambivalences of parental care among young adults in Germany, in K. Lüscher and K. Pillemer (eds), *Intergenerational Ambivalences: A New Perspectives on Parent–Child Relations in Late Life. Contemporary Perspectives in Family Research*. Oxford: Elsevier Ltd, Chapter 4, pp. 225–252.

Lowenstein, A. (2007) Solidarity-conflict and ambivalence: Testing two conceptual frameworks and their impact on quality of life for older family members. *Journal of Gerontology: Social Sciences*, 62B(2): S100–S108.

Lüscher, K. (2002) Intergenerational ambivalence: Further steps in theory and research. *Journal of Marriage and Family*, 64(3): 585–594

Martin-Matthews, A. and Phillips, J. (eds) (2008) *Ageing at the Intersection of Work and Home Life: Blurring the Boundaries*. New York: Taylor & Francis.

Margiotta, P. Raynes, N., Pagidas, D., Lawson, J. and Temple, B. (2003) *Are You Listening? Current Practice in Information, Advice and Advocacy Services for Older People*. York: Joseph Rowntree Foundation.

Means, R. (2007) Safe as houses? Ageing in place and vulnerable older people in the UK. *Social Policy and Administration*, 4(1): 65–85.

Meucci, S. (1994) Death-making in the human services, in R. Enright (ed.), *Perspectives in Social Gerontology*. London: Allyn and Bacon. pp. 267–272.

Milligan, C. (2005) From home to 'home': Situating emotions within the caregiving experience. *Environment and Planning*, 37: 2105–2120.

Minkler, M. (1996) Critical perspectives on ageing: New challenges for gerontology. *Ageing and Society*, 16(4): 467–87.

Moody, H. (2006) *Ageing: Concepts and Controversies* (5th edn). Thousand Oaks, CA: Pine Forge Press.

bibliography

227

Murray, P. D., Lowe, J. D. and Horne, H. L. (1995) Assessing filial maturity through the use of the Filial Anxiety Scale. *The Journal of Psychology*, 129(5): 519–529.

The National Council for Palliative Care (2008) Available from: www.ncpc.org.uk

New Zealand Ministry of Social Development (2007) *The Social Report 2007: Social Connectedness*. Available at: www.socialreport.msd.govt.nz/social-connectedness/index.html (accessed 24 October 2007).

O' Hanlon, A. and Coleman, P. (2004) Attitudes towards ageing: Adaption, development and growth into later years, in J. Nussbaum and J. Coupland (eds), *Handbook of Communication and Ageing Research* (2nd edition). London: Lawrence Erlbaum Associates, Publishers. pp: 31–63.

Oldman, C. (2002) Later life and the social model of disability: A comfortable partnership? *Ageing and Society*, 22(6): 791–806.

Oliver, M. (1996) *Understanding Disability: From Theory to Practice*. London: Macmillan.

Olshanky, S. J. (2006) Don't fall for the cult of immortality, in H. R. Moody (ed.), *Ageing: Concepts and Controversies* (5th edition). Thousand Oaks, CA: Pine Forge Press, pp. 68–70.

Onwuteaka-Philipsen, B., Muller, M. and Van Der Wal, G. (1997) Euthanasia and old age. *Age and Ageing*, 26: 487–492.

Peace, S., Wahl, H. W., Mollenkopf, H. and Oswald, F. (2007) Environment and ageing, in J. Bond, S. Peace, F. Dittmann-Kohli and G. Westerhof (eds), *Ageing in Society* (3rd edition). London: Sage. pp. 209–235.

Phillips, J. and Bernard, M. (2008) Work and care: Blurring the boundaries of space, place and time, in A. Martin-Matthews and J. Phillips (eds), *Ageing at the Intersection of Work and Home Life: Blurring the Boundaries*. New York: Taylor & Francis.

Phillips, J., Ray, M. and Ogg, J. (2003) Ambivalence et conflit dans les familles vieillissantes: perspectives européennes. *Retraite et Société*, 38: 80–103.

Phillipson, C. (1993) The pensioners' movement, in J. Johnson and R.Slater (eds), *Ageing and Later Life*. London: Sage.

Phillipson, C. (2006) Ageing and globalisation, in J. Vincent, C. Phillipson and M. Downes (eds), *The Futures of Old Age*. London: Sage. pp. 201–207.

Phillipson, C. and Walker, A. (1986) *Social Policy and Ageing*. London: Gower.

Phillipson, C., (2004) Work and retirement transitions: Changing sociological and social policy contexts. *Social Policy and Society*, 3(2): 155–162.

Phillipson, C., Ahmed, N. and Latimer, J. (2003) *Women in Transition: A Study of the Experiences of Bangladeshi Women Living in Tower Hamlets*. Bristol: Policy Press.

Pifer, A. and Bronte, L. (eds) (1986) *Our Ageing Society: Paradox and Promise*. New York: W. W. Norton.

Pillemer, K. and Luscher, K. (eds) (2004) *Intergenerational Ambivalences: New Perspectives on Parent-Child Relations in Later Life*. Amsterdam, Boston: Elsevier.

Plath, D. (2008) Independence in old age: The route to social exclusion? *British Journal of Social Work*, 38: 1353–1369.

Preston, D. (1984) Children and the elderly: Divergent paths for America's dependents. *Demography*, 21(4): 435–457.

Preston, M. (2008) *Disability in Older People*. Available at: www.patient.co.uk/showdoc/40000147/ (accessed 19 February 2009).

Priestley, M. and Rabiee, P. (2001) *Building Bridges: Disability and Old Age* (End of ESRC Award Report). Leeds: University of Leeds, Centre for Disability Studies.

Priestley, M. and Rabiee, P. (2002) *Building Bridges: Disability and Old Age.* (Summary). Available at www.leeds.ac.uk/disability-studies/projects/olderbridges.htm (accessed 19 February 2009).

Ray, R. (1996) A postmodern perspective on feminist gerontology. *Gerontologist,* 36: 674–680.

Ray, R. (2007) Coming of age: Critical gerontologists reflect on their own ageing, age research and the making of critical gerontology. *Journal of Ageing Studies,* 22: 2.

Ray, M., Bernard, M. and Phillips, J. (2008) *Critical Issues in Social Work with Older People.* Basingstoke: Palgrave.

Riley, M. W. (1988) The ageing society: Problems and prospects. *Proceedings of the American Philosophical Society,* 132: 148–153.

Riley, M. W., Foner, A. and Riley, J. W. (1999) The ageing and society paradigm, in V.L. Bengtson and K. W. Schaie (eds), *Handbook of Theories of Ageing.* New York: Springer.

Roberto, K., Blieszner, R. and Allen, K. (2006) Theorizing in family gerontology: New opportunities for research and practice. *Family Relations,* 55: 513–525.

Robine, J.-M. and Michel, J.-P. (2004) Looking forward to a general theory on population ageing. *The Journals of Gerontology Series: A Biological Sciences and Medical Sciences,* 59: M590–M597.

Rubenstein, R. (1989) The home environments of older people: A description of the psychological processes linking person to place, *Journal of Gerontology: Social Sciences,* (44): 45–53.

Scharf, T., Phillipsons, Smith, A. and Kingston, P. (2002) *Growing Older in Socially Deprived Areas. Social Exclusion in Later Life.* London: Help the Aged.

Scharf, T., Phillipson, C. and Smith, A. (2005) *Multiple Exclusion and Quality of Life amongst Excluded Older People in Disadvantaged Neighbourhoods.* London: Social Exclusion Unit, Office of the Deputy Prime Minister.

Schneider, E. L. and Brody, J. (2006) Ageing, natural death and the compression of morbidity: Another view, in H. R. Moody (ed.) *Ageing: Concepts and Controversies* (5th edition). Thousand Oaks, CA: Pine Forge Press. pp. 51–4.

Scourfield, P. (2007) Helping older people in residential care remain full citizens. *British Journal of Social Work,* 37(7): 1135–1152.

Seale, C. F. (1997) Social and ethical aspects of euthansia: A review. *Progress in Palliative Care,* 5: 141–146.

Seale, C. F., Addington-Hall, J. and McCarthy, M. (1997) Awareness of dying: Prevalence, causes and consequences. *Social Science and Medicine,* 45: 477–484.

Shakespeare, T. and Watson, N. (2002) The social model of disability: An outdated ideology? *Research in Social Science and Disability,* 2: 9–28.

Sheldon, J. H. (1948) *The Social Medicine of Old Age.* Oxford: Oxford University Press.

Sixsmith, A. (1986) The meaning of home: An exploratory study of environmental experience. *Environmental Psychology,* 6: 281–298.

Stephenson, P .H., Wolfe, N. K, Coughlan, R., and Koehn, S. D. (1999) A methodological discourse on gender, independence, and frailty: Applied dimensions of identity construction in old age. *Journal of Ageing Studies,* 13(4): 391–401.

Sundstrom, G., Johansson, L., and Hassing, L. B. (2002) The shifting balance of long term care in Sweden. *The Gerontologist*, 42: 350–355.

Surr, C. A. (2006) Preservation of self in people with dementia living in residential care: A socio-biographical approach. *Social Science and Medicine*, 62: 1720–1730.

Thane, P. (2000) *Old Age in English History*. Oxford: Oxford University Press.

Thane, P. (2005) The age of old age, in P. Thane (ed.), *The Long History of Old Age*. London: Thames & Hudson. pp: 9–29.

Townsend, P. (1957) *The Family Life of Older People*. Harmondsworth: Penguin.

Townsend, P. (1962) *The Last Refuge*. London: Routledge and Kegan Paul.

Townsend, P. (1981) The structured dependency of the elderly: the creation of social policy in the twentieth century. *Ageing and Society*, 1(1): 5–28.

Townsend, P. (2007) Using human rights to defeat ageism: Dealing with policy-induced 'structured dependency', in M. Bernard and T. Scharf (eds), *Critical Perspectives in Ageing Societies*. Bristol: The Policy Press.

Tronto, J. (1993) *Moral Boundaries: A Political Argument for an Ethic of Care*. New York: Routledge.

Tuan, Y. (1977) *Space and Place. The Perspective of Experience*. MN: University of Minnesota Press.

Tunstall, J. (1963) *Old and Alone*. London: Routledge and Kegan Paul.

United Nations Organisation (2002). *Report of the Second World Assembly on Ageing*. (A/CONF.197/9) New York: United Nations. Available at: www.unngls.org/pdf/MIPAA.pdf. (accessed 5 November 2008).

United Nations (2005) Population Division of the Department of Economic and Social Affairs of the United Nations Secretariat, *World Population Prospects. The 2006 Revision* and *World Urbanization Prospects: The 2005 Revision*. Available at: www.esa.un.org/unpp (accessed 9 June 2008).

United Nations, Department of Economic and Social Affairs and Population Division (2006) *World Population Prospects. The 2006 Revision. Fact Sheet: World Population Ageing*. Available at: www.un.org/esa/population/publications/wpp2006/wpp 2006.htm (accessed 20 July 2009).

United Nations Population Division of the Department of Economic and Social Affairs of the United Nations Secretariat, DESA (2007a) *World Population Prospects: The 2006 Revision*. Population Ageing. New York: United Nations.

United Nations Population Division of the Department of Economic and Social Affairs of the United Nations Secretariat, DESA (2007b) *World Population Prospects. The 2006 Revision Highlights*. Available at: www.un.org/esa/population/publications/wpp 2006/ WPP2006_Highlights_rev.pdf (accessed 20 July 2009).

van Gaalen, R. I. and Dykstra, P. (2006) Solidarity and conflict between adult children and parents: A latent class analysis. *Journal of Marriage and Family*, 68: 947–960.

Vickerstaff, S. (2006) Entering the retirement zone: How much choice do individuals have? *Social Policy and Society*, 5(4): 507–517.

Victor, C. (1994) *Old Age in Modern Society: A Textbook of Social Gerontology*. London: Chapman and Hall.

Victor, C., Grenade, L. and Boldy, D. (2005a) Measuring loneliness in later life: a comparison of differing measures. *Reviews in Clinical Gerontology*, 15: 63–70.

key concepts in
social gerontology

Victor, C., Scambler, S. J., Bowling, A. and Bond, J. (2005b) The prevalence of, and risk factors for, loneliness in later life: a survey of older people in Britain. *Ageing and Society*, 25: 357–375.

Victor, C., Westerhof, G. J. and Bond, J. (2007) Researching ageing, in J. Bond, S. Peace, F. Dittmann-Kohli and G. Westerhof (eds), *Ageing in Society. European Perspectives on Gerontology* (3rd edition). London: Sage. pp. 85–112.

Vincent, J. A. (2003) *Old Age*. New York: Routledge.

Walker, A. (1980) The social creation of poverty and dependency in old age. *Journal of Social Policy*, 9(1): 45–75.

Walker, A. (1981) Towards a political economy of old age. *Ageing & Society*, 1(1): 73–94.

Walker, A. (ed.) (2005) *Growing Older in Europe*. Buckingham: Open University Press.

Walker, A. and Maltby, T. (1997) *Ageing Europe*. Buckingham: Open University Press.

Walter, T. (1993) Sociologists never die: British Sociology and death, in D. Clark (ed.), *The Sociology of Death*. Cambridge: Blackwell: Part 3: 264–295.

Wiggins, R. D., Higgs, P. F. D., Hyde, M. and Blane, D. B. (2004) Quality of life in the Third Age age: Key predictors of the CASP–19 measure. *Ageing and Society*, 24(5): 693–708.

Wiles, J. (2005) Conceptualizing place in the care of older people: The contributions of geographical gerontology. *International Journal of Older People Nursing* in association with *Journal of Clinical Nursing*, 14(8b): 100–108.

Wright, M. (2006) A voice that wasn't speaking: Older people using advocacy and shaping its development. Available at: www.opaal.uk

Yeandle, S., Bennett, C., Buckner, L., Fry, G. and Price, C. (2007) *Diversity in Caring: Towards Equality for Carers*. Report No. 3 Carers, Employment and Services Report Series. Leeds: Carers UK with University of Leeds.

Zimmermann, C. and Rodin, G. (2004) The denial of death thesis: Sociological critique and implications for palliative care. *Palliative Medicine*, 18: 121–128.

bibliography

name index

Adams, R. 48
Ajrouch, K. J. 59, 88, 184,
    195, 197, 200
Akabayashi, A. 93
Akhtar, S. 88, 89
Akiyama, H. 99, 111, 196
Aldous, J. 116
Andersson, L. 149
Andrews, G. 20
Antonocci, Toni C. 58,
    59, 60, 99, 102, 111,
    196, 200
Aranda, M. P. 88
Arber, S. 169, 174, 178, 201
Arkani, S. 188–9
Askham, J. 97
Atkinson, D. 7
Attias-Donfut, C. 11,
    169, 201

Baars, J. 56, 205, 206, 207
Bacerra, R. M. 89
Baillie, J. 64–5
Ball, M. M. 132
Baltes, M. M. 14
Baltes, P. B. 14, 214, 216
Barer, B. M. 110
Barnes, M. 193
Barresi, C. M. 89
Becker, G. 90
Becker, M. 116
Beham, B. 176
Bengtson, V. 26, 28, 57, 97,
    98, 111, 116, 204, 205,
    207, 208, 218
Bennett, K. 37
Bernard, M. 86, 129, 137
Best, F. 9
Birren, J. 1, 14
Black, H. K. 185
Blenkner, M. 102
Boldy, D. 20, 31
Bond, J. 71, 129, 176, 177,
    179, 180
Bonnie, R. J. 79, 80, 81
Bornat, J. 39, 40, 41
Bourne, V. 202
Bowlby, J. 36
Bowling, A. 176, 177, 178,
    210, 211, 212
Bradley, G. 47
Brenton, M. 34, 129
Bridgen, P. 168
Brighton, P. 106
Brody, E. M. 116, 155
Bronfenbrenner, U. 86
Bronte, L. 215

Burgess, E. 205
Burholt, V. 98
Butler, R. 21, 155
Butt, J. 178, 180
Butts, D. M. 138
Bytheway, B. 22–3, 127

Calasanti, T. 206
Cantor, M. H. 196
Capro, L. M. 154
Carstensen, L. L. 196
Chaaya, M. 184
Challis, D. 46, 47, 48
Chamberlayne, P. 40
Chambré, S. M. 51
Chan, F. 105, 106
Chaplin, R. 32
Chappell, N. 45
Chen, H. 159
Chen, P. C. 88, 89
Choi, L. W. 88, 89
Chow, N. S. 63
Christensen, K. 153
Clark, M. C. 108
Clarke, A. 39, 40, 41, 42
Clayton, V. 14
Cohen, E. S. 23–4
Cohen, J. 93
Cohen, S. 196
Cole, T. R. 62
Coleman, P. 129, 154
Comas-Herrera, A. 158
Connidis, I. 27–8
Corden, A. 36
Corner, L. 71, 176, 177,
    179, 180
Coupland, J. 14
Croucher, K. 129
Crowther, M. R. 211
Croxall, J. 37
Cuddy, A. J. C. 22
Cuellar, I. 89
Cumming, E. 97
Cummings, E. 22, 205

Daatland, S. O. 197
Dalley, Gillian 43
Dannefer, D. 141, 198, 207
Darton, R. 32
Davidson, K. 178
De Jong Gierveld, J. 148,
    149, 150
Dewilde, C. 141
Dharmalingam, A. 98, 159
Dieppe, P. 210, 211, 212
Dittman-Kohli, F. 216
Dobbskeepel, D. 32

Donlon, M. M. 22
Dowd, J. 205
Dowd, J. J. 218
Downs, M. G. 74
Draper, P. 176, 178
Dunning, A. 5, 6, 8
Dyer, C. 77
Dykstra, P. 27

Easterlin, R. A. 173
Edelman, P. 33
Edgerton, R. B. 41
Ekerdt, D. J. 64
Elder, G. 56, 140, 142, 143
Elford, H. 41
Elkholy, A. A. 63
Espinoza, S. 105, 107
Estes, C. 119, 120, 191, 206
Evans, S. 175, 178–9, 179
Evans, W. 105–6
Exton-Smith, A. 118
Ezekiel, J. E. 93, 95

Farmer, M. M 219, 220
Farquhar, M. 177
Fennell, G. 132
Ferraro, K. F. 51, 219, 220
Finch, J. 43, 101, 103,
    104, 132
Foos, P. W. 108
Forrest, R. 127
Franks, P. J. 164
Fried, L. P. 105, 108
Fries, J. F. 154, 155, 214
Fuller-Thompson, E. 116
Fulmer, T. 80

Gabriel, Z. 176
Gallagher, D. 37
Galloway, S. 176, 180
Gans, D. 101, 102, 103
Gaugler, J. 32
Gavrilov, L. A. 122
Gee, S. 64–5
Genevro, J. L. 37, 38
Giarrusso, R. 28
Gibson, R. C. 112
Gilleard, C. 206, 216
Ginn, J. 168, 174
Glasby, J. 158
Glaser, B. G. 68
Glendinning, C. 158
Glick, P. C. 98
Goldenberg, J. L. 22
Gough, I. 125
Gough, O. 189
Grant, B. 159

name index

subject index

subject index

key concepts in
social gerontology

key concepts in
social gerontology